Blades of Grass

Blades of Grass

The Story of George Aylwin Hogg

MARK AYLWIN THOMAS

authorHOUSE

AuthorHouse™ UK
1663 Liberty Drive
Bloomington, IN 47403 USA
www.authorhouse.co.uk
Phone: 0800 047 8203 (Domestic TFN)
+44 1908 723714 (International)

Published by AuthorHouse 06/04/2019

ISBN: 978-1-7283-8884-7 (sc)
ISBN: 978-1-7283-8883-0 (e)

Library of Congress Control Number: 2019942711

Print information available on the last page.

I dedicate this book to my Aunt Rosemary, who forever held so dear the fond memory of her remarkable brother, and to my maternal grandmother, Kathleen, who brought them both into this world. Also to my great aunt, Muriel Lester, who took her nephew to China.

Contents

Preface

A police Land Cruiser, gleaming white in the hot late-April sun, with every imaginable light flashing and siren shrieking, sped ahead of us to herald our coming. The heavy traffic had already been halted at every junction and crossroad on our route. The centre lane of the crowded main street had been cleared for our unhindered dash from the Jincheng Hotel at one end of Lanzhou to the railway station, which lay at the far end of that long, thin industrial city on the upper reaches of Huang He – the great Yellow River.

We had started on the third and last stage of a truly amazing week in the spring of 1988, which started with a memorial meeting in Beijing's Great Hall of the People followed by banquets and speeches, and much VIP treatment for us foreign guests amongst whom were, for instance, delegations from the New Zealand government and their embassy in Beijing, delegations from China Friendship Societies of New Zealand and Australia, members of the International Committee for the Promotion of Chinese Industrial Cooperatives and a delegation of the New Zealand press. A three-hour flight whisked us over the provinces of Hebei, Shanxi, and Shaanxi, following the line of the Great Wall of China to the northwest to Lanzhou, the sprawling capital of Gansu Province where there were more greetings and meetings, more banquets and speeches. Now we were to travel by special train up onto the edge of the Gobi Desert, following the route of the old Silk Road, to the ancient oasis towns of Zhangye and Shandan; to Shandan, where my uncle, George Aylwin Hogg, had died forty-three years earlier.

As the monstrous pair of steam locomotives hauled our special train on its fourteen-hour journey up over snow-covered mountain passes onto the Gobi and into the narrow Hexi Corridor between the wide steppe of Mongolia and the high Tibetan massif of Qinghai, there was time in the otherwise-hectic schedule at last to think and reflect. I recalled a vivid dream that I had had when I must have been only five or six years old. I had thought about that dream many times over the years, but especially when I was preparing for this trip – this pilgrimage – to China. In my dream, I had been seeking my uncle's grave. The image was still vivid in my mind: an arid, sun-baked hillside in a mountainous landscape, harshly bright in the high-altitude sun. There stood a simple headstone set beside a stream, shaded by a few small trees.

As I looked out of the carriage window waiting for my call to breakfast, there were certainly plenty of sun-baked slopes, but not a sign of water and only sparce vegetation such as for saltwort and *jiji* grass. The colours and forms of the loess hills and the rocky mountains in the early morning sun were something to wonder at. Totally dry river beds were frequently in evidence, and in the ones that were close to the railway embankment, one could see immaculate masonry work reinforcing the would-be river banks and jutting into the river from the outside curve of a bank to break the force of water in case of a flash flood that could otherwise wash out the railway embankment in no time at all.

In the months prior to this trip, I had had another dream. I had dreamt of playing the part of my uncle in a film about his life in China. I had woken up thinking how fantastic it would be, but of course laughed it off as a wild impossibility. When I was actually invited to do exactly that, I could hardly believe my ears, but I had no hesitation in accepting. Ye Huan, my personal guide and minder, came excitedly into my compartment as I sat on my bed sipping at the ever-present cup of green tea – the best way to prevent dehydration in that extremely dry North China dust-laden air.

"I tell you, Mr. Thomas," he said. "Your luck is in. How would you like to return to China for a few months?"

"Well, of course I would like to, but how on earth is it possible?" I exclaimed.

"There are some guys from a film company on this train. They have been observing you for the past few days, and they would like to make you a proposal," explained Huan. "Come and meet them!"

Later that year, I returned to China and spent about three months making a six-part television miniseries acting the part of my uncle.

In Memoriam

"George Hogg was one of the few foreign friends of China who really penetrated into the life of the Chinese people. Though he was called Ocean Secretary by his colleagues and friends, they never treated him as a foreigner because they never felt that he was in any way foreign to them. He really set one of the best examples of the new type of missionary." These were the words of Lu Guangmian, known to his Western friends and colleagues as K. M. Lu, written shortly after my uncle's death.

"I am still stunned by the news of George's death. It is like the story of the early missionaries all over again – the men most needed, and in George's case irreplaceable, go. What matters to me is to get men who will take up his work and catch his spirit." Thus wrote Bishop Ronald Hall, Anglican Bishop of Hong Kong.

In pursuance of this, the Bishop and the Rev. George Woods, MP, wrote to the *News Chronicle*, which published this appeal on 14 September 1945:

Wanted: Six men ready to risk their lives

Six courageous young men are needed at once to go to China to work for the Chinese Industrial Cooperatives. They are to take the place of one who did the work of six – George Hogg, brilliant thirty-year-old Oxford graduate who died recently of tetanus at Shandan, in northwest China, one thousand five hundred miles from Chongqing, and beyond the reach of medical aid.

If they are willing to take the same risk of disease, endure discomfort, eat only Chinese food, learn to talk the language like a Chinese, they should offer their services immediately to the secretary, Anglo-Chinese Development Society, 34 Victoria Street, London SW1.

Hogg, who worked with Rewi Alley, the inspiration of the Chinese Industrial Cooperative movement, was headmaster of the Shandan Bailie School, which trains junior technicians.

These schools are named after an American missionary, who introduced the system, which is helping to produce a democratically industrialised China.

This remarkable young Englishman lived as a Chinese and shared the food of the boys in any place they could find to set up a school - it might be a cave, an old temple, or a roadside depression roofed with canvas.

Anyone not prepared to take a similar risk need not apply.

The response was overwhelming. Several hundreds of young men offered their lives. The Shandan project continued to develop. Contributions sent in my uncle's memory came from faraway countries. One from Oregon in the United States bore the hope that it might be used to start a small medical centre to save other lives. This and other suggestions materialised. A clinic consisting of a two-bed sickroom, a dispensary, and a clinical laboratory was set up in connection with the school. In 1947, a young New Zealand doctor and his wife, Bob and Barbara Spencer, went out to Shandan to set up a hospital with generous funds donated by the Women's Cooperatives Guilds of England and Wales. The Spencers spent three years in Shandan during which time they achieved no small number of miracles. Their story is told in Barbara Spencer's book entitled *Desert Hospital in China*.

In August 1945, Rewi Alley wrote, "I shall do my best to stay here and carry on, though there are all sorts of people calling me. George would never forgive me if I did not stay and do my best with this most basic work."

Rewi Alley, a New Zealander, died in Beijing on 27 December 1987 soon after his nintieth birthday after living in China for sixty years. The memorial events that brought me to China as a representative of my family were in commemoration of the life and work of Rewi Alley, China's long-standing number-one foreign resident - a much honoured and respected gentleman. As the week progressed, packed with activity, it became increasingly obvious that we were not only remembering the life of one man, but of two. The second was George Aylwin Hogg, my Uncle Aylwin, who died in July 1945 at the age of only 30 after an action-packed seven years in China. All the time during that week of speeches, Aylwin's name kept coming up, and I began to see that the Chinese people held his memory in equally high esteem as they did Rewi Alley's. These two men had worked together in the chaotic years of the Sino-Japanese War and the Chinese Civil War to create a unique form of industrial training on which to base the reconstruction of industry for the New China that they believed was to come.

By drawing on the memories of family and friends about his childhood, boyhood, and his development into the young graduate who went on a visit to China directly after coming down from Oxford, never to return, I shall follow George Aylwin Hogg's movements to the Far East via America and let his own letters and other writing form the bulk of this book.

The name *Aylwin* is of ancient origin derived from the earliest of all baptismal names, *Aelfwine*, which predates written history and most probably is rooted in the Gaelic and Celtic cultures. The name is translated as "noble friend" or "wise friend", an apt name indeed in this case. He was a wise and noble friend to the people of China.

Chapter 1

Home, School and Oxford

"M y son did not die on July 22nd, 1945," his mother once wrote. "He just passed through the doorway of death to a life of further possibilities." George Aylwin was born on 26 January 1915, to Kathleen and Robert Hogg at Red Gables on Leyton Road in Harpenden, Hertfordshire. Robert Hogg was a successful merchant tailor in business with his brother in Hanover Square, London, and Aylwin was the youngest of a family of six children. The first memories are of an aureole of curls like a pale gold cloud about Aylwin's head; he loved to put on his brother's cricket cap and black school waistcoat, which looked ridiculously incongruous on him.

He repudiated the idea of death at the age of four. He had been distributing drawings with great pride, and one of his brothers, to tease, said, "I suppose when you're dead you'll want us to frame them and stick them on the wall?" To which Aylwin replied in astonishment, "I shall never *die*, Stephen! When my body gets old and worn out, I shall go to God's land. He'll have the window open. He'll be all ready, and He'll pop me into a new body." Another time he was overheard saying to his sister, "If heaven isn't much nicer than earth, Rosemary, I shall ask God to let me come back."

Aylwin was fortunate in having for his nurse and first governess Gladys Owen (Soney, for short), who later worked with Aylwin's aunts, Muriel and Doris Lester, at the Kingsley Hall Settlement in Bow, the heart of London's East End. After some years in London, she went to dedicate her life to the "untouchables" of India, working for the International Fellowship of Reconciliation. She started to teach Aylwin when he was six by the Dalton Laboratory Plan, an educational concept created by Helen Parkhurst and inspired by the Montessori way, and so set him thinking things out for himself at that early age. One morning, in the year that Émile Coué popularised autosuggestion, Soney was awakened by the following conversation between Aylwin and the minute teddy bear he took to bed with him: "Now, Tiny Tim, what is your worst fault?" After a pause she heard, "Oh, swank! Well, Tiny Tim, before you go to sleep, and directly you wake up in the morning, you must say to yourself: 'Every day in every way I am getting less and less of a swank.'"

Aylwin was nearly ten when he showed a feeling for words. His father had been reading aloud Tennyson's "The Eagle", and then asked: "How would *you* describe an eagle, Aylwin?" After a moment's thought, he replied, "A whirring mass of fierce glory."

Soon after this, Aylwin's parents decided to send him to Switzerland to an international school which had been inspired by the International Fellowship of Reconciliation and was run on Montessori principles at Gland on the shores of Lake Geneva. Rosemary was returning there for a second year and begged to take her little brother with her. The school's aim was to break down barriers of age, sex, class, and nationality. All the staff shared the housework with the children, and the cook, the only one who was not a teacher by profession, taught Italian as it was her native language. The gardener came in to school meals and was waited on by the children, as everyone else was. Indicative of the style of discipline at the school, the bursar one lunchtime tapped on his glass for attention. "Anyone wanting pocket money for the midnight feast tonight, call in at my office after lunch." That particular feast, of course, didn't materialise. What is the fun of a midnight feast when the powers that be know all about it in advance? On another occasion, just as a midnight feast was beginning to get into full swing, one of the teachers popped her head around the door to wish everyone "Bon apétit!" Once a week, there was a school meeting at which the girls and boys were free to criticise the teachers and even the head, and to express their views on anything that they thought unfair or wrong. All this is bound to have influenced Aylwin's subsequent work.

Before their departure, Rosemary, in schoolgirl fashion, was describing and discrediting someone at the school, but Mother intervened and declared it was not fair to prejudice the boy's mind and that she must let him judge for himself. On the night before departure, Aylwin's mother sat on his bed and tried to prepare him for the sudden severance of home discipline. "You will no longer be able to hear my voice, or Soney's voice. You must learn to listen to your *inner voice*. It will always tell you what is right, if you make a practice of listening to it."

The following week, two letters arrived from Switzerland. Rosemary's recounted, "Aylwin's inner voice is coming along just fine. Yesterday it made him wash out his own pants and vest." Aylwin reported, "I have looked at Miss ¬ from my own point of view, and I also think that she is a silly old fop."

After this emancipating year abroad, Aylwin went, at the age of eleven, as a dayboy at first, to St. George's School, a co-educational school in Harpenden. Here, his three brothers had established a tradition, which meant Aylwin had considerable living up to do. He became the ordinary English schoolboy, going through the normal stages at the normal ages.

Two other families who had children of the same ages as the Hoggs lived just across Harpenden Common. The Hunters, with six children in all and father abroad most of the time in the Rumanian oil fields, provided a second home to the younger four Hoggs. They and the Hunters' older four were all best friends right through school. The house was always full of youngsters, including frequent visitors from the orphanage across the road. The Hunter family had left Russia in haste during the revolution, leaving all their worldly possessions behind, and the youngest son had been born in a truck on the hazardous journey. Mrs Hunter seemed to hold open house for just about everyone. She was a remarkable woman whose very practical Christian way of life made a great impression on the Hogg children. It was so different from their own home environment, and made much more sense to them than all the preaching and church-going that went on at home.

In 1928, Robert Hogg bought a plot of land from Mrs Hilda Salisbury of Gables End, just down the road from Red Gables, where he built a slightly smaller and very beautiful house, which they called Wayfarings. By this time, the elder children, Gary, Barbara (my mother), and Daniel (Dan'l) had grown up and gone out into the world.

Rosemary and Aylwin, supposedly attending school chapel along with their brother, Stephen, who was in the choir, would regularly sneak off to spend Sunday mornings at the Hunters. They would decide between themselves on their story, knowing that Mother would want to know all about the sermon at lunchtime. Stephen never let on. Once, when imparting the "vital information" for Mother's benefit, Aylwin became so carried away with his own inventiveness on the arranged story that he "retold" the supposed sermon in intricate detail. Stephen, true to form, displayed remarkable self-control and managed not to choke and splutter on his lunch in his totally suppressed amusement.

The second home-from-home for the Hoggs was the Nelson household. There was Muff, who was in Aylwin's class at school. Winifred Nelson, known as Muff, remembers that, at about the age of nine, she met Aylwin for the first time. Aylwin was out on Harpenden Common with his brother Stephen. Muff was inquisitive. She already knew the older Hoggs, who were friends of her older brother and sister, Robert and Cicely. After due introductions, Muff rushed home in great excitement to announce: "There's another Hogg – a smaller one, with a funny name – Neptune or something." Thereon in, Aylwin was always known as Neptune to Mr Nelson, who insisted that the boy didn't like being called Pig. Rosemary remembers the Nelson household as a wonderfully happy home with "just the right hospitable but keep-out-of-the-way parents." Everyone there had a pet name. Aylwin, almost without exception, called Mrs Nelson by her nickname, Arab, but on occasions by her first name, May, which apparently amused them both as though they had a private joke going that no one else was allowed to share. Why Arab? Because Mrs Nelson's daily help boasted the same surname as the legendary T. E. Lawrence!

Aylwin, known as Pig, was a very close friend of both of Muff's brothers, RP and Bosh. He spent most of his weekends and holidays at their home where cricket, tennis, touch-rugger, and strange games of hockey were hilariously played. The girls would join in everything, even the rugger. These energetic bouts would be frequently followed by blowouts at Bunty's, the nearby café, and evenings were spent listening to records and playing riotous card games. Muff recalls Aylwin's lovely singing voice and tremendous sense of humour, along with a very serious, conscientious, thoughtful side to his nature. She and Aylwin became head girl and head boy together in their final year at St. George's, in the same way as Cicely Nelson and Stephen Hogg had been five years earlier.

Aylwin also followed a family tradition by becoming captain of the Rugby XV. His sixth form master wrote:

> I was very wide awake to his possibilities for I sensed in him great reserves and a high sense of purpose. He was modest to a degree and had true humility. Quiet and unassuming, he nevertheless was a dominating influence in the form. It was a joy to observe, in the years after he left, a new generation of prefects showing traits of character

which they had unconsciously copied from him, so his influence lived on. It was equally
a feature of his rugger that, in the hardest game, he always seemed to have something
in reserve to call upon in an emergency.

Reports in the school magazine reveal further apparent admirable qualities, but he *was* prone
to an occasional lapse of his sense of high purpose. On one such occasion, while a prefect in the
fifth form, he and a few similarly mischievous friends "borrowed" a little car belonging to the
French teacher, Miss Terry. Late at night they secretly drove a few miles out into the country to
where the St. George's scout troop was camping, and let down all the tents onto the unsuspecting
occupants. There was a terrific row the next day back at school. The headmaster, Cecil Grant,
gave the culprits a sound caning, and they were all deposed from their positions of prefect for
a couple of weeks. Muff got all the details of the escapade from a very shamefaced Pig. "He was
a very upright boy and usually kept out of Roger's and David's ridiculous behaviour", recalls
Muff. "While being very amused at Roger's and David's doings, Aylwin worked hard and did
well. He was very kind and gentle, and very understanding." Roger Hunter was in the same class
as Aylwin, as was his other good friend David Proctor, known as Dippy. They were a very tight
threesome all the way through school. Dippy remembers Aylwin as "a man of few words who
strove for personal perfection. He never said anything without seeming to think carefully first
about what he was going to say. Those few words always made sense."

When the time came for him to follow his three brothers to Wadham College, Oxford,
Aylwin walked into the Wadham 1st XV, was elected secretary of the Rugby Football Club in
his second year, and captained the College in 1937 just as his brothers had done in their turns.
He also played regularly for the Oxford University Greyhounds Rugby Football Club and went
on tour with them. The warden of Wadham, Maurice Bowra, wrote of Aylwin, "He has great
reserves of character and seems to have some inner vision of his own which shows him where
to go and what to do."

During the long vacations, Aylwin would visit the various countries of Europe, with little
money in his pocket and expecting adventure. In 1935 he spent some weeks at the home of a
German undergraduate friend whose father was a member of the Nazi Party. He was a landowner
of considerable influence, and he took Aylwin about with him, explaining the various ways in
which they were working for "the betterment of the people". Aylwin, naturally, had a good deal
to say on the other side, and lively discussions followed.

In the summer vacation of 1936, Aylwin set out on a hitchhiking tour through central and
southeastern Europe with £4 in his pocket and a Rhodes Scholar for a companion. En route
to Dresden, via Cologne and Berlin, they gathered some interesting sidelights on events and
opinions in the Reich. From Dresden they hitched to the Czech border and the Sudetenland
and thence to Aussig and Prague on practically anything that had wheels, asking searching
questions of all and sundry. Their route took them through Bohemia to Austria; to Hungary,
along the Szeged road to Arad in Transylvania; to Poland, through the High Tatra region; and
so to Krakow.

The time had come for Aylwin to return and prepare for his last year at Oxford. So, bidding farewell to his companion, who had decided to go on to Russia, he set out alone on the return journey. At one town, which he reached so late that the workhouse was the only available sleeping place, he had the experience of being stripped of clothing and marched naked along the aisle between the rows of beds, whose occupants raised their heads to watch his slightly embarrassed progress.

After a few more days of hitching, he reached home in high spirits and with a keen realization of the rivalries and factions in Europe and a fairly representative knowledge of the poverty and dissatisfaction among the people, which augured ill for the future.

Chapter 2

America

When Aylwin left Oxford in 1937, after taking his degree in modern greats, philosophy, politics and economics (PPE), his aunt, Muriel Lester, was planning another of her round-the-world tours in connection with the Fellowship of Reconciliation. One day, in the garden as he helped his mother with weeding the flowerbeds, they discussed the possibility of his joining her. It was a fine opportunity. His elder brother, Dan'l, had gone with his aunt on her first visit to meet Mahatma Gandhi in India a few years previously, but as that was before he was to go to Oxford, there had not been the question of his future work. Could Aylwin postpone his choice of career? And what about money? There was none to spare after educating the family, but such an opportunity was not likely to occur again. As the weeds came out and the flowerbeds were straightened, difficulties were got rid of one by one, and they came to a decision. The future must be left to take care of itself. The experience would add to the value of his work, whatever it might ultimately be. Aylwin would draw out the small legacy left to him as a child. With any luck, this would get him to the Far East, and then he would have to fend for himself.

His Aunt Muriel was delighted at the anticipation of having such a congenial companion, but asked if he had enough money to pay his passage over the ocean and across the United States, 3,500 miles by train from the Atlantic to the Pacific coast. "I've enough for a single ticket to Shanghai and a bit over," he answered. "After that I'll have to find some way of earning my passage home via India, and I'll hitch-hike across the United States."

So it was settled that they would sail on the *Queen Mary* in September. He was so engrossed in the recently published *Gone with the Wind* that he had to be fetched from the armchair where he was reading and hardly noticed he was leaving home as they set off from Harpenden by car for Southampton. He must have been more excited than he appeared, for when at the quayside, he left the driver's wheel and the family got out after him. His brother jumped back in very quickly as Aylwin had forgotten to put on the handbrake, and the car was gliding sedately towards the sea!

In the States, he was inundated with invitations, and he thumbed his way by car or lorry far to the north as well as to the Deep South. It was a good way of getting to know America and its people from many angles. He revelled in the long, swift night rides by lorry; he ate with all sorts of folk; he slept where he could. An obliging policeman gave him a cell one night. Every now and then he joined his aunt in the house of one of her friends. People were eager to find a corner for him in the sleeping porch, a camping ground, or their garage, for he seemed to add something to every group he entered. It was not only his vitality as a healthy young man who loved singing, laughter, and good conversation; he seemed to carry about with him a sense of completeness, which evoked serenity and assurance in others. An out-of-practice old pianist who never performed in company but loved playing, surprised herself at a party when Aylwin asked her to repeat the Mozart Sonata he had overheard that morning. She found she could do it without nervousness or apology. His power of perception was keen enough to make him a penetrating critic. "Often in his presence," Muriel once wrote, "one's hitherto unnoticed gaucheries, absurdities, or petty meannesses became apparent to oneself; how, I don't know, because he never found fault with you, never implied your wrong by his right." Was it his freedom from the tyranny of egoism that enabled him to communicate a sort of quiet confidence to other people?

He often found that ice had to be broken before a driver could trust his hiker. "See that bridge ahead?" one of them asked him. "That's where I shot the last passenger I picked up. He started some funny stuff with a gun." Here is his own account of his travels, which Aylwin wrote in the form of an article that he entitled "An Englishman Goes American":

What does it mean to be a "new country"? Concrete edifices, automobiles and emancipation, yes; but tumbledown shacks, itinerant hoboes and the defensive attitude of *proud youth before age* go to complete the picture. There is no better way of acquainting oneself with the many complementary aspects of life in America than to go hitchhiking. Idle men and business men, doctors and salesmen, dentists and labourers, lorry-drivers and school-children, white or Negro, gentile or Jew, drunk or sober, are all on the road and all willing on occasion to accommodate a clean looking body. How unpleasant to be taken into the country before discovering that one's host is drunk, and to face the choice between drunken drive and a long walk! How charming on the other hand, to be carried at the end of a hard day by six pretty misses on their way home to Boston from school, or to pile into an old Ford packed with high-school boys discussing football prospects! If you get bored with the upper crust, and yearn for the conversation of a crude realist, a visit to an all-night café or a petrol station will yield some friendly lorry-driver. If you wish to discuss economics or the current trade depression, you will find an itinerant salesman at any commercial hotel; and if you want to take pot luck, go and stand in the road and wave your thumb at any likely looking car. Long stretches of concrete road make companionship almost necessary to safe driving, so you will not be the only one to gain.

In no other country is the individual experience so rich in its variety. In the Tennessee Valley, a man drew up for me, unsolicited. He was bursting, sweating, hat pushed back off his brow, with the need for someone on whom to release his mind; the things which fate had incredibly done to him, and not, for once, to somebody else, reiterated themselves before his exasperated attention. The look on the face of the little girl he had run over that morning (I saw the marks on his car); the three hundred dollars he had given to the hospital doctor (he was not liable, but her people had nothing), just about all the money he had, now not enough to get him home; his insurance, on the other car, not this; his wife ill, and not to be worried. What was he going to do next? Well, when he had left his government job in New York three years ago, he had thirty-seven thousand dollars. This he invested in a nightclub, two gas stations, a farm in Georgia, and his house in Indiana. Now he guessed he was about all square, with the house as his only asset, and he would try to get back his old job in New York.

In Missouri State I became friendly with another whose life had held many different pleasures. In early life he had been a deputy sheriff. One night the sheriff and his boys were out on a manhunt. The sheriff could not think what he had left behind. After hours of searching, the bloodhound discovered their quarry sleeping under the hollow of a riverbank. It was a tense moment. "Stick 'em up" bawled the sheriff who was leading; only then did he discover what was missing. Lights flashing in the victim's eyes prevented him from noticing the absence of a gun! Later my deputy turned speed cop. Having his own machine, he was given a uniform and told that he was "in control of all traffic". Unfortunately, in his code of morality, the conception of an "honest living" prevented him from causing others to be fined while he himself received a two-dollar commission. He would therefore limit himself to remonstration with reckless drivers. One day he halted a car, which seemed particularly bent on perdition. As he drew alongside he caught sight of a sub-machine gun menacing him from the rear seat. Gangsters from St. Louis! Did he run them in, singlehanded? Did he give them a surreptitious puncture? His own story was much more human. He explained to them that his only interest was in their safety and that some of them were going to get hurt if they went on driving that way. Then he wished them God-speed. Far from calling up headquarters, he took good care not to mention the affair to anyone. Nowadays my friend is married, and proud of a job which is honest even to him, as a salesman. He took the orders, I helped him sort things out from the back of the car and carry them in: "one alarm clock, three tea sets, five small trays and an umbrella"; so his life continues along this even tenor.

Who would be a long-distance lorry driver! In America these men must often drive for two and even three days and nights without sleep. Coffee and cigarettes seem to be their staple diet. Yet no more cheerful individual is to be found; perhaps it is the continuous jolting, which prevents chronic indigestion and liver trouble. Their constant fear is that they will fall asleep at the wheel; the hitchhiker takes advantage of this to offer his services as a conversationalist. Though conversation is often difficult above the roar of the motor, especially when one is handicapped by an *English accent*, I would always fight against sleep in my corner, because the driver in his had to keep awake or kill us both. It is indeed infinitely exhilarating to roar along between fifty and sixty miles an hour, high above the road, watching the deft yet strenuous and muscular movements by which these monsters are controlled. A combination of two levers gives the driver a choice of nine forward gears and two reverse gears. Every fifty miles, or more often, we would stop for coffee and companionship. Others of these great men would be straddling the round stools or would drift in. Road information, friendly jokes and even hitchhikers are freely exchanged. Perhaps the drivers would join in a dance or two before leaving; the hour means nothing to them. I remember a certain wayside café girl, bulging out of her scarlet silk dress. She was enough to give ordinary men a headache at any time of the day, yet here was my driver at seven in the morning careening round with her to the blare of slot music as a preliminary to breakfast!

Perhaps I am unduly prejudiced in favour of lorry drivers, because they were my means of escape from two very awkward situations. The first was in Arkansas, the hitchhikers' terror. Other states have laws against hitchhiking, but none enforce them so strictly. Two boys were even arrested while sitting quietly under a little poster, which showed their desired destination. Once I was landed on the Missouri-Arkansas line at four in the morning. Nothing existed there but a café and a few petrol stations. It was bitterly cold, with a strong wind. Big round metal *Esso* signs clanged dismally. As I walked down the road I shrank into myself with the frozen feeling that I had really come to the end of the world. But inside the café I found a cheery fellow, driving a pair of linked vans down from Toledo to Memphis; I had only to show him my credentials (Passport? Good enough!) and we were away from the terrible place. On another occasion, travelling from Boston to Washington: I reached New York at dusk, and decided to make a night passage. Having crossed the Hudson River by the George Washington Bridge, I came by devious ways to be stranded along a skyway that bypasses the industrial district around Newark, New Jersey. The footpath was only just wide enough for one, but the pack on my back was as wide as the path. The trucks which rushed by were turned from friend into foe as their overhanging bulk threatened to crush me against the concrete wall of the bridge. In the glare of oncoming lights it was often impossible for them to see me at all. When I had walked to the far end of the skyway, the aspect of things turned from the nightmare back to the normal, and I was able to find a friendly lorry driver on his way to Baltimore. He was a cheerful laconic fellow from Indiana. We discussed New York. It had gotten, he said, so that he plain didn't like to go to New York any more, the way people hustled him around there.

A study of human nature is very important to the hitchhiker. Many different techniques have been evolved to overcome the motorists' reluctance to halt. Of course there are certain blessed individuals who make a point of stopping in all circumstances, but for most rides the suppliant must rely partly on the creation of favourable conditions by his own art. Personally I like to take up a stand about thirty yards on the far side of some obstacle, to make sure of attracting attention well in advance, and then to stand back, trying to look as if I don't care and am very happy anyway. When one has sufficient money for food and even for a bus fare, it is quite easy to preserve this attitude, even after being fooled by practical jokers who slow down until one runs after them and then go off in a cloud of dust. But it is different for the poor fellow who has not had a good meal, and whose next one will be when he reaches home the other side of the continent. Abject and drooping, feebly motivating his arm and thumb long after the need for attention is past, he hangs over the road like an old bent lamp-post. His hopelessness adds to his lack of success. The roads in America are peopled with migrating families following the crops, young people without homes, old men looking for billets and old women looking for their husbands. Often their hard-luck stories are untrue, but the truth is crueller if less dramatic than the story.

The hangover from pioneer days is still very apparent. The *hail fellow well met* spirit, which stands on no ceremony, is a relic of the day then the pioneers must help each other freely, or perish. There is also the jungle wariness that trusts its own strength and cunning before it trusts the forces of law and public opinion. The fact that drivers stop at all proves the existence of the one, and that in many cases they will take care to carry a gun points to the other. A pasty-faced man of forbidding mien stops for me. He is a dentist. Last week he killed a man, apparently neither by running him over nor by dentistry, but by shooting him through the head. A hitchhiker whom he had picked up made him hand over his purse, and then got out and walked off. The dentist simply reached for his own gun from the pocket of the car, and shot him dead from behind. "Accident hell!" he said in answer to my enquiry, "I would have been disappointed if I hadn't killed him." Perhaps he only made this story up to frighten me, but from the way in which he told it, with righteous indignation at outraged hospitality, and from the look on his face as he recalled his action, I believed him. He was half sorry, half proud of his exploit. Perhaps he was more sorry than proud when even the excuse that he was ridding society of a dangerous criminal went with the discovery that the hold-up was done with a piece of stick!

Circumstances peculiar to the country destined America to give birth to the hitchhiker, but nowadays criminal exploitation of road hospitality is making him an unwanted child, and people are becoming less and less accommodating. It is significant that only two women stopped for me in three months; one of them really didn't count as she had an enormous dog! But after all, the chances of a bad nut are not so great. A steel worker from Massachusetts, who picked me up on his way home from work, told me that he stopped for anyone day or night. "If you've got it coming to you, you've got it coming to you," he said, "and there's nothing you can do to stop it." In support of this theory, he told me how one night, long ago, he was driving his then Ford (a Model T) when three gunmen jumped into the back without any of the usual courtesies. He drove on at their command, knowing that not far ahead lay a barracks, at which he intended triumphantly to deliver them with a swift turn of the wheel. Just before attempting this difficult manoeuvre, he was disappointed to find that they had jumped out just as they had jumped in, without ceremony.

The hospitality of American jails has been made famous by many literary bums. I resolved to try it while in the South. My introduction was made easy by a friendly driver who picked me up on the road between Savannah and Macon, Georgia. It was dark when we reached his home and, after showing me extreme kindness, he took me first to a petrol station which would help me get the night ride I desired and second to the police station where, on his recommendation, the boys would be glad to look after me. I sat all the evening on a box in the petrol station, reading and drinking *Coca Colas*. By ten o'clock no ride was forthcoming, so I returned to the police station. I was given one compartment of an iron cage set in a concrete cell; it contained a clean mattress and bunk, and a clean quilt. "What time would you care to be unlocked?" enquired my jailer. The next night was not so pleasant. In conversation with a couple of policemen in a town on the Georgia-Alabama line, I told them of my previous night's adventure and was invited to try their jail. Having escorted me in their radio car (they were imperturbably off duty to the exciting monotone of the messages), they left me to the sergeant. He was a most sinister man. A steel tube took the place of his severed right hand and he was driving nails into the wall with it; no hammer was necessary. The bare room contained a few people standing round the stove; they spat expertly and frequently. "If you're in more of a hurry than I am," said the sergeant after a time, "there's always the sidewalk outside." Only pride forbade an immediate retreat. His face was about as hard as his steel tube hand; eyes blue, when you could see them, hollow cheeks and an Irish jaw. This time my "good-night", as he showed me a musty pile of blankets in a filthy cell, was answered by "Up at four and we don't feed anyone, get that straight." But next morning I learned that people are not always as tough as they seem on first acquaintance; he let me sleep until six and then took me out along the road in his own car.

To compare and contrast, to find the links and the wedges between my host country and my own, was a source of great amusement both to me and to the Americans who helped me. Language is supposed to be a major factor holding us together, yet I would often have difficulty in making myself understood. A New England doctor stops for me on his way to visit an outlying patient. "Have you come far today?" I ask, by way of making conversation. "Pardon me?" he replies. "Have you come far?" I repeat. "I didn't quite catch that." At the third attempt he says "Yes isn't it?" and we drive on in silence. Though language may differ, certain types of individual are apparently still common to the two countries. A lorry driver who took me into the northern part of New York State would at intervals repeat incredulously: "Gees! But you might just be an American college boy!"

The first word that comes to the average American's mind after "Englishman" is *conceited*. It seemed to me that this idea is perpetuated by misunderstanding. When an Englishman goes to America he is a little awed by the facility with which Americans express themselves, and is driven further than usual into an assumed attitude of superciliousness. Meanwhile the American too is awed in the face of what he takes to be breeding and the veneer of an "ancient" civilisation, and hates the Englishman in his heart for not letting him forget his newness. Oxford, to the American man in the street, spells aristocracy, top hat and morning coat, so that when asked where I studied I would always add "but it's not so bad as it sounds" if I wanted the conversation to continue on a friendly basis. Strange twists will often determine the direction of friendly impulses. I was sitting in a rough roadside café in illiterate Alabama; a sordid looking group was gathered in the middle of the room; every few minutes a sharp-faced woman would blow a minute globule of spit through a hole in the stove, with the air of a self-conscious schoolboy who had learnt a new trick. They seemed to be predisposed to dislike everything, so I was surprised and relieved to find that Englishmen were *personae gratae*. The explanation turned out to be that Tommy Farr (English to them) had nearly beaten "that damned black bastard of a nigger Joe Louis, who came from around these parts. Wish he'd killed him!" A sort of inverted pride of locality!

It is one of the joys of hitchhiking that anything may happen at any time. One morning when I was still in Texas ....

When there were only two more weeks before he was due to sail with his aunt from San Francisco, Aylwin was still a long way to the east, in the plains of Texas where he found motorists none too willing to stop and take up passengers. One after another shot by him, glad to be free of the low speed limit in the city where thumbing was not allowed. A slight feeling of apprehension was beginning to steal over him when a car slowed down a hundred yards ahead, and with great relief he got in. Silence, as they sped along. After half an hour, the driver asked, "Where 're you going?" Aylwin replied, "To Japan and China with my aunt." After a further fifty or sixty miles, the motorist remarked in a casual way to test this tramp with an English voice, "I'm on my way to China too. I'm travelling with the Englishwoman, Muriel Lester."

"Oh, she's the aunt I was telling you about!" So he was taken by Dr Lacy and his wife the whole sixteen hundred miles to San Francisco.

Chapter 3

Mississippi Co-op

Perhaps what Aylwin gained from most in the United States was the time he spent on the cooperative farm in Mississippi where a gallant venture was in progress. Sharecroppers, both black and white, had been living wretchedly for generations, always in debt to the landowners, many unable to read or write or keep account of what was owing to them. Through this cooperative farm, they were now becoming free, building rainproof cabins, and cultivating their own fruits and vegetables as well as the owners' cotton fields. This made a great impression on Aylwin. This account of his first introduction to a cooperative venture was published in *The Japan Times & Mail* on Sunday, 20 February 1938:

> The sharecropper keeps no accounts, no books; it is useless to do so. When at the end of the year, the little slip of paper is handed to him bearing figures in black and red, he makes no comments, goes home to his wife, dejected, downhearted and hopeless. Another year has come and gone; he has worked hard – hard as a slave – and what has he now; nothing but a slip of paper with little figures in black and red. Another year of grinding toil faces him; maybe he will do better next year. There is hope for a while, but not for long; he knows deep down in his heart that the future is hopeless. A great loneliness and despair seizes him, and he sits down with hands grown large from heavy work, brushes away tears from eyes glued to the cotton stalks in his doorway.
>
> This is a southern minister's picture of the condition of nearly two million families, ten million people, in the heart of America, the richest country in the world.
>
> At the end of the Civil War in America, not only was the prosperity of The South destroyed, but also the means by which it had been produced was gone with the freeing of the slaves. A new system had to be found, which would bring together the property-less freed slaves and the penniless land-owners. It was under these circumstances that the sharecropping system, which now accounts for more than sixty percent of the cotton production in the USA, was first introduced. The planter supplies land and equipment, the sharecropper supplies the labour, and at the end of the year the proceeds are divided in agreed proportions. But meanwhile the sharecropper must live, so the planter lends him the bare means of subsistence at a high rate of interest. The charges for this, and for many other services which the planter is supposed to supply, are deducted from the

cropper's share of the crop. All figures, both of crop sales and of loans and charges, are kept by the planter; in many cases the sharecropper has no access to the accounts even if he is able to read. All too often he is told after a year of hard labour that he is still in debt, legally bound to another year of labour. Under this system the South recovered none of its former prosperity; but rather, as competition from South America, China, India, Egypt and finally Russia grew, and as the universal adoption of tariffs hurt export industries all over the world, the position there has grown worse. Until today nearly two-thirds of the sharecropping class is composed of poor white people. It is primarily this mixture of the races that has prevented any movement of these people to free themselves. Without unity they can achieve little, and it has been the policy of the planter class to use one racial group against the other, and so to keep both in poverty.

Politically, the Negro has never, since the days immediately succeeding the Civil War, had any power in the South, and the means used to prevent his attaining it in a country where all men are nominally equal, has also disenfranchised the poorer classes of white people. White croppers are unable, even if they have sufficient interest, to meet a poll tax in the spring of the year, when their fortunes are at lowest ebb. Perhaps a final reason for the quiescence of the sharecropping class is fear; fear of violence, used sometimes in the name of the law. So, spread over an area about as big as the main island of Japan, are two million families, ten million individuals, poor, divided in race, oppressed to the point of political annihilation.

Some years ago, national interest in America was aroused by press reports of a struggle on the part of these "forgotten men" to form themselves into a Farmers Union. Their efforts were met as usual with violence and eviction, but this time two things worked in their favour; it was the first time that the black and white croppers had organised jointly, and public opinion in the rest of the States was on their side. Brave people of an enquiring nature began to visit the effected areas to see conditions for themselves. On one such expedition went Dr Sherwood Eddy and Sam Franklin, formerly a missionary in Kyoto, Japan. They were told frequently to get out and to mind their own business; instead, Mr Franklin camped beside the roadside with evicted families. Finally he and Dr Eddy were jailed for enquiring too deeply into the doings of a sheriff, who was using his official powers to get forced labour on his own farm. The sheriff was afterwards convicted on a charge of peonage; but it was perhaps his action in arresting Mr Franklin that finally caused the determination to take an active part in helping these people. Two things had to be done. First, immediate relief must be given to those in greatest need. Second, some lasting improvement had to be found in the whole system of cotton production. Mr Franklin is not the kind of fanatic who thinks all poor people are angels, and all their employers are villains. Landowners and workers alike are caught in the same fossilised system, linked to a failing industry. The planters are powerless to help the sharecroppers to any great extent unless the whole system is reorganised.

The need for such a change may be looked at from another point of view. There is present in the South a combination of factors which in other countries has proved particularly amenable to the growth of fascist forms of government; economic insecurity is the first essential, and a tradition of violence in the attainment of ends, and a popular indifference to its use bred by three thousand seven hundred lynchings between 1889 and 1929. A planter class of leaders, educated to a sense of their own superiority. The poor whites, ignorant and bigoted, also convinced of their own superiority; men such as they form the lower bureaucracy under every dictatorship in the world. Lastly, a scapegoat race; even religion in the South, being rather of an "otherworldly" type, would suit the book of a fascist leader wishing to divert people's attention from the present day.

The answer to all these difficulties came to Mr Franklin as a cooperative farm, later perhaps to be extended into a chain of such farms. There were many difficulties besides the economic in such a venture. Rugged individualism has always been an important part of American make-up. The Negro race, with whom the attempt was partly concerned, had never developed a sense of responsibility such as would be indispensable to the success of a cooperative. The sharecropping class as a whole had been taught to look only to the present, to this year's crop. For most people the present is a rounding-off of the past and a preparation for the future; not so for the sharecropper mentality. If the present can be improved by lying and cheating his way out of past obligations, or by mortgaging his entire future, he will not hesitate to do these things. The present is the only thing that counts; all else seems hazy and unimportant. How to give such men a sense of building, something of their own which they can help to grow, and in the process to build up their own characters, is one of the chief tasks, which Mr Franklin is attempting. Whereas under the old system a man and a mule cooperated to farm a cotton patch, Mr Franklin is uniting thirty-two families, white and black, into one productive community. The field of operations has been extended from a cotton patch to a farm of over two thousand acres, near Clarksdale, Mississippi, yielding a complicated crop by modern scientific methods.

Leadership on the farm comes from above, but control is growing from below as the cooperative meeting and elected council become more confident. At the beginning of the year the crop is decided upon and profit assessed. Five-sixths of the anticipated profits are distributed in weekly wages to the workers, the proportion which each man is to receive in accordance with the value of his work, being fixed by the men themselves at cooperative meeting. At the end of the year, the one-sixth, which has been held back is distributed, plus or minus any difference between actual and anticipated profits.

Beside this producers' organisation is a consumers' cooperative store. The profits on this store are redistributed among the buyers in proportion to the amount of their purchases through the year.

This year a credit cooperative is to be started in addition to these two other organisations, so that the community is becoming ever more self-sufficient.

Over twenty houses have been built, and a large community house used for Saturday socials, Sunday services, and meetings of various sorts. There is a clinic with a visiting doctor and full time nurse, a Negro and a white kindergarten, and Sunday schools. A *Good Neighbour* organisation distributes second-hand clothes, and helps those in special need.

As to the success of the farm at present, a distinction must be made between the producers' and the consumers' organisations. The store has been doing a fine business. At present, membership is limited to the members of the farm for legal reasons, but it is hoped in the near future to open it to the public, when it is likely to become the main store in the district. But the farm itself as a producing unit is having a difficult time. Cotton prices are bad, and the government restriction scheme has hit this particular farm very badly. This has led to the need for a drastic alteration in the agricultural policy of the farm, under the advice of a professional agronomist from Georgia University. Partly so as to tide over while this transition is in progress, partly to make the cooperative a better economic unit, Dr Sherwood Eddy and Mr Franklin have gone to the country to ask for means to buy a second farm, near the old one, which is in a more favourable position with regard to the government regulations. The two farms are supplementary in several ways, overheads are cut, and more families are given homes and security. By December of last year they had raised twelve out of the thirty-six thousand dollars needed to pay for the newly acquired tract of land.

Mr Franklin's task is a hard one. He must plan widely for the farms as a whole; he must listen to the individual grievances of each member. He must act as minister for the farms, and at the same time be touring the country to interest people in his work. He must try to instil a spirit of mutual trust and idealism in a people which has been moulded into ways of mistrust and selfishness. To succeed needs great patience, great faith and great love. Mr Franklin has these things. It also needs help from the outside: one cooperative farm is such a very small drop in the bucket that it may be lost, overwhelmed by the reactionary pressure from around it, unless it can be helped through its earlier stages to grow into a bigger and more self-sufficient unit.

Chapter 4

Two weeks after leaving San Francisco, on Christmas Day 1937, they arrived in Yokohama and became the guests of Doctor Kagawa in Tokyo. Dr Kagawa had been developing the cooperative movement in Japan for the past twenty years. He took Aylwin over the cooperative banks, restaurants, market gardens, and farms that he had founded. There was even a cooperative pawnshop. These and a cooperative hospital caught Aylwin's imagination. Realising his interest, Dr Kagawa invited Aylwin to stay on for a while longer to study the movement. Aunt Muriel went on to China, on her tight schedule, to meet her Fellowship of Reconciliation friends in Shanghai.

Aylwin learned a lot about the Japanese. He found that the ordinary people really believed that their country was fighting "to free China from banditry, warlords, and the oppressions of the Kuomintang". They were incredulous when faced with reports of successful Chinese resistance and the evils of Japanese imperialism. They urged Aylwin to return and tell them what he saw for himself in China.

He had found no Japanese enthusiastic for the war, though there was plenty of flag waving in addition to victory marches and propaganda. Refusal to serve with the forces was almost unheard of. Such a stand would bring disgrace on one's parents, one's family, and one's ancestors, but numbers of men had joined the China draft, determined to drop their rifles at the battle, preferring to be shot by their own officers than to fire on the Chinese. This attitude he found to be widespread.

On 30 December, Aylwin wrote home from Kobe, Japan:

I'm afraid it is ages since I wrote. San Francisco wasn't it? Well we had a middling journey across the Pacific on a French boat called *President Doumer*. You can travel third class in good comfort on these boats. Typhoid injections and periodic very rough sea kept us to our beds on several occasions. Aunt wrote an article on the "Preconditions of Peace", and I wrote up my experiences hitchhiking, which I will send you later.

Honolulu was grand. There was some fellow there who'd been to Bow in the summer. He took us swimming in beautiful warm sea. Shallow water with coral underneath reflecting a bright jade colour and high green mountains, very different from the dusty and rocky ones I saw in America.

We had some excitement on board when a stupid young officer took ciné film of the fortified zone in the Inland Sea, and was spotted by the Japanese through binoculars. They rushed after the boat and got to it just as the pilot was getting off, and bawled at him through a megaphone to get back on again. There was then a terrific fuss because they wanted to arrest the officers but weren't allowed to because it was French territory, and so had to get the consul all the way from Kobe while we stayed at anchor and ate.

Aunt didn't think she would be welcome in Japan, but messages invited her and we found that high quarters had agreed it would be a good thing for Anglo-Japanese feeling. Feelings against England here are very strong. Reading magazines, it is often difficult (so we are told) to know whether the war is fought against England or China. Feeling against America, on the other hand, is friendly. This is very queer since anti-Japanese feeling in the States is much stronger, I think, than it is in England. Explanations vary: the British are the chief rivals in China; British Naval help for China cost many thousands of Japanese lives (so the story goes); the USA is in a much stronger position to interfere than Britain who is divided in attention; trade with USA is much more important to Japan than that with England; possibly there are designs against Hong Kong. It is important to remember that all this anti-British feeling and friendliness towards USA is manufactured by government, which has complete control over press, radio (sets which can receive foreign stations are illegal) and mail. People in Japan have not yet the critical and objective attitude necessary for the working of democracy. Fascist coups have been defeated, but on the other hand the civil government means nothing, and the people believe everything that is told them by the military controlled government. I find much to compare with Germany. Only the really thinking people here are I think more gullible than those in Germany. It may be compromise and bluff however. Very difficult to tell what is gullibility and what is fear of consequences. Not necessarily fear for self, but fear that if one is "completely silenced", the means of future and potential good is gone. Another thing is that Japanese people are not as disillusioned about war as are Westerners – so far easy victories and commercial success.

Some streets of Tokyo are decorated with groups of three flags – German, Japanese, and Italian, as New Year's bunting!

Dr Kagawa is a great man on cooperatives. We visited a cooperative food factory in Tokyo slums which puts out sixty-five thousand nutritious meals every day at a cost of 28 Yen (about 32d) for *three* meals, not only nutritious but good quality! That is the second factory. Now they are building a third for higher-priced meals. Just now they are busy baking compressed rice cakes for New Year. The meals are delivered hot in cans to homes, factories, shops, and so on within a three-mile radius. There is also a co-op savings bank and pawnshop, farm co-ops, hospital, clinics, and others. Dr Kagawa thinks that international co-ops are the only basis for world peace. There is to be a conference in 1939 at The Hague, which he has been asked to preside over. He says co-ops are still a strong underground in Italy, Germany, and Austria.

Aunt leaves for Shanghai day after tomorrow. Dr Kagawa has asked me to stay on as his guest to study co-ops and Japan in general. I like him very much. He is a good man with an enormous sense of humour, and sympathy for people. He has a finger in so many pies, and his brain works in so many different directions that he finds it difficult to make all his little schemes practical, so that many people call him a dreamer with a certain amount of justification. Other people accuse him of getting married, but I suppose one can hardly blame him, poor man; certainly his life has become a lot less colourful since his marriage, although his wife is an excellent person and works almost as hard as he does.

Consumers' Cooperatives, such as the stores you see around, are theoretically groups of people who agree to divide the profits, keeping a certain amount for reserves, in proportion to the amount that each one has spent at the store. There are many other systems, but that is the most successful one essentially. Producers' Cooperatives are much harder to manage because modern production calls for disciplined performance of monotonous tasks under very skilled leadership, and any time wasted is very expensive owing to the expensive plant. So there is little chance for democratic processes of discussion and so on to work.

The way the farm worked – assessing the year's profit, dividing five-sixths amongst the members as wages in proportion as fixed at a democratic meeting, then dividing the rest at the end of the year – gives democracy a chance really to work for the poor people who are only interested in the things that immediately concern them, and cannot be expected to judge on complicated political issues. They really get a kick out of managing their own little farm, and this farm is one of a federation of farms, and the federation of farms is joined to federations of mines, ship-makers, cotton producers and everything else you can think of, so that in the end you've got a sort of national parliament of cooperative representatives. Parallel with it is a similar organisation of consumer cooperatives, and the two combine to co-ordinate supply and demand.

Maybe I have a job teaching at Hankou University, from February till June, but very doubtful now as Japan is in charge. Expect to stay here about one month then find some sort of job in China till summer.

I saw the worst slums anywhere today in the Korean section of Kobe; swarms of people living in houses without shape or form, seen to be just piles of wood and junk.

A week later on 8 January 1938:

Here is a version of my hitchhiking story, which I sent to America. I am going to make up another one for England – certain alterations – as soon as I find out about copyrights. Also I'm thinking of a couple of other ones about here, but nothing very definite yet. It is a very curious situation here. People are proud of believing what they are told, and we know who controls what they are told. Propaganda is *very* strong against Britain. The leading paper had three four-column instalments on the subject of how Britain is to them the real cause of the "incident" and Jiang Jieshi [Chiang Kai-shek] is only a tool in the hands of London and Moscow. The object is, they say, to "save China and Asia from Britain". The Chinese people really want to be saved, but some of them don't know they do owing to anti-Japanese propaganda, which Jiang Jieshi carried on at the instigation of his controllers. This one among many such articles openly claims prospects of conflagration between my whereabouts and yours.

At a Buddhist temple on top of a hill in Nara, I saw a very curious thing. It is surrounded by a balcony. People get hold of a bundle of prayer sticks, one prayer on each and run round and round the balcony. Completion of each lap is marked by dropping a prayer stick into a bag provided. Old women hobble, and young men rush round with furious zeal pushing each other out of the way. It is also advisable to mumble prayers to yourself as you go round. A bench is provided to put coats on and strip for action. No hot showers though! A very healthy religious exercise – it was frosty and cold when I was there.

I spend a lot of time reading about Japan, and also Huxley's *Means & Ends*, which is a wonderful book, I think. Japanese restaurants don't hurry one away, so I can sit over meals reading. It is a blessing to get cheap food and everything after the US.

I wonder how things are over there – I haven't seen one English newspaper since I left Southampton! Not even managed to discover who won the varsity rugger match.

I suppose you are at winter sports now? I think I may get some here. I shall go to stay with a friend of ours at a place which is not far from skiing.

It is really very hard to get to know the people of a country whose language one can't speak at all. I've never experienced it before – always people would understand German or French before.

On 1 February 1938, from Kyoto:

I put off writing this because I thought I might be going to get some mail soon and hear from you. But it doesn't seem to materialise, so you'll have to wait for an answer to the many letters, which must be piled up for me somewhere. I haven't had anything that reached America later than December 1st!

I stayed in Tokyo about two weeks and then came to Kyoto to stay with some friends of Aunt Muriel's, a young American who married an American-born Japanese girl. They are the best people, and I am having a fine time. I have given a combination talk about America, the Oxford education system, and the boycott movement, three separate times, and on Sunday evening I gave a talk about the co-op farm I visited in Mississippi, USA, if you remember. The man who runs that farm was a missionary here for some time, and so people are very interested. I am to give my combination talk at least twice more, and tomorrow I'm to talk to a girls' school about something or other, and on next Sunday I preach the sermon (only I told them it wasn't going to be a sermon) at the Union Church here – about the co-op farm again. So I am getting to be quite a public speaker! I will leave here southward and Muriel-wards end of next week.

It is a most beautiful country as you can imagine. Everywhere you go there are twisty pine and cypress trees, grotesque in some moods, delicately odd in others. Today, mine host plus an American boy and I took bicycles up mountains into the heart of the country. We reached a little village buried in the hills ....

This article that Aylwin called "The Other Japan – a day in the country" tells of one of his encounters with the *real* Japanese:

Mine host is a city missionary in Japan and needs a weekly change of scene. I am not a missionary and have had a continuous change of scene ever since leaving England five months ago but I am glad when he suggests a day in the country for the good of our livers. So we rope in a friend because two's company and three is fun, and start off up the river from Kyoto on bicycles, armed with peanuts and peppermints. Strapped on the carrier of one of the cycles is a large package of luncheon. The day has begun.

The day *has* begun! It is now snowing and rather cold, so that our jollity as we challenge the tram to a race out of town is a little forced. But as we get away from the city, the weather lifts and the sun comes out, and after this surprising change has occurred several times we grow used to the snow when it comes, noticing only the fresh bloom of beauty each time the sun breaks through.

Before long we have struck a village; winding through its mud (but the houses look clean and many of them new) we come to the shrine called Kamigamo. We look through the graceful arch of one big *Torii* [gate] across a wide space to an identical one opposite, with outlines now blurred by the slant of softly falling snow. Dismounting from our cycles, we walk them over the intervening space. As everywhere in Japan it is the trees which attract my attention. Whether they are gnarled and grotesque, or twisted daintily, there is always something arresting about them; each one seems to have been planted individually and tended with care. From the freshly ochred Torii and the new gold paint much in evidence, this must be an Imperial shrine; our surmise proves correct when we come to the front of the shrine itself where a beautiful low bridge across a stream is railed off for the Emperor's especial use. In front of the shrine a mother is piously clapping hands and bowing. The baby on her back has an early indoctrination! At her side a little girl solemnly goes through the same motions. We watch them go off, the mother walking lithely on her high *geta* [thong-type sandals with high soles to keep the feet off the ground], and the little girl trotting beside her. I wonder if the baby must not be restricted inside the little cubby-hole made for him on his mother's back. Anyway, there can be no doubt as to his warmth, for his mother acts as a fine windbreaker, and many folds embrace him. I wonder too at the close folds of their religion, begun so early, so binding in later life.

Now comes the hard part of the day. The hills are steepish for cycling, the wind is against us and sometimes the snow gets in our eyes. The bicycle wheels sink into yielding mud. We steel ourselves a little to the effort with the thought of how nice it will be on the return journey. Now and then we put on an especially strenuous spurt, holding our breaths until we can get to the windward of a fertiliser cart, drawn by swaying oxen. The fastidious-nosed must find it difficult to lose themselves in beauty of the eye, in Japan, being constantly pulled back to reality by their noses!

After all, there's no sense in overdoing this exercise business even if we are out for our health, so stops are fairly frequent to look at the view and to whet our appetites for lunch with peanuts. The river still runs below us, though bends in the road often take us away from it; steep and wooded mountains rise on either side. Once we could look over the valley, across the river glittering in newfound sunshine, to snow-covered pine slopes topped with rolling cloud. We compare the beauty of Japan with that of our own countries. Though such scenery or at least scenery equally beautiful of a different kind, maybe found in England or America, you have to go a long way to find it there; whereas in Japan it is almost typical. This is the conclusion at which we arrive; thus, although national pride is satisfied, we really feel we must hand it to Japan on the whole!

Before reaching the village of Kumogahato (which means Field of Clouds) that we have selected for lunch, we get another glimpse of sunlit beauty. Emerging from a wood, we come suddenly upon a denuded slope rising sheer up from the road. Lying at all angles to one another, as though they had been matches scattered from above, are pine trunks, ready to be piloted downhill into the stream. Already stripped of their bark, the exposed sap has given each one a yellow jacket, so that they stand out brilliantly against the soil beneath. Behind them is a light green foliage, and behind that again the dark green of renewed forest. Down beside the river is a pair of foresters smoking long pipes in front of their open fire.

The village itself is a monument of Japanese perseverance, thrift and natural artistic sense. Fields must be levelled from the hill-side, unruly mountain waters must be checked and guided as they are needed into the irrigation channels, walls must be built to retain falling stones and earth. The houses are perched on odd ledges, or hewn out of the mountainside, and if a few feet of space are left over, a garden makes them beautiful. How would such a piece of land be used in England, America or even in Switzerland? At best it would be left to grow wild: more likely used as a dumping place for cans and junk. In Japan nothing must be wasted. At meals *en famille*, it is customary for tea or hot water to be poured into each rice bowl after meals. When the bowl is soaked clean, each swallows his own brew.

When we arrive at Kumogahato we are very thirsty after our stiff ride, and think to find a teashop in which to eat our sandwiches; but the village has none apparently. Mine host is a resourceful fellow, and moreover he has his reputation as leader of the expedition to consider. The temple yields him nothing, though he says tea and temples often go together, but at length he finds a friendly farmhouse. We jubilantly park the cycles and kick off our shoes. Entering the house, our first impression is of smoke and darkness. Gradually however our eyes get used to the gloom and we can look about us. The house is built into the side of a hill, and the hillside immediately behind the window prevents much light from entering on that side, though the purpose of ventilation is well provided for by a row of slits above the window proper. An open fire burns in the middle of the room, reminding me of many similar fireplaces I had seen in Swiss mountain chalets. Smoke escapes into the loft above through holes left in the bamboo ceiling, and the thick bamboo poles are blackened now by the smoke; there must be some sort of moisture however, for they glisten darkly in what light there is.

Only Granny, Mother and Baby are at home out of the household of eleven. It is the first of February. All the men folk have gone to the village schoolhouse to begin festivities connected with what used to be the New Year's Day, at the beginning of February, on the old Chinese calendar, now in disuse since the Meiji restoration. At home the women had marked the first day of the month by placing a vase of fresh *Sakaki* [an evergreen] boughs on the rice boiler. On each first and fifteenth day of the month it is the custom thus to invoke the God of Rice, that he may expedite the boiling. There was little other furniture in the room, but a large frame was slung over the fire, from which pots could be suspended over the flame if desired, and a few clothes hung on the wall. The floor was of straw matting, kept scrupulously clean; the walls lacquered below, and a dull blue finish above. Incongruously, an electric light hung over one corner, apparently used only in cases of emergency.

Granny is a very cheery old lady of seventy-seven. She tells us that she has recently been unable to work any longer in the fields. However, the burden of the entertaining must fall on her, for Mother is a little shy, or perhaps just preoccupied with the Third Generation. Granny performs her tasks as hostess unimpeachably; a large cauldron boils on the fire, and she has soon ladled the boiling water from it into the teapot. Mother and Baby try some of our sandwiches, though very dubiously. The Old Lady declines for gastric reasons, but regards their variety with a growing wonder, which is transformed into housewifely curiosity as their ingredients are explained to her. Not to be outdone in generosity she brings us freshly baked *Kagami Mochi* ("mirror cake" made from a paste of pounded rice and used especially for New Year's Festivities) which are roasted in the fire, and two little bowls each of sugar and pickles. No apprehensions need be entertained about the cleanliness of the roasting process, for the fireplace is kept scrupulously clean; here no-one would think of throwing any unclean matter into the hearth. We are enjoined to eat the pickles and the Mochi together, or Grandma will not answer for the consequences. I eat the whole of mine except for the uncooked lump in the centre of the cake, but the others have to resort to much surreptitious paper-handkerchief manipulation. After lunch, prolonged by innumerable cups of tea, Baby has to be put to bed. It is a very warm bed, although there is only a thin mattress between Baby and the floor, for the quilt, which covers him and covers also a small charcoal stove, protected from the covers by a wooden frame. I wonder if the blood will not be drawn from his head, which sticks out into the cold, by the heat from the stove, which is under the quilt by his feet. Maybe it is a form of baby-craft unknown to western mothers. Baby is no sooner in bed however than he has to be brought out again for my camera. I would have taken the picture without him, but Mother would have none of it. Grandma is told to keep still for the time exposure, but she looks at the camera so intently as to be oblivious to the fact that she is swaying at least two feet on her knees. When at last we prepare to go we feel that we have really been accepted as friends, and that they are sorry to lose us. She tells us we are the first foreigners ever to have been entertained at her house, and we are honoured to be so. Foreheads touch the ground as we bow to each other from the kneeling position, and nothing will do but that Grandma herself must see us off the premises and on our way, with all ceremony. Baby is the only one who does not seem particularly interested, but even he has softened to the extent of taking several bites from his sandwich. We have left behind some half-dozen sandwiches, some peppermints, and a chocolate cake, so we can imagine the men folk having a good feast off our exotic foodstuffs! Also a *Yen*, carefully and ceremoniously wrapped in a piece of paper so as not to hurt anyone's feelings.

The snow has now set in, in real earnest, so we are blinded by the driving flakes as we coast downhill towards home. It is all good fun however, and we feel that we don't much mind what happens to us after our session of warmth and companionship in the farmhouse. Indeed, excitement is not yet quite over for the day. The jolting of the downhill ride on a country road has loosened the frame of one of the bicycles. Fortunately, no disaster occurred, but it meant that one of us had to sit on the steel struts of his rear carrier so as to take the weight off the weak part, much to his criss-crossed discomfort. The people we met must have been surprised. "If these mad foreigners must go out pleasure-bicycling in the snow, why don't they at least sit on the saddle?"

Sitting comfortably at home again with the newspaper, it occurs to me that if the boycott is to be effective against the Japanese army regime, it must first hurt such simple kindly people as we have met today; *C'est la guerre? C'est la guerre* that out of that lonely mountain village of eighty-seven inhabitants, ten young men have already been taken to the army, three of them already killed.

In mid February, he wrote home:

Tomorrow I leave for Shanghai, very sorry to leave this nice country and grand people. I am glad to have seen them here first. According to Japanese papers five hundred people per day are dying of exposure in the streets of Shanghai.

February 6th used to be New Year's Day on the old Chinese calendar out of use here since 1868, and many of the old customs have remained to this day, instead of being transferred to the new New Year's Day. I went to a festival, and saw them throw the "god-boxes" onto a bonfire, to be burnt up at twelve midnight, while the people go away and buy new ones for the coming year. Also went to Nara, which is one of the ancient capitals, and filled with old temples and shrines, and stone lanterns. On this night, five thousand of these lanterns were lit, all along the winding paths covered with tree arches.

Then, the day before yesterday, we went skiing which was simply grand; only one day, unfortunately. I felt so energetic I climbed way up the mountain by myself, and then found I had forgotten how to come down properly, so it was quite frightening until the old technique came back a little. Meanwhile of course I had sat down on several rocks. I suppose you all went to plutocratic Switzerland as usual.

We stayed one night up at the skiing place with some friends of mine host. They were grand young American people. There wasn't quite room for me at their house to sleep, so they parked me off on a young couple from Wales, schoolteaching at that town. It was nice to meet people from home again. When we were alone, I asked them what they thought of Americans. "Well, they're a little overpowering sometimes". As Americans on the other hand think the English are very quiet. The trouble is that the Americans can't wait long enough for the English to get going, so they have to strike up some patter to avoid silences. It was very amusing to see how the English were sort of reposed and retired within themselves during the conversation, while the Americans were floating along on community waters. Americans all seem to have a particular idea of English people. Certainly they have met some queer examples. For instance there is a nice American couple living down at some very isolated beauty spot which tourists sometimes, but not often, get to. The Americans are the only foreigners in town. Whenever any tourists arrive it is customary for the natives to tell the American woman, who then goes to meet them and make them feel at home, gives them a guide and so on, and even has them to magnificent tea. Well, one day word came that a party of English women had arrived at the station. So of course she went down to meet them. When she got there, they were all standing about looking lost at the station, so she found the leader and said "Is there anything I can do for you?" No answer. So she repeated; this time a haughty "We're quite comfortable thank you."

During the voyage to Shanghai, Aylwin attempted to analyse the complex conflicts within Japan as he had come to see them during his seven weeks in the country by writing the following article which he called "The Japanese People and the 'China Affair'":

National regimentation of opinion takes many different forms. The propaganda of anti-propagandists has constantly warned us that in case of war our feelings will be scientifically stirred to hate against the enemy people. Japan is at present undertaking a vast modern war, she has the most rigid censorship, most successful insulation of any country in the world; yet the Japanese people neither hate nor are taught to hate the Chinese. Not only are Chinese people living in Japan well treated, but government propaganda makes a feature of this. It features also the essential goodness of the Chinese people, and the kind way in which the Japanese soldiers are supposed to be treating them. "The enemy" in Japan is represented sometimes as Russia, sometimes as Great Britain, sometimes as Jiang Jieshi in person, never as China.

Historical background is largely to blame for the extraordinary unity of the national will to win along these lines. "Morale is created by the right dogmas, symbols and emotionally potent oversimplifications"; whereas in Germany, national conformity had to be created in the people, in Japan it already existed and had only to be directed. The

Symbol of the Emperor and the *Dogma of Nationalism* were perfected, and the emotionally potent *Oversimplification* was easy to put over on a people which had none of the western tradition of *critical loyalty*; to be loyal in Japan means to believe what you are told; to believe is part of one's duty and a thing to be proud of.

The Throne without doubt is the central unifying factor. It is essentially the institution, embodying the religious awe-fullness of individual Emperors in unbroken succession since 660 BC that retains the homage of the people; the individual is sacrificed to the institution, insulated into atrophy lest he shall destroy the symbolism of his person. Paradoxically, although the people are universally and unquestioningly loyal to the Emperor, they yet know that he is not a free agent. The only group, which does not realise this fact, is the group which happens at the time to be controlling him. Historically the crown had always been controlled until with the Meiji restoration of 1868 it emerged apparently supreme over the Tokugawa Shogunate. Fire followed frying pan. The victory over the Tokugawas was only obtained with the help of the Satsuma and Choso clans of the south, who in return for their help were made the nucleus of the Imperial Forces, independent of the government and with direct access to the Throne. The result was a continuation *de facto* of the Shogunate, now cloaked with the sanctity of the Emperor's name. The question arises whether the people's complete loyalty to the Emperor might not result in a reaction against the military, which they know to be controlling him. The strength of nationalistic spirit and the conviction of the war's messianic nature seem, for the present at least, to have ruled out this possibility; it is nationally unthinkable that the Emperor should not be of like mind with his mentors.

The dogma of nationalism in Japan, though largely imported, has certain indigenous features. It is commonplace to refer present aggressive spirit back to Japan's rude awakening to western methods by the gunboat of Commodore Perry in 1853. Pertinent to this relation is the East's notorious disregard for time. The evil nature of the phenomenal world in the Buddhist metaphysics pervading Japan makes chronological history unimportant. Thus, coupled with the emphasis on power politics, which Perry gave to their slant on Western ways, is incapacity to understand any change in political method which may have been attempted in the west since that time, and particularly since 1918. Japanese nationalism was formed on the 19th century European model, coupled to the ancient *Samurai* tradition of intense personal loyalty. It received spiritual nourishment from successful wars against China (1894) and Russia (1905), both enormously superior in size, and the latter in reputation; from its own very smallness and from the American and British Exclusion Acts, which discriminated against Japan. Finally, if any doubts existed as to the wisdom of its course, they were dispelled by the growth of fascist ideology in Europe, and by the consequent hardening in the practice of the Democracies. It has never suffered the demoralisation of defeat, nor even sufficient wartime hardship at home to cause the disillusionment increasingly common in the west.

The conscription of idealism by *emotionally potent overstatement* was under these circumstances made simple. The war is represented as a campaign to save China, and hence contiguously Japan as well as ultimately the rest of Asia, from Communism, from Western domination, and from a clique of unscrupulous oppressors of the people centred around Jiang Jieshi, which intrigues for its own gain with either or both of these powers. Communism is a tremendous bugbear; the sacrilegious of its menace to the Emperor's safety is especially stressed. The second potent cry was directed exclusively against British and Russian interests in the east; America could do nothing wrong, at least until the naval co-ordination between Britain and the United States was revealed at the Singapore defence manoeuvre in January 1938. Finally, the conception of a powerful Jiang – Soong – Sun Yat-sen family connection embroiling an impoverished and divided population in war is readily acceptable to a people which, except for the small Christian minority of one in two hundred and fifty and an even smaller group of intellectuals, know nothing of the new China. The poor and ignorant Chinese people are supposed to be the dupes of propaganda against these would-be friends, and they must thus, this quite seriously, be forced into a *cooperative attitude*. Naturally the Japanese are told nothing of the horrors perpetrated in China; nor can they be expected to guess at them with no jumping-off place in their own past experience.

The extraordinarily general belief in the divine mission of Japan may thus be ascribed to historical background both ancient internal and modern European, to its perfect insulation, and finally to an exclusively subjective psychology which prevents them from the imaginative wearing of other people's shoes. Moreover fear, for family or for institution, has successfully prevented much open opposition even on the part of those who are aware of falsity. The furtherance of an ideal, as apart from leader, family or nation, by an example of self-sacrifice is foreign to Japanese mentality. The martyrdom of the Japanese Christians, which began at the end of the 16th century and lasted until 1637 lacked nothing in nobility, yet it was completely successful in wiping out Japanese Christianity. In the present crisis, compromise has been the almost universal reaction of the Christians in their various stages of disillusionment, afraid of nationalisation if not of liquidation. Yet in almost none of the churches has compromise gone so far as to pray for victory, as was done from 1914–1918 in churches all over the West.

Perhaps an over-gloomy picture has been painted. Under conditions of national unity unequalled anywhere in the world, there is a growing discontent and a fear that however righteous the war may be, Japan has bitten off more than she can chew. Cost of living has risen thirty percent since the opening of hostilities, and is likely to rise much further. The past three years have been times of unrest. Changing opinions, the clash between groups manifested in the February 26th 1937 incident, the conflict between *Westomania* and *Westophobia*, the difficulty of preserving the good of Japanese culture without also excluding much that is good in Western culture, have all contributed to a vague but general discontent. Yet in company with this discontent is the conviction not only that Japan's cause is a right one, but that her position of heroic sacrifice was forced on her through no fault of her own, and that her conduct of the war has been befitting a nation of high principles. Until these convictions are destroyed there is no conflict between discontent and loyalty, but rather the one supplements the other. Returning soldiers would destroy them; the inference is that the soldiers will not be allowed to return. Extreme economic distress or the continued non-fulfilment of promise, for example *that the fall of Nanjing will bring the end of the war*, might have the same effect. Possibly the boycott may ultimately help create a reasoning discontentment in the place of an unreasoning loyalty, though at present the reverse seems to be the case. Whatever the cause, disillusionment when it comes will have a devastating effect on virgin political consciousness.

It is perhaps appropriate to introduce at this point some background history of the internal upheavals within China and of the conflict between China and Japan.

Warlords, each controlling large sectors of the country, jostled for power following the fall of the Qing Dynasty in 1911, which was brought about by a popular revolution. A republic was inaugurated in 1912 by Dr Sun Yat-sen, and under his leadership the Nationalist Party (Kuomintang) based in Guangzhou (Canton) made progress, slow as it was, in achieving some hope for a united China. Sun Yat-sen soon yielded the presidency to General Yuan, who ruled until 1916, after which the country fell into administrative chaos. Anti-Japanese agitation in 1919, following Japan's aggression against China during the First World War, developed into a movement for complete political change. It was out of this movement that the Communist Party was formed in 1921 with Mao Zedong as one of its founder members. They formed a close alliance with the Nationalists and in fact were an integral part of the Kuomintang with Dr Sun Yat-sen as acknowledged leader.

Following Dr Sun's untimely death in 1925, his military commander-in-chief, General Jiang Jieshi, emerged as the leader of the Kuomintang Party, but the Kuomintang and the Communist factions each claimed to be the true disciples of Dr Sun Yat-sen's ideals. The Three People's Principles – nationalism, democracy, and the people's livelihood – were accepted by all. The Communists were gaining increasing support. The famous triad of the families, Sun, Soong, and Jiang, was put asunder. Soong Ching Ling, the widow of Sun Yat-sen, was in support of the Communist faction while her sister, Soong Mei Ling, the wife of Jiang Jieshi, remained solidly behind her husband. In 1926, the Kuomintang and the Communists appeared to join forces in order to overthrow the Beijing government, but in 1927 Jiang Jieshi turned his army against the Communists in Shanghai and many other places, massacring thousands in a few days, and he executed several of the Communist leaders. The Communists themselves were split into two main groups, one of which was indisputably led by Mao Zedong. This group devoted its energies to revolution in the countryside, setting up a Soviet-style government in the provinces of Hunan and Jiangxi. Here they redistributed the land among the peasants and built up a self-sufficient base with their own Red Army.

At the same time, a powerful warlord, General Feng Yuxiang, who was known as the Christian General for his kind nature, came down on the side of Jiang Jieshi. Together they planned to take Beijing, which was under the control of the former Manchurian Bandit, Zhang Xuolin. The so-called Northern Expedition defeated Zhang's army at Shijiazhuang, in Hebei

Province. Zhang's army retreated northward to Dingxian where they stood again against the Northern Expedition. Zhang was finally driven out, but at great expense to the surrounding countryside.

Beijing was at last taken, and so by early 1929 most of China was united, ending a thirteen-year period of anarchy. Nanjing was declared the new capital, and Beijing (then known as Peking) was renamed Peiping, meaning "Northern Peace". Jiang Jieshi was declared president of the Republic, with Feng Yuxiang as vice-president of the Executive Yuan (cabinet). Peaceful unity was, however, short lived. Warlords whose armies had not been disbanded engaged in a succession of clashes across the country creating the instability ideal for the Japanese grand plan. Jiang Jieshi next turned his attention to the Communists, and from 1930 to 1934 he conducted as many as five military campaigns to put them down. By 1934 they were almost crushed, but at this desperate point some one hundred thousand, led by Mao, burst out from encirclement and embarked on the Long March, a long circuitous route through many provinces towards the northwest. They were mercilessly pounded and harassed by Jiang's forces, but a year later less than one-tenth of their original number reached the safety of mountainous Shaanxi Province where they built their new base, in Yan'an. Their epic journey gripped the imagination of the people throughout China, and they soon made their presence known throughout the provinces of Shaanxi and Shanxi.

In the minds of the Japanese militarists, it was necessary to conquer China as a first step to conquering the world, but in order to conquer China, they first had to take Manchuria, China's northeastern provinces. Much of China's internal conflict was most probably engineered by Japan, but certainly they took advantage of the situation in 1931 by creating an incident in Manchuria to justify their intervention by force, ostensibly to protect their interests in the Manchurian railway system. The Japanese had earlier blocked a number of Russian incursions into Manchuria and were moving in to gain control of the region's plentiful coal and iron, which Japan sorely lacked. This became known as the Mukden Incident. A small explosion was arranged on the railway track at Shenyang, at that time called Mukden, which was blamed on Chinese troops. The Japanese Kwantung Army, originally sent to the Kwantung Peninsular to the south of Shenyang to protect Japanese rail and shipping interests, was moved in to gain control of the coal and iron supplies. Soon they had overrun almost the whole of Manchuria. China and the League of Nations, to whom she appealed, were powerless to stop the takeover. Despite calls for sanctions against Japan, outgoing American President Herbert Hoover had no enthusiasm for a crisis, and the incoming President Roosevelt was occupied with the onrushing Great Depression.

Following the murder of the Chinese Manchurian warlord allied to Jiang Jieshi, by ultranationalist Japanese officers, Tokyo installed a puppet regime in March 1932 and declared the independence of a new state they called Manchukuo. They named as chief executive the last emperor of the Qing Dynasty, Pu Yi. They now had control of virtually all of China north of the Great Wall. Manchukuo was recognised by only Japan, Italy, Germany, and the Vatican.

Another event of momentous significance took place and became known as the Xi'an Incident. Clearly, Jiang's preoccupation with the Communists was undermining national unity in the face of Japanese aggression, and it was plain that the Japanese were taking advantage of the split. Many of Jiang's subordinates were intensely frustrated when they were ordered to refrain from attacking the Japanese and to turn instead against the Communists. Some refused to fight, and even high-ranking officers negotiated an unofficial truce with the Communists. The demand for an end to civil war and for unity in defence of the nation was beginning to sweep the country.

Becoming alarmed, Jiang Jieshi went to Xi'an where he had established a headquarters for the campaign against the Communists. In a move that electrified the nation, in December 1936, he was kidnapped by a group of his own officers and forced to face the facts. The Communists intervened as mediators, offering to accept Jiang as leader of the nation if he dropped his campaigns against them and turned resolutely against the Japanese. Manchuria had long been under complete control of the Japanese, but now even in many areas south of the Great Wall, their army was able to move about at will. On the night of 7 July 1937, they held a field exercise outside Beijing near Lugouqiao, the famous Marco Polo Bridge. A Japanese soldier apparently wandered off to relieve himself. His comrades later claimed that they thought he had been kidnapped. On this pretext, they clashed with Chinese troops and then bombarded the nearby city of Wanping. It was undeclared war, and Japanese reinforcements rushed in from Manchuria. The Japanese were poised to attack Beijing, but the Chinese army evacuated it in order to save the historic city from destruction.

China appealed once again to the League of Nations, which met to consider the call for international sanctions against Japan, or at least explicit condemnation of such unprovoked aggression. In countless sessions, all resolutions for collective international measures against Japan were voted down with, in most cases, only New Zealand and the Soviet Union in support. Times were hard in the United States, and American ships continued to supply Japan with oil and steel. Business was business.

During July 1937, the Japanese amassed eight divisions and hundreds of aircraft in the vicinity of Beijing. The Chinese Twenty-Ninth Army withdrew to the Nanyuan (south barracks) and was ordered to resist if attacked. On 27 July, squadrons of aircraft attacked and bombed them continuously for twenty-four hours supported by heavy artillery. The Chinese forces were peasant infantrymen without air or tank support and almost wholly lacking artillery, and they had no training or experience in mechanical warfare. They fought heroically, but were slaughtered in their thousands. The next day it was all over; the area was a wasteland of dead and dying soldiers, mules, and horses. There was nobody to care for the wounded, for the Chinese army had no such organisation. Sometime later, several Beijing hospitals sent out work parties to the ruins of Nanyuan to rescue as many as they could. There was much panic in the region south of Beijing as the North China Plain was now wide open to any advance the Japanese might care to make, and this was the obvious direction for them to attack. However the aggressors first moved by sea, opening up a new front around Shanghai; they also drove westward towards Suiyuan. But the big drive southward was not delayed for long. While the eyes of the world were on Shanghai, which was being bombed mercilessly, the Japanese advanced southward along the Beijing-Hankou railway. The Chinese made another stand along a line north of Baoding.

Once again, peasant armies resisted desperately but were no match for the highly trained and superbly equipped enemy. Towards the end of 1937, the Japanese forces, under the command of General Iwane Matsui, took Nanjing. During the next few months, appalling atrocities took place there noted in the history books as the Rape of Nanjing. Some historians say that three hundred thousand people were killed in two months, and thousands of women were reported to have been raped. Others placed the fatalities at anywhere between tens of thousands to two hundred thousand. Still America continued to supply oil and steel to Japan.

Chapter 5

Shanghai and Hankou

On joining his aunt in Shanghai towards the end of February 1938, Aylwin saw the appalling conditions for himself. The Japanese military, so unlike the people he had just left, had burned down the surrounding villages and bayoneted the farmers so that the city was full of hungry and homeless folk who had to watch each other become thinner and colder until they died, unless they would submit to the invader and help him collect scrap iron to be made into bombs for killing other Chinese folk inland. The Japanese flag was flying everywhere. This was China's main industrial metropolis, now in tattered ruins, the people living in the streets glad of a newspaper to help keep the frost off their bodies at night. From their house in the International Settlement, Muriel and Aylwin could see the uninhabited area on the other side of the river that had, till recently, been an especially cheerful city. On three previous visits, Muriel had seen the happy, bustling, crowded network of narrow streets lined with little houses where tradesmen, craftsmen, and their families lived, each a hive of good-tempered industry. Now it was desolation. Crowds of workmen would stand on the Settlement side of the bridge, staring across at what used to be their homes. No house could be seen with four walls and a roof. None was inhabited except by the dead soldiers and packs of dogs – like wolves, over-nourished and bold with their unusual human diet. On one occasion, finding an area where the dogs had not yet reached, they found the streets strewn with dead Chinese soldiers, lying as they had fallen, arms flung out, hands relaxed, and peaceful expressions on their faces. Strewn around were pieces of shrapnel – pieces of British and American scrap, sold at three times its normal price by people who, at home, showed moral indignation against the actions of the Japanese.

Japanese sentries with fixed bayonets would allow those to pass who had a stamped card, and who took off their hats to bow low before them. Thousands of Chinese civilians were crowded into refugee camps. In one camp they visited, they found 122 families in one room. A Chinese family more often than not consists of three generations. Their worldly possessions were with them, mostly just bedding. Every inch of the floor was occupied. Only rice was provided in many camps – a quick route to malnutrition and death.

It wasn't only the civilians who were starving. Muriel and Aylwin visited hospitals full of Chinese soldiers, all dying of hunger as well as from their wounds.

The alien soldiers in Shanghai were reminiscent of the Black and Tans in Northern Ireland. They were lonely, knew themselves to be hated, and wanted to go home. How glad they were if they were greeted with a "good morning" in their own language, or after they answered a question, one were to say "thank you" in Japanese. They were bewildered too. They would enquire of pressmen, "Is there any news? Shall we be going home soon?"

As for the policy of starvation of the populace, how could one in all conscience stand back in horror and indignation? After all, the British Army had prepared the way for such happenings: during the Boer War, British policy had dictated that the homes of the Boer farmers should be destroyed and their families put into concentration camps where death claimed a high percentage.

Aylwin decided to stay on in China for a while to get to know the people and their problems. He had, after all, promised his friends in Japan to return with the truth of what was happening in China. With only a few pounds left, he made his way by a devious route to the Kuomintang wartime capital of Hankou from where he would get to see China from the inside.

His next letter home was written aboard the *Suwa Maru* on 9 March 1938, as he was bound for Hong Kong:

> I left Shanghai yesterday, rather gladly. It is quite exhilarating in a way, being packed with seething humanity – refugee children who will follow you a mile for a third of one cent repeating "no papa, no mamma, no whisky soda" until you buy them off – street stalls selling anything from fountain pens to fried eels – beggars lying full length on the pavement exposing sores and whining – women with groups of children all crying artificially, but with real tears and crowds of jostling laughing people. I met some nice people but was really rather bored after the first week.
>
> I am sorry that we, Aunt and I, now travel on alone – she is a good egg! There was nothing much for me to do in Shanghai – the artificial limbs Aunt wrote about are being made elsewhere; the place is packed with refugee missionaries who are only too willing and anxious to do anything that there is to be done. Aunt gave me a cheque for £10 from you. She isn't quite sure what it's all about apparently after receiving your last letter. She understood it was for me to be able to stay in China and do work for which nobody is able to pay me, there being many hands but no money; if this is the case, good. Thank you *very* much, and I will write and tell you what I do with it. If not, it had better be part of the loan you are going to make me.
>
> On this boat going to Hong Kong, I am travelling third class – it's a Japanese boat – very bad principle but no other boat of reasonable price going for some time. In my cabin are two Indians, a German, a Scotsman, and a Japanese. It is rather fun, a great big clean cabin – except that the first thing they do in the morning is to light cigarettes!
>
> I haven't given up on the idea of going to India by land yet. They are building a new road from China into Burma and another into French Indo-China I think. This is becoming the front door to China, now that the Japanese have closed the coastline. When the Japanese finally make fast in North China and along the coast they may find they haven't got much after all, as all the trade will go out by the back door, or should I say new front door. But if I find something useful to do in China, I'll stay here for a bit, as it probably is one of the most interesting places in the world just now.

Haven't had any more mail yet except one nice letter from Daddy the other day, for which many thanks – written just after your return from Crans.

Good show about the Marmite! Did "the Arab" help you over that? I had a letter from the Nelson family the other day. Half a ton should cure quite a lot of people I should think! Did you interview the Lord Mayor?

Chinese meals are absolutely enormous! Dish after dish comes in, and the idea is only to take a very little of each. This has great effect in preventing indigestion, but is rather unsatisfactory otherwise – I prefer a good tuck in on a few things. Dr Lacy, the nice fellow who picked me up in Texas, gave us a Chinese banquet the other day.

Newly arrived in Hankou, Aylwin wrote home on 20 March 1938, on a business letterhead belonging to Van Reekum Bros. Ltd of Amsterdam. It read:

I'm a businessman now, and this is my firm! I came up here from Hong Kong after staying there for a bit. It is really the most interesting place in the world now I should think. I have been staying in the house of an American, Bishop Logan Roots of the American Episcopal Mission, who Aunt Muriel knew vaguely and with whom some other friends of ours had close connections. He is a very good fellow. In his house live two young missionaries, one lady journalist, a Pole, and an American woman authoress [Agnes Smedley] who at one time rode all over the place with the Eighth Route [Red] Army, and Frances, the Bishop's daughter aged about twenty-four, who is a good sport and recently led an expedition up to the communist China country. She and all the people who went with her say it is the most marvellous place, and the communist spirit at its best there under hardship and the binding force of a common enemy. You need not be afraid I am becoming bellicose. If ever I was a pacifist it is now coming to China and hearing bellicose statements from missionaries and others, quite justified in a way by the genuine appallingness of the Japanese atrocities (not propaganda as during the war, and apparently not reciprocated) after being in Japan and seeing how nice the people there really are.

Last night we had a party in the bishop's house. He is a very sporting bishop. We sang, and a fellow played jazz on a cornet, and the daughter accompanied marvellously. We found there was a pretty good quartet, and we are going round to the hospitals of wounded soldiers and play for them, sing I mean.

I have found a place to live permanently now. It will be grand to have a real base after having hardly unpacked my bags since leaving England and always going on from one place to the other. It is on a missionary compound belonging to the Lutheran Mission in a house with a couple of youngish fellows; very nice indeed – a tennis-court, and nicely out of the city. I shall buy a bicycle, and it will take about ten minutes. I shall also I think manage to get a job for an hour or two a day teaching English to some people at the Russian Embassy. It will be interesting to get those contacts, and will give me more than enough to take Chinese lessons myself. My job just about covers my living expenses at the house. Oh, I forgot I hadn't told you about the job. I got talking to a young Chinese fellow in the train coming up. He was all alone in a first-class carriage, so you see the advantages to be immediately secured by getting to know him! It was much nicer than my third class bunk, very hard and not room to sit up. Well, I found that he was going to Hankou to sell paper for his firm from Shanghai, and it came out he wanted a secretary, not really because he would have very much secretarial work, but to impress prospective clients with the firm's opulence. So I got the job. He lives in a good hotel and I come round every morning at nine, and stay till twelve. In the afternoon I can come back if I like and sit there to be on hand for visitors and read or do my own stuff, study, write or whatnot. It is very good experience in practical business, and training for the absent mind.

I can go round to the bishop's house whenever I like and meet all the interesting people that are always coming around to see him. He is quite a close adviser of General Jiang Jieshi.

And I have time to study the language so I can go travelling without getting arrested all the time. I was arrested on arrival here, and in Formosa; not properly arrested but required to follow someone to the police station to be examined!

I tried to get a job teaching at the university here, but no good because it is halfway through the term already. But they think they'd like someone maybe next term to teach philosophy, or maybe economics, which would be an admirable opportunity.

Just now things look pretty hopeful for China, and it's Japan that will suffer most in the end. This is saying something too. The bishop says there are fifty million people wandering about, homeless in China. There are some people working out schemes for them, agricultural and others, notably Pearl Buck's husband John who came to dinner with us the other night. Today at lunch there is to be a man commonly known as "the Christian General". The story goes that in times past he baptised his army with a hosepipe!

The newspapers here are terribly provincial, which is to say they are concerned only with Chinese happenings. I wonder if you couldn't like to take the *New Statesman* or the *Guardian Weekly* and send it on to me. I'm afraid when you write you will have to send it via Hong Kong and airmail in China, as the trains from here to Hong Kong are quite uncertain, and the mail might never get through at all. The newspapers of course may be sent ordinary mail, and hope for the best.

We are to have a truck from the Red Army to take us round singing at the hospitals on Saturday!

Bishop Roots became a strong supporter of the Eighth Route Army in the United Front era of 1937–38, and it was at his house that Aylwin got to know such people as the American journalists Edgar Snow and Helen Foster Snow (Peg Snow), Agnes Smedley, John Foster, Evans Carlson, and Rewi Alley. He began to learn a lot about China, and to see that the northwest was the cradle of Chinese Civilisation, not just in past millennia but perhaps also in the present day. As he wrote in the preface to his book, *I See a New China*:

It is known as an historic scene of racial and political struggle; as a vast economic hinterland only recently being opened up as Japan drives Chinese initiative out of the coastal cities; as a military base of vital strategic importance, in which guerrillas and young students are teaching the people to live new lives of resistance, as a place where modern social influences are trying to establish themselves under conditions much the same as existed for tens of centuries before China ever admitted Western civilisation. For all these reasons, the Northwest is an ideal place from which to watch New China taking shape. Here the nation's stirrings are at its lustiest. Here is seen at its best the Chinese people's amazing adaptability.

Aylwin's imagination was caught by the enthusiasm of those who had visited Red China, so, with the help of the Eighth Route Army headquarters in Xi'an, and of Agnes Smedley in Hankou, arrangements were put in hand to travel to the northwest border region, the stronghold of guerrilla resistance, and Yan'an in particular: Yan'an, Mao Zedong's mountain headquarters since the end of the Long March in October 1935. In May 1938, Aylwin wrote home from Hankou:

> The sponsor of the trip will be Agnes Smedley whom I have heretofore mentioned I fancy. She is tall and rather grim and Eton-cropped, about forty, an ardent supporter of the communists of the Chinese not Russian variety, formally dogged all over the place by the "White Terror". She was in Xi'an at the time of the kidnapping of Generalissimo Jiang Jieshi, thought it was a fascist plot, and spent the whole day burning her precious papers in the hotel room, only to find that it was her own friends who were carrying out the coup! She is a real revolutionary. It is surprising how much revolutionaries, whether Christian or other, have in common. She has given away every penny more or less to her pet projects, has collected thousands of dollars for them, but made no provision for herself. She is regarded as a communist by the foreigners, so they won't have much to do with her. She cannot have Red Army status because they don't accept any foreigner's except doctors. Because she is known to be connected with them, however, she cannot even get a job in the Russian Embassy, who is afraid of getting in bad odour with other consular and ambassadorial staffs. Her new passport, which she got after great trouble from the American officials, was stolen on delivery by Chinese fascist agents who have official recognition from the Chinese government; if the Japanese come, they will undoubtedly kill her, through gangsters if not able to get at her any other way. She can't get out over land without a passport, and hasn't money to get to America. The British won't let her into India because she fought with the Indian Nationalists during the war. But maybe it isn't as bad as it sounds, and someone is bound, maybe, to help her when the time comes.

Some indication of how his ideas were beginning to form also appeared in those same letters home:

I don't know about the next term job yet. I can't make up my mind. You see, if something turns up to do with relief work, or a chance of teaching up in the northwest, I should like that better. The trouble is that I should probably decide about the whole thing before leaving here.

Three weeks later he wrote:

I've got a job at the university for next year, not much salary, but enough to pay living expenses. I'm looking forward to it very much, beginning in September. Before then I have to work up three courses on English history, Western history, and economic history, periods unspecified.

The war also took an interesting turn about that time:

I expect you were thrilled about the nature of China's first air raid over Japan proper the other day, leaflets instead of bombs. It was pretty good, I think. The Japanese people are undoubtedly becoming a bit suspicious of their government, and it will serve to disillusion them about the lack of truth about the brutality and lack of principles of the Jiang Jieshi clique, controlled by England and Russia hand in hand, which they are told is carrying on the war against the heroic Japanese troops who are helping the Chinese people revolt.

By the beginning of June, it was nearly time to leave on the trip north to Yan'an.

Things don't look as good as when I wrote a few days ago .... The road from Xi'an to Chengdu and from here to Chongqing is bound to be open; that is to say not under Japanese occupation, so no anxiety need be felt whatever you read in the newspapers. I hate to get out of here in a way, and leave my friends to take things like what happened in Nanjing [Rape of Nanjing] last year, but I do want to see what's happening up in the former Red Army, and if I don't go soon there may be no way of getting up there. Also, I have no set place here as my job at the university is only in case the Japanese do *not* come. Of course everything may turn out all right, and I'll come back here and teach as prearranged, but I somehow don't think so. The newspapers here still keep up a perfectly normal attitude .... There are quite a lot of League of Friends and Red Cross doctors up where I am going, so I might get something to do helping them, or in connection with one of the refugee schemes. I get all the way from here to Xi'an, about two days by train, for sixteen shillings!

Aylwin and Stephen with
Mother in the garden at
Red Gables, Harpenden

Aylwin and Stephen
having tea in the
garden with Father
at Red Gables

The young
George Aylwin Hogg
as a student

Hitchhiking in Hungary,
summer vacation 1936

A visit to the country with friends in
Kumogahato, Japan in February 1938

George Aylwin Hogg with Agnes Smedley
and friends in Hankou in 1938

Chapter 6

Journey to Yan'an

It took four days on an evacuation train, instead of the promised two, to reach the massive-walled, ancient, one-time capital of China. The Kuomintang had decided to move their capital from Hankou to Chongqing, and to make a stronghold of Xi'an. The following article by Aylwin appeared in the *Manchester Guardian*:

Local gossip had it that the Chinese Government was beginning to evacuate Hankou; that the Japanese would approach the city from all sides; that indiscriminate bombing would soon begin; that poison gas would be used on the city; that the dikes would be cut for defence purposes regardless of the low-lying Chinese dwellings; and a hundred other things. Anyhow, for those who wished to make the Northwest their new home it was time to get moving; rumour had it that Zhengzhou had already fallen. Time for bundle and basket, string and strap; time to sell what you had, take up baby and bedroll; time to go.

Tired refugee eyes looked out from the train as it rolled slowly over the flat plains. "Not much to stop the Japanese here," they seemed to be thinking. More people pile in at every station until there seems to be not an inch of space left uncovered. The floor is already quite taken up with people sitting on their luggage. Late at night a smiling face appears at our window, then a man's whole body, then case after case, roll after bale after box, each new imposition on us being made with a nervous laugh and *Bu yao jin, bu yao jin* (It doesn't matter, not at all). As though he were the one to decide what mattered and what did not! For a time I refused to cooperate having been bred to the belief that you should stick to your rights for a seat if you have paid for a ticket. But after a time I thought that maybe this doesn't apply to China in wartime, and by the time he had begun to bring his whole family through the window, from toothless mother-in-law to squawking baby, I was helping to stow away his belongings with a certain zest. He was pulling in an old lady by the hands as a final instalment. One tiny "golden lily" [bound] foot feebly pawed the air in the attempt to find a purchase. I could with decorum grasp this tiny thing in my two hands and guide it gently on to the seat. An ample reward for discomfort to have handled this lady's most treasured most useless, possession!

At half past four next morning the train pulled into Zhengzhou. All was scurry and bustle. But it was not the prosperous activity of a big station, which stands and watches the coming and going of busy people. The station itself seemed to have an air of hurrying desertion. The office buildings were gaunt and unoccupied; there was no one to carry and no one to bother with tickets. Groups of soldiers lying tired or wounded on the platform provided the only static element.

A crowd of dark figures was disappearing over the rails, and I must lose no time in following them. A diminutive boy appeared, to carry my bags and assure me that the train for Xi'an was waiting up the line. Sure enough, ten minutes' walk brought us to a long train whose two locomotives were steaming impatiently. All around the train moved a milling throng. Like ants over the body of a dead snake, they swarmed over it, through it, under it; like ants they staggered under burdens twice their size. Camps were formed on top of each coach; food supplies and weaker members were raised and lowered with baskets and rope. The whole train resembled a crocodile of wagonettes making their way off on an old-time Sunday school treat. Umbrellas of oiled green and brown added to the picture. Beneath, muddled up with the springs and supports, dynamo and steam brakes, many a soldier had strapped himself and his rifle; a false move or a bad knot would mean a fall between the wheels onto the rails below. Taking a leaf from the book of my last night's visitant, I selected a window through which willy-nilly to bundle my stuff and myself. Soldiers occupied most of the seats, and stretched their bulk along the wide luggage racks lining each side. Refugees and their belongings took most of the floor, but I was able to squeeze a place for my bags and to climb atop them.

At one station a groomed and silk-gowned scholar entered the train. There was still sufficient prestige attached to his class for him to obtain a seat, but it was unwillingly given, and he must fawn and smile his sweetest to ingratiate himself with the dispossessed soldier and his mates. Time was when the scholars were the most highly respected class in China and the soldiers had no class at all. Things have changed since then.

A thin-faced soldier sitting next to me begs among us for food scraps. Calling under the seat, he produces first a little brown dog that eats what he is given and disappears again with wag-tailed thanks. Then reaching up to the luggage rack he brings down a covered basket and draws out a singing bird, which sits chirping on his hand for its morning crumbs. The bird is put back, and the pet-keeper himself, apparently, turns soldier again.

A second night passes in fitful sleep. There was a driving rain, and the crush was increased by those people from the top of the train who would force their way inside. A bowl of water at a country station and the crisp dawn air soon removed dust from within and without. At Luoyang, reached by mid-morning, half-penny bowls of rice and egg soup cooked individually on a brazier while you wait, ripe peaches at twelve a penny, hard-boiled eggs, tea and bread of dubious cleanliness could be purchased from picturesque characters along the platform. Here there was an air-raid warning. As we leapt from the windows three planes were already circling over the city and the anti-aircraft shells bursting around them. Rough trenches had been prepared beside the line, into which those who could get off the train in time flung themselves. The campers on top were mostly left to the mercy of machine-gunners from the air. I was glad enough to be at the bottom of a pile of others. Bombs exploded on the station as we lay face downwards, breathing deeply the scent of the damp earth. Then we could hear the drone approaching us until it was low overhead. Would they attempt to bomb the train and the line? Would the quantity of soldiers on the train tempt them to sweep it with machine-gun fire? Timeless seconds of apprehension passed before we were cautiously turning our heads to watch them fly away. Back at the station we found the line quite unharmed. But some distance away a column of smoke spelt homelessness, death and a numb hate for these inaccessible and all-powerful visitants from the sky.

The train now travelled swiftly westward out of the area threatened by the Japanese. The countryside took on the aspect of the Pyrenean foothills in Catalonia. Hills and houses were of a dusty brown; arid terraced fields yielded sparse crops of wheat, potatoes and turnips. Donkeys and mules appeared in place of water buffalo and oxen, light green and brown for the luscious rich green of the rice in the river beds, geometrical shapes of mountains in purple, green and brown for the uniformity of the plains.

News on arrival told them that Zhengzhou, through which they had passed, was now surrounded and that trains were no longer running past Luoyang. The following is from another article Aylwin wrote for the *Manchester Guardian*, describing his journey to Yan'an:

There was plenty of material for romance among the occupants of the lorry which was to take us nine hundred miles northward, from Xi'an to the capital of Communist China. Sprawling over the piled goods and baggage inside were a honeymoon couple, the bridegroom's sister, two runaway young girls, a migrant student, a group of Red Cross war nurses, and other interesting but less definable persons. The pair of runaways – one stocky like a boy, the other slight and delicately formed – had run before the advancing Japanese and was now on their way to join Yan'an's army of students. They were inseparables: their eyes shone with youthful idealism, and they were fired with a passionate desire to help their country – but they fell short of glamour in their baggy green uniforms. I was later to see the Red Cross nurses at work in Yan'an. Conditions were primitive, and there were none of the city diversions to which they had been used. They too must have been fired, less obviously, with patriotism.

We passed over a plain studded with the giant mounds of ancient mausoleums, over rivers red with the rains. Later, as we reached the mountain country, each climb was a gamble as the lorry slowed from a roar to a grind and from a grind to an angry growl, with the block-bearer crouching anxiously behind the rear wheel. Deep-cut valleys and crenellated skyline, geometrical fields in light greens and rusty red, terraces rising in regular proportion to plateaux in relief, gave the whole scene an air of detached symmetry which is common to all loess country.

By the afternoon of the third day the tyres and the driver had quite given up. The fifty-mile walk to Yan'an was enforced but it provided a fine opportunity to see country life at close quarters. I could sit outside a little roadside inn, built of mud and straw with a mat-roofed porch, and wonder at the strange, gaunt people, whose main crop was hemp, whose bare babies played in the dust, and whose unvarying diet was a kind of noodle. I could leave the road to inspect more closely the ancient deserted temples, with their stilted plaster figures ranged in robes as though for a court scene. Once I climbed a hill to a beautiful temple, which seemed at first to be deserted but in which lived two old men, aged sixty-five and seventy-two, as guardians. "Eighth Route Army, good not good?" I asked in Chinese. Their affirmative answer was made unnecessary by broad and toothless grins.

The road itself was by no means empty. Military trucks passed in both directions. There were convoys of mules carrying locally produced matches to be sold in Xi'an. Processions of screeching wheelbarrows pushed their dusty way with flour supplies for Yan'an. Sometimes a gentlewoman and her baby, seated comfortably on a donkey's packsaddle, would pass on their way to visit some relation. Migrating students and volunteers for the Eighth Route Army were hiking, penniless, often equipped with little more than toothbrush, tin mug and towel, to Yan'an.

At five o'clock one evening we descended suddenly into the city's extra-mural activities. The scene was strongly reminiscent of a London park on Saturday evening. Basketball and football were being keenly played on the wide parade ground; the whistles of the referees cheeped officiously, and a happy crowd was looking on. Anxious amateurs were riding ponies, in turn, up and down beside the road. Booths selling tea and noodles added to the holiday spirit, their proprietors would take nothing for my tea; they called me *Peng you* (friend) and very soon I graduated to the *Tong zhi* (comrade) class.

Next morning, from conversations with my interpreter and with local government officials in Yan'an's encaved *Whitehall*, I began to understand something of the changes in *Red China* since cooperation with the Central Government began. The laws of the *special area* are the same as those of the rest of China, though, claims local pride, *a little better enforced*. The system of government is also the same, though *a little more democratic*. Local economy has no longer to strive for self-sufficiency, and local industries have consequently lapsed in the face of cheap *imports*. To offset all this there is quite evidently a great pride in the national unity of resistance to Japan. *Whitehalls* are apt to be dull, but this one, and the conversation it produced, was a complete exception. In its subterranean cool I sipped tea and looked, in the intervals of translation, across the valley to cave-ridden mountains on the other side of the river.

There are as many students in Oxford as in Yan'an, four thousand men and a thousand women, comprising the Anti-Japanese Academy, the North Shaanxi University and the Yan'an Art Institute centre in Yan'an, while they have many thousands more students in decentralised units throughout the area. The students live for the most part in caves which they or their predecessors have hewn from the soft mountain-sides; they are provided with two uniforms yearly, two meals of millet daily, and an allowance of seven cents (¾d.) weekly to pay for cooking fuel, salt, vegetables and other alleviations. Their hardy life is shared by instructors and by Government officials and Army leaders themselves. Their morale is high and affects the whole city with a spirit of fine, self-confident gaiety.

Letters home revealed more about his Yan'an experience. On 24 June 1938 he wrote:

Here I am in the heart of Red China. It isn't very *red* just now because everything is subjected to the one end of anti-Japanism, of which movement it is undoubtedly the dynamic centre of the whole country.

Since the war there have been no soviet assemblies, though some of the officials have been elected; the trades unions are not engaged in class war because there is a united front of the classes against Japan; instead they conciliate between employer and employees on occasion, but direct most attention to political and military affairs, training people in the objectives and antecedents of the war. The former Red Academy is now called the Anti-Japanese Academy; a certain brand of very cheap cigarettes, locally made, is called Anti-Japanese cigarettes; art and drama have the same motif.

The war is expected to last ten to twenty years, and there is not much planning for the postwar period. In spite of all the anti-Japanese feelings, it is apparently not forgotten that it is Japan and not the Japanese people – the system and not the individuals – that is wrong. It is the aim of the government that everyone in the area shall be able to speak a few words of the Japanese language so that, when Japanese soldiers are in a position to surrender, they can explain they will be well treated, and that they are friends. Schools to this effect are already established. There are six Japanese prisoners in town; they live in quarters on their own, and are free to walk around the city quite unguarded. They are educated people and are allowed to read. They are not very happy, but they scarcely would be under the circumstances, would they?

The town of Yan'an is situated in the valley and up its sides, three hundred miles north of Xi'an. It took us six days to get here in a Red Cross lorry. The tyres were bad and finally, after many bursts and punctures, we had to walk about fifty miles of the way. Marvellous loess country terraced and cut into amazing geometrical figures by the water on its soft make-up. This loess is believed to be composed of the dust blown from the Mongolian deserts. People have lived for thousands of years in caves cut out of this soft, half-mud-half-rock substance, and still do. In Yan'an itself the government offices, trade union headquarters, hospital, university, and many other important places, as well as the ordinary dwellings, are in caves! Cool in the summer and not too cold in the winter. Looking out from one of them you see right over the city roofs to hills across the valley, whose outer surface is also honeycombed with rows of caves at various levels. There are many most beautiful old temples on the hills round about. One most startling thing is the Printing Press – it turns out a couple of newspapers a week, and many books and pamphlets. It is situated in some massive caves called the Buddha Caves; very gloomy as you go in. When your eyes get used to it, you see first a huge Buddha high up at the back, gazing meditatively in front of him. Then, far underneath, scurrying printers' devils, bales of paper, and huge presses in clanking motion.

During his stay in Yan'an, Aylwin met and interviewed Mao Zedong, Zhou Enlai, Generals Nie Rongzhen and Zhu De, Dr Ma Haide (George Hatem), and many others. About a week later, on 3 July, and still in Yan'an, he wrote further:

It is a good place to be in, especially now when there is a big week of festivities from June 1st–7th to celebrate the 17th anniversary of the Communist Party in China and the outbreak of war which, to them, is an inevitable and long-sought-for event. On the first day there was a marvellous theatre performance given by the art school. They had composed a modern Chinese opera, and have some wonderful singers. The scene opened on domestic happiness. Enter, after some songs, a sobbing lady who turns out to be refugee from war zone, sings songs of woe for lost child and husband. The village, including a cocky villain who afterwards turns out to be a traitor, namely in Japanese pay, turns up to listen and strikes poses of commiseration and invitation to live with him. Next act, husband-refugee, by strange coincidence, turns up with fresh stories. Meanwhile the hero of the original domestic happiness is gradually (*very* gradually! after the manner of Eastern drama) working himself up to a high pitch of determination. In the final act, things strangely move quite quickly. First, amid sounds of approaching war, the refugee-son turns up and sings songs of reunion with his mother. Then there is a torch hunt, by night, for the villain who has been found out; finally, a cock crows, a bell rings, and the hero with a last joyful and triumphant look at the heroine goes off with his lance to join the militia! That's the climax and propaganda, but everything here is propaganda.

There are about eight thousand students feeding on nothing else but millet and propaganda. It is a fairly good type of propaganda, however, not based on hate. The whole machine is directed against Japanese imperialism, and the Japanese people are represented as potential friends and allies. It is amazing, the number of students and young people of all classes – from all parts of the country as well as from Singapore, Manila, New Zealand, and Hawaii – who are attracted here. There are two women ex-film stars for instance! Only about ten percent of the students, or less, are communists. They come largely because of the enormous reputation which the Reds gained when fighting the Kuomintang before the Xi'an Coup; because the Red Army at that time originated the guerrilla tactics which are now recognised as the only way in which to fight Japan; and because the Reds are the leaders of ant-Japanism.

If you are not a pacifist you could hardly wish to find a better place. If you are, it is difficult to know what to say. Most of your arguments about war leading to fascism, and so on, don't work here. This war will lead increasingly to democracy, if it is carried out as these people want it to be. Their ideal is a new kind of totalitarianism; not that of a highly organised super-capitalistic country working like a machine in centralisation, but that of small groups of de-centralised units, part-time soldiers, part-time peasants, the whole politically conscious of the need for democracy and for breaking the Japanese lines by surprise attacks.

The orthodox communist wouldn't find very much to please him here – no communist industry or agriculture, nor even a communist form of Soviet government. Everything of this kind has been subjected to the supreme end of nationalism (I think without hate) and how to stop Japan. However, the spirit of communism remains. The government officials and the chiefs of the army get less pay than the students or the patients in the hospital. In fact, I shouldn't call it pay, just an allowance. Everyone in public service, also all the students and soldiers wear government-supplied uniforms and eat government-supplied millet. Some have private money (rich-parent students for example) but the only way it shows is perhaps as a coloured shirt on Sundays, or extra food, which is shared with the table.

Owing to it being near the rainy season, I haven't got time after all to go up and look at the refugee outfits we gave our money to. I'm very sorry, but I think it's all right.

When I get to Xi'an I will airmail to Hankou to see about my job and proceed to Hankou or Chongqing accordingly. I will probably leave here about June 7th. There is a nice Swiss League of Nations doctor here who will travel with me.

He realised that he was still very green – new to China and all its deep cultural complexities – so he restricted his writing to the simplest form. Based on what he had seen and learnt in Yan'an, Aylwin put over the Chinese attitude to the Japanese soldiers in a short story, which was published in the *Manchester Guardian* later that year, entitled "Prisoner's Return":

Private Fukuda remembered what his officers had often told him: "Chinese soldiers keep no prisoners; if you are taken, they will torture you mercilessly to death," and crouched lower behind the mound that served him as cover. He and the five others remaining from an ambush party one hundred strong were fighting crazily; partly from natural courage, partly from the thought, "Death in any case for us: better by bullet than torture." For a moment they stopped to listen. The Chinese soldiers surrounding them were shouting in unison, and the words sounded familiar. "Lay down your arms," the chorus came, in strange but recognisable Japanese; and then, "Chinese and Japanese soldiers are brothers; only the Japanese Militarists are our common enemies." Private Fukuda and his comrades looked at each other as they loaded their rifles. "What new trickery will the sly Chinese be up to next?" exclaimed one of them. But somehow the shouted slogans ate into them, and when it came to the end they didn't keep back cartridges to finish themselves off, as they had meant to do.

For days they walked west over the bare brown Shanxi mountains. After getting over his first surprise at these laughing, friendly Chinese soldiers of the Eighth Route Army, Private Fukuda had opportunity to think for the thousandth time of the greenness of grass and pine trees, the richly yielding, well watered terraces and the rounded hills of his native Kyushu. The mountains here were grotesque and menacing; they seemed man-made in their regular geometrical bases topped with queer sphinx shapes or malformed ominous idols. They were dry and arid, and the terraces, which the peasants had so hardly hewn from their flanks, seemed to yield nothing but stones.

Some time after reaching Yan'an, capital of the Eighth Route Army territory, Fukuda began to open his eyes. For one thing, the place was full of military students. There were men and women. They had come to this corner from all parts of China, and from overseas. They wore simple cotton uniforms, just as the students at the poorer schools in Japan did, ate the coarsest food, and slept in bare caves. Yet they seemed happy and entered enthusiastically on the stiffest of schedules. These could not be the running dogs of China's warlord oppressors, nor did they give the impression of being pressed men from the ranks of the suffering masses. What reason was left for their coming? Private Fukuda's chain of thought stopped there for the moment. Afterwards it occurred to him that the peasants in the villages through which they had passed had not been slavish, but had gladly helped the soldiers. And another thing: he and his companions were allowed to go freely out of the city, without guard. That seemed to point to a pretty good understanding between the people and what he had thought of as their inhumanly selfish rulers.

For several hours a day, a young Manchurian from the Eighth Route Army's Enemy Works Department instructed them on the official Chinese view of the war. They heard for the first time of Japan's imperialism, her greedy robbery, and her unscrupulous militarists who in their lust for power and money had involved two peoples in bloodshed. It was a picture of such simple villainy that Fukuda failed to be convinced. Some of his officers, who were supposed to be in league with the arch-villains, he remembered as being hated by their men; but mostly they didn't seem to fit the part. He knew them for decent enough men, who loathed the muck and cruelty of war as much as he did himself, and asked nothing better than to return to Japan. But Fukuda remained impressed with the things he saw about him, and with the little kindnesses that they, as prisoners, received. He was grateful for sometimes being given rice, rare and expensive in these northern parts, instead of having to fill his stomach with unaccustomed millet. So when invited to give a dumb-show play on theatre night, Fukuda and his comrades decided to put their tongues in their cheeks and give what was wanted.

The plays before theirs were strangely moving. Stories of simple village folk, and the way the war affected them. Fukuda and the others giggled nervously among themselves and sucked much air between their teeth at the way the Imperial Japanese Army was pictured. But often, forgetting nationality, they were carried along by living stories of love, and bereavement, refugeeing and reunion. The songs were haunting, and the stage-restored beauty of the girls, whom they had been used to seeing as sexless students in baggy blue uniforms, touched chords of tenderness and home in their hearts.

The six prisoners had resolved that their own turn should be short and snappy. Dressed in Japanese uniforms, four of them walked onto the stage, which had been arranged to suggest a barracks. While they were whispering conspiratorially, the remaining two strutted in, dressed as officers, and began shouting orders. The men turned on their officers and killed them. *Finis*. It was as simple as that! The audience roared and cheered and stamped their feet. Chairman Mao Zedong, sitting amongst them in his shirtsleeves, laughed with the rest. Fukuda rather despised their appreciation of such crudity, but it did occur to him that there certainly weren't any of the Welcome Japan as our Deliverer attitudes about them! And suddenly he felt sick, and fuller of disillusionment than ever before. Were these people not fired with the same spirit of patriotism, which he had believed to be Japan's own monopoly?

There came a day when it was decided that their re-education was complete. They were taken back to a place not far from where they had been captured, and released. All that they had seen and heard faded into the background and became unimportant, as they walked down the railway line to headquarters with their old comrades. Once more they were integral parts of a venerable human machine, ready though rusty to bow again to its almighty purpose. Old thoughts, old reflexes, slid soft-shod back into their minds as they prepared to enter the presence of the commanding officer.

There was no look of inquiry or welcome in the shifting eyes of the men who sat around the little table. Their chief looked up, one hand still trifling with some object on the table. "You Japanese soldiers," he said, "have for several months been prisoners of the Communist armies of China. You have now been freed. We can only conclude that you have in some measure adopted their vile principles. In any case you are dangerous men. We cannot allow you to mix with true Japanese soldiers. Tomorrow morning you will all six face the firing squad."

Time is a personal thing. What for some men are blank, unremarked seconds, are for others seared deep with slow drops of eternity. For a long time, as it seemed to Fukuda, he felt no emotion. Only, he saw himself and the five others; facing them, seated, was *Fear*, which in self-defence must kill. He saw the whole machine, of which he had just now felt himself a part, as oiled by ignorance, and knew at least his Chinese brothers had much more than half the truth on their side. Saluting, he turned to leave the room.

Chapter 7

Evacuation

Aylwin returned to Hankou where the situation was approaching a climax. It was at this point that he started as a journalist for the American United Press Agency. The next letter home was dated 12 August 1938, and mentions, for the first time, the Chinese Industrial Cooperatives:

> I am having an extremely interesting time. At first fairly quiet, I didn't have much to do except make polite conversation once a day with the British Consulate in case they had any news that would come out in a natural, easy way; also at Navy HQ. The rest of the time I could work up stories of my own. The first thing I investigated was the cholera situation, with a view to discovering if it would become worse on account of the evacuation of health officers and so on. Answer no, but it took me a long time and lots of interesting interviews to find out. Second, the government and relief organisations' efforts to clear out refugees and poor residents; I found they are making terrific efforts to get people away, three boats running regularly, a special train every day, and a walking party of a thousand men every day. The latter have tea-halts every four miles along the way, and food places every ten. They are provided with tickets for two meals daily. This led to what the refugees are going to do in their new homes, and I found the most interesting line of all, which I am following up, about small mobile industries organised cooperatively.
>
> Today and yesterday have been very heavy; terrific air raids on the cities Wuchang and Hanyang across the river, and about three miles at either end of Hankou. Afterwards, we all go out in different directions to get the news and take pictures. It is both gruelling and gruesome. Yesterday and today I got the big news of foreign property hit. One of them was on the compound of the Hua Chung College where I had the job offered me, and might have been teaching.

The following is an article by Aylwin which he called "Wuhan Waits", concerning the imminent fall of Wuhan, the collective name for the three close neighbouring cities of Hankou, Wuchang, and Hanyang:

Today, September 25th, there were three air-raid alarms. Each time we went onto the roof; the city seemed to sleep below us, but we could sense its vigilance. The flags of the nations waved their warnings, ships idled in the river, and the factories had to stop work; rickshaw pullers rested in their rickshaws and people from the streets were crowded in doorways. Each time the city waited silently; nothing came. We have had no bombing raid for over five weeks now, and the Japanese have broadcast from Shanghai that they will not bomb Wuhan again. People who fled into the country after the mid-August raids (one thousand five hundred killed on August 10th and 11th) are now returning. In the country there are no anti-aircraft guns, and the planes can fly low to sweep the roads with machine gun fire. The country is noisome with end-of-summer filth and swarming insect life; the chances of catching malaria, cholera and typhus are as great as those of being hit by a piece of shrapnel, or of being caught in the wreckage of ancient wooden buildings.

The Japanese have shown that they want to take Wuhan over as a going concern. For this reason also they have been encouraging the idea of a demilitarised Safety Zone in Hankou. They know that, given the risks and uncertainty involved in leaving, any Chinese will prefer to stay if there is hope of protection. Those concerned regard the *Safety Zone* as a purely temporary affair, for *the period of transition*. After the occupation it will receive no special treatment. There will merely be a nicely preserved piece of China ready for Japanese exploitation, with an enormous supply of foreign-supported labour for Japanese factories and of foreign-fed women for Japanese soldiers.

Perhaps for this reason, the Chinese Government is at present refusing to give any assurances about demilitarisation; preparations for defence continue uniformly through the city. Meanwhile the foreigners take the Japanese at their word, and continue their plans to protect the Chinese who, but for their own presence, would have left. They hope that at the last moment the Chinese command will either agree to demilitarisation or retreat from the city.

The general opinion seems to be that the large number of foreigners in Wuhan will be sufficient to preserve it from the fate of Nanjing. But there is also a strong radical element which denounces the *Safety Zone* as the more or less explicit scheming of foreign capitalists to protect their own property under the guise of international philanthropy. Why, it asks, should the Chinese Government destroy morale by tacitly admitting the probability of Wuhan's capture, weaken its own defences, and help to preserve a valuable future base for Japanese economic and military activity? The Japanese have never respected their promises in the past; in this matter they are quite unable to do so, because the Japanese army depends on debauchery for the opiate and inspiration of its soldiers.

Hankou is gradually taking on a more warlike air. Flags painted on every foreign building for previous scares, notably at the beginning of January and the end of May, have been re-painted and every conceivable excuse for a foreign flag is sought by the Chinese. The inscription: *This property is mortgaged to a Belgian company* painted across broad red, yellow and black stripes frequently catches the eye. A double row of stout posts intertwined with barbed wire lines the centre of the main streets. Fortifications and machine-gun emplacements are appearing at key points, and massive reinforced wooden gates set in concrete beds are ready to be closed across the main streets.

Wuchang across the Changjiang (Yangtze) River and Hanyang across the Han River are dead cities. You can walk for hours between ruined houses in the musty smell of rotten woodwork and plaster rubble. Here and there you will find a family camping in what was once its own home, or an old woman mumbling to herself as she pokes among the ruins of her past. But the great majority of the people have either evacuated or are living on the streets of the foreign and ex-foreign concessions.

As a result, Hankou itself is exceedingly active. Government officials, foreign missionaries, rickshaw men, beggars and refugees have all moved to Hankou. Buildings which had long been standing idle are now being used for dwellings and offices. Traffic, liberally sprinkled with military trucks and generals' shiny cars, jams in bottle-necks caused by the barricades. The rickshaw pullers, whose ranks have been swollen by *foreign* labour, vie with each other for fares even more strenuously than usual. Often the weird chant of a hundred coolies in unison floats over the city, as a large piece of machinery from an outlying Chinese factory is lifted on poles and human shoulders into a foreign go-down.

After dark, activity becomes more marked than ever. The pavements are crowded with beggars and their children. The night-clubs and cinemas are packed every night, both with Chinese and foreigners. Recently a *Thrift Campaign* was inaugurated, and many a rich Chinese was startled to see an accurate account of his last night's doings in the local paper, the amount of money he had spent in entertaining, and possibly the amount of mileage which he had covered in his official car on official petrol. Accompanying the description was the threat to disclose identities next time!

A large colony of journalists tries to get to the centre of all this activity. Permanent or itinerant, special or staff, free-lance or attached, book, article or *spot news*, pen or camera, they are all busy, or busy waiting. The majority of them eat together in the alcohol-free Navy YMCA. Here they meet several times a day on the best of terms, and the dining room is often occupied long after meal-times by little groups engrossed in serious talk or lost in uproarious laughter.

Hankou waits in various ways. The authorities are trying to thin out the seven hundred and fifty thousand sediment of population which still remains. Madame Jiang Jieshi concentrates on evacuating factory girls, and on mobilising officials' wives into war service groups. The Chinese people wait stoically, hoping personally to escape. The foreign business and official class is busy organising food and fuel rations for emergency, special police to function during the interim period, special concentration points for foreigners, and the management of the *Safety Zone* in case it becomes possible. The reinforced British naval force, nearly three hundred and thirty in all, keeps itself occupied with games, lectures and the erection of a barbed wire barricade round the top of the Consulate wall. The missionaries are too busy working out ways in which to protect or evacuate their flocks even to think very much about protecting their enormous properties. Everyone is trying to live as normally as possible in an abnormal city.

Outside the cities, the peasants in the country had their share of the horrors of war. One day, the following comment entitled "No Damage" was noted in the British press:

> Enemy bombers approached at dusk yesterday. Weather conditions favoured defence however, and they were prevented from finding their objective. Apparently confused as to their whereabouts, they released their bombs over the open fields before turning back. No material damage was done.

Aylwin had a different angle on the same story:

> The little Chinese house of wattle and straw stood alone on a dry patch of ground among the rice paddies. Through years it had seen nothing but the daily lives of its farmer folk and their domestic capital. Men and women scarcely distinguishable, a succession of children, a few pigs, ducks, and water buffalo, had been indiscriminately sheltered – from the oldest toothless one down to the latest baby, litter, or calf. Jagged cracks ran slantwise down its walls, and it was perched askew on its raised hillock like an old and disreputable hat. Evidently it had achieved sudden fame, for a crowd of excited people was milling round it, and more could be seen coming from all directions along the paths between the rice paddies.
>
> Nicely arboured between the two projecting wings of the house and almost entirely filling the courtyard the huge carcass of a water buffalo lay; this seemed to be the centre of interest, but some way off a small group had discovered a pair of hairy hind legs, emerging from a bundle of red crushed meat. Attention was suddenly diverted from these as a woman raised the side of an overturned wheelbarrow to reveal a mangled human body. She held the barrow up for the crowd with one hand, using the other to help her in a mumbled incantation. The crowd peered curiously at the remains and went off in little groups to swap emotions at a safe distance; some of them threw the woman a few pennies before leaving. Meanwhile a mourner's dirge and the smoke from burning paper money came from a half-open door into the house itself, where the body of a woman, perfectly unhurt save that it had no head, was lying fully clothed on the floor. The sight of her un-shrouded body, headless and thick with child, excited only a sort of pitying wonder. It was at once too near the ordinary, and too far beyond the limits of ordinary experience, to bring horror.
>
> Outside the door two policemen were talking with the men of the family. The words: "Lights, showing lights," kept recurring. Gradually the whole story was pieced together.

Last night as Father pottered about putting things to rights for the night, the soft rise and fall of the sirens came to him over flat miles of planted rice and green vegetables. Air-raid – what of it? There had been many before.

At night they are especially beautiful. Red flames lit up the horizon and outlined the houses and trees between. White streamers chased each other across the sky, joining sometimes to catch the silvered fly in the round patch of light at the end of their beams, but more often dancing solo. The red tracer bullets from the machine guns flowed regularly, as an illuminated ticker tape projection, from one plane toward another, the dotted straight lines in the sky contrasting strangely with the curves of nature's motion. Occasionally there was a flash of light as a burning plane fell like a glowing meteor to the ground. Or the ghostly white of a parachute swayed softly in the moonlight.

But such pretties as these are for people who have time to stand and watch. Farmer folk have other things to do. That these strange sky-birds should have any connection with him and his farm was unimaginable to Father; he and they were in different worlds. That which has never happened, never will. Why should it? What would it be like if it did? No answer possible. So Father held the light above his head, counting in his pigs for the night.

High in the sky the invading airmen cursed the evening mist and the murky moon. They cursed the glare of the clever searchlights and the worrying attention of the defending pursuits. Perhaps their wish was father to the thought that they were above an airfield. Anyhow, when they saw a speck of light below them they dropped their bombs in a shattering line, four miles from their objective, and headed back for home.

Father dropped the light, suddenly frightened, and turned to run in. He and several of his animals were massacred where they stood. One small piece of metal flew through the house window and beheaded a woman standing inside. But the soft mud received the force of the explosions, so that the old house stood battered and displaced, like the Chinese people, but still serviceable.

Twelve hours later the surviving part of the family was still dazed and stupid. Death they had accepted as a part of life, but *this* – this was out of the picture. For the first time in their lives they had been shocked into detachment. While the crowd thronged curiously about them, they stood passive and sullen, as spectators before their own debacle. But soon the urge to renewed action gripped them. With a *Mei you fa zi* (It can't be helped) and a *Sheng yi ge fa zi* (We'll find a way) they prepared to take up their old struggle for existence from the lower vantage point. Without Father, wisest and strongest of them all, without a woman to toil in the fields and cook their meals, economically perhaps worst of all – short of a draft animal, they must wring from the land enough to pay the rent, provide a decent burial for the dead and a minimal subsistence for themselves. They must get used to the idea of more sirens, more raids, tomorrow and the next day and the day after that. They must work and work so as to keep their battered home and their home's soil at least until invading armies followed the planes.

Already, a quarter of a mile away, the country life was going on as usual. A water buffalo more fortunate than its fellow sloughed patiently through the mire. Little pig-tailed girls looked up wide-eyed from their squatting in the fields. Three smiling fellows, sheltered by broad grass hats from the sun's hot rays, leaned lazily into the cross-bars of a treadmill that scooped water into their irrigation channel; each pair of legs seemed divorced from a body in complete repose, as they walked interminably over the spokes. This was the life to which the little house and its depleted family belonged, and from which they would soon again be indistinguishable. Almost – but never quite. In a moment, they had lived through the fury of a war, seen the snuffing of hopes and happiness, felt the birth of bitterness.

As the weeks passed, life in Hankou was becoming more difficult, as this letter, written on 13 October 1938, describes:

I haven't had anything from you since yours of September 13th. I don't suppose it's your fault. The air service was stopped for a bit, and is still very irregular, so sometimes the post office people get fed up waiting and send stuff off by rail. The other day a train left here Sunday, for the south. On Monday it came back again, started off again Monday night, and on the following Saturday it still hadn't even reached Changsha, less than two hundred miles down the line! We have two or three air raid warnings a day quite often here, but no raids. Instead, the planes go off and bomb villages and stations down the line.

The city is building a tremendous amount of fortifications both within and without. Big gates with barbed wire, sandbags, and machine gun emplacements, walled up alleyways are common sights. Most of the shops are in process of moving, and many have already done so. The ones that can afford to do so wall up the windows and doors when they leave.

I don't get time to learn any more Chinese now, but can sometimes get on all right for small friendly conversations with the people I meet. Later I hope I'll be able to learn to speak well enough to cover ordinary needs.

Many people think that when the time comes there won't really be much fighting around the city, that the fortifications are either wishful thinking or just to keep order. Most people give it at least another month before they get here, anyway. It's difficult to tell whether the South China expedition is really serious or if it's meant just as a diversion from the main drive on Hankou.

After the fall of Wuhan, just across the river from here, I still don't know. I feel I'll have to teach in the University of Guilin, though I don't want to at all. I would much rather try and get something with Rewi Alley, or something like John Foster, or I've been offered a job with the Chinese Red Cross unofficially, which might still be there.

The war is coming closer. Everyone is dashing off with bundles and bales slung over shoulders, often with no money. Now we are pretty well cut off. The Japanese have practically cut the railway to Guangzhou about forty-five miles from here, whatever else they may be doing to it down below in the south. They have already cut the railway to the north not so far away. A Chinese boom is being put down, upriver from here, so no more boats after tomorrow. Airline to Hong Kong suspended, and so on. Everyone is very calm though.

On the night of October 24th the mayor reports that a population of about half a million remains in Wuhan. That means that over a million have evacuated. A week ago, movement was desultory. Children still played familiarly among the trenches and sandbags of the city defences; dance halls were filled with haymakers in the last sun; flowery girls whose limbs peeped provokingly from their side-split skirts, and businessmen profiting by the times. But for the last three days the roads have borne a steady stream of traffic.

At night the automobiles of the fortunate bump uncomfortably into the country; they travel in the dark to avoid Japanese planes flying low over the road to strafe anything that doesn't take cover quickly enough. In daytime the poorer citizens set out. Carrying spring beds, tables and chairs, cooking utensils, invalids on litters, babies in baskets, all slung on stout poles across their shoulders, their rhythmic *Ho-hee ho-ho* will echo with every step for hundreds of miles along the refugee trails. The government has also organised a scheme by which each rickshaw takes five refugees, and each caravan of rickshaws a hundred yards in length has three evacuating policemen as guards and controllers. Today the last boat left upriver; disconsolate families who were unable to push their way aboard in the seething mass of people and baggage, sat on the fore-shore watching their hopes of safety sail away.

Meanwhile those who are staying behind – including over a thousand foreigners – were either frantically busy, or keeping themselves artificially busy to avoid thinking of the guns that could sometimes be heard down the river. There was tremendous relief today when it was announced that a Safety Zone, to be kept free from hostilities, had finally been agreed to by both sides. Plenty of excitement too, when we opened the morning paper to find a warning from the Foreign Residents Association headed in big black type "Danger from Demolition of Buildings" which said, "Open all windows, shut doors, keep clear of windows. Do not stand on rooftops to watch or photograph results .... Spend the day in the Race Club Grandstand", which is outside the city.

Whatever their advice to their protégées, the committee members of the *Safety Zone* and the Foreign Residents Association themselves spent a day of feverish activity in the city. Plans for food kitchens, mat sheds, special volunteer police both foreign and Chinese had to be completed, inquisitive and persistent newspapermen continually to be foisted off. Father Jacquinot in plain black habit, his *Nantao Safety Zone* badge as his sole ornament and a hopeful emblem for the whole city, moved sure and dignified among them.

Meanwhile the British Navy was having a busy enough day bringing on shore the hundred and eight men of a special landing force, to man the gates and police the ex-British Concession, now called *Special Administrative Area Three*. Then the news that

Japanese planes had that morning attacked the gunboat *Sandpiper* in Changsha came through, to add grimness to the preparations in Hankou and irony to the recently expressed Japanese gratefulness for third power cooperation in avoiding incidents.

Now the night is deep and dark. We are in the heart of a great city, the capital of a people which loves noise; but it is as quiet as midnight on the plains of Arizona. Wounded soldiers are lying along the Bund hoping to be evacuated in junks. Groups of farmer folk hurry through the city driving their cattle in front of them. Small pathetic lines of refugees pass quickly in no set direction, like sheep; soon they will lie down fatalistically to wait in the street. If they wait here they may not be worse off than those who have left; the countryside has malaria, scouring Japanese planes, bandits; it will be overrun by a food-less perhaps money-less crowd which will sweep it clean of food as thoroughly as a swarm of locusts.

Sleep is uneasy in Hankou tonight. At any time it may be interrupted by the violent explosions of scorched earth policy; and what of tomorrow? The Generalissimo is gone! Long live the Emperor Meiji!

Shortly after this, all journalists were evacuated from Hankou, and the next letter is dated 4 November 1938:

Here I am back in Shanghai. We came back in two hours and fifty-seven minutes; it took me about two weeks to go the other way, from here to Hankou. The answer was in a magical aeroplane supplied by the Imperial Japanese Navy to take all journalists out of Hankou. So we had a grand flight over the country scarred with trenches and battlefields and bomb craters and over the towns about which we've been reporting for months – but which were just names as far as I was concerned.

Of course we were thankful not to have fighting around Hankou. The Chinese made a wonderful withdrawal, and it was they that saved the city from war. They also tried to blow up the big Japanese buildings and also their own big buildings so that the Japanese wouldn't be able to use them, but in many they were prevented by the British Navy, which seems to have got the plans, and after the Chinese had gone, began to move out all the dynamite from the buildings, thus handing over invaluable property safe and sound to the Japanese, which is all very strange. In a way you can't blame them, because the explosions could have endangered foreign property and lives. But what are the foreigners doing there anyhow? And what right have they to hand over Chinese property to the Japanese? And where the plans for dynamiting were carried out without interference, they proved to have been well laid and didn't harm surrounding property much.

In an open letter to the *Manchester Guardian*, Aylwin described how United States Navy gunboats, berthed in Hankou harbour, were moved in front of the National City Bank and down to the Standard Oil installation in a similar attempt to ensure preservation of property for the Japanese. He saw how the Italian Consul welcomed the Japanese Army, which marched past an Italian guard of honour ... each was doing only what seemed right to him in the immediate circumstances. But circumstances being what they were, the combined result stank. Even the eighteen newspapermen, who regarded the situation so cynically, were themselves not free from opportunism. Though staunch followers of the Chinese government and many of them on their way to rejoin it, were they not at present enjoying the luxury of an airliner provided for them gratis by his Imperial Japanese Majesty's Navy?

The safety of civilians from actual warfare, which had been the main avowed object of the safety zone, was ensured by the Chinese withdrawal. The Japanese had, within a week, occupied all available buildings in the zone and begun the forced evacuation of Chinese householders in the former Russian Concessions; several cases of rape were reported by foreign eyewitnesses nightly. As to the foreigners themselves, even consular officials were not immune from the most stringent control of personal movement within the ex-British concession. Japanese were also reliably reported to have entered the administrative offices of this ex-British concession area and smilingly replied to a naïve explanation of the governmental system, "You have a majority of four to three, eh? Soon we are four to three!"

As to the four hundred thousand refugees who crowded into the zone and were encouraged by the business element on the zone committee to expect protection even after the occupation, they were kicked out unmercifully at the order of the Japanese. Before the occupation, their presence within the property belt had been indispensable to the latter's protection. Now they were no more than an insanitary nuisance to the foreigners no less than to the Japanese. A new zone (no longer graced with the name *safety*) was arranged for them in deserted slums not wanted for billeting troops. Long trails of them – all the oldest and feeblest that were unable to evacuate – could be seen struggling along the road to the new quarters: pregnant mother led blind grandmother; grandfather bent almost double under the weight of the family belongings, small daughter carried the baby. Their misery was extreme, and they bore it with typical Chinese stoicism. As they walked through thin driving rain, I myself within a few minutes saw one Japanese soldier try to take a family's bedding, another begin to take away a refugee woman, and a little girl lying desperately ill on the pavement.

In a letter home about the Chinese who waved Japanese flags and let off firecrackers, carried Japanese officers' personal equipment, to welcome the troops into the City, he wrote, "Amazing! I never believed all the stuff one hears about Chinese *traitors* before." Later on, no doubt, they did it from fear. But these were quite unnecessary – obviously trying to *suck up*.

Chapter 8

Return to Japan

In another letter home dated 9 November 1938, Aylwin wrote to say "I hope to see Tommy in Japan, maybe spend Christmas there, hence to Beijing which I mentioned in my last letter." The letter continued:

What I didn't mention before, for fear of censor (this one is carried to Hong Kong by a friend), I hope from Beijing, to go through the Japanese lines into Northwest China – see some of the government within government that the Chinese carry on so successfully in so-called "occupied areas". I think there will be useful things to be done there. Maybe I'll find this man Rewi Alley of the Industrial Cooperatives up there – nobody here seems to know where he is a present.

The United Press gave me a whole month's salary bonus because we did a good job in Hankou, and they say in the future when I make trips they'll be glad to buy contributions. I'm staying at the Foreign YMCA here for the present. It is an absolute palace. The best of all the delights of civilisation in Shanghai is an enormous gymnasium in the YMCA with a squash court attached which is free for guests!

Aylwin wasn't able to enjoy the luxuries of the YMCA "palace" for very long, however, before being struck down with a severe attack of paratyphoid, which landed him in hospital for nearly three weeks, using up his US$80 bonus. On 6 December he wrote home from his place of convalescence, the house of some good friends in Shanghai:

Here I am all fine and dandy chez Aimee and Frank Millican, who are proving quite the experts on feeding up after illness, which is now what I need. Frank is also an expert bath attendant, invalid-in-bed washer, chambermaid, bed maker, and rubber-down. There's no end to his talents; in short, clover. And it's free. The hospital where I have been sleeping day and night for the past nineteen days cost seventeen dollars each day, which would worry me in my rare waking moments. These were usually during the night, through which I sweated with monotonous regularity to the tune of four or five changes per night. It didn't used to happen in the daytime, I don't know why. Last night I hardly perspired at all for the first time, so I am definitely better. I have now passed three and a half normal temperature days. When it is seven, I'm allowed to start getting up. Now I have plenty of pep, read all day, and eat like a wolf.

On 21 December, Aylwin wrote home to say, "I am fit as a fiddle, and can even go downstairs with some degree of confidence that my knees won't give way." Then, a few days later:

Today I went to the Chinese city, Nantao zone, where the Goodwill Industries, for which Aunt Muriel collected quite a bit, are going. Today was Christmas holiday, but we are going out to stay there on Boxing Day, and I hope to get some pictures. All the children in the kindergarten are being given two suits of fresh underwear for Christmas, but they are not allowed to wear it till two days after Christmas, when they are all to be given the first bath they've had for ages! There has been no water supply – so they're going to carry enough up for this occasion; also no coal, so they have carried enough wood over from a half-burned house to heat the water. The inhabitants of the city are beginning to come back; that is the bravest of them who dislike being fed for nothing, by charitable foreigners. Incidentally, the International Red Cross is still spending seventy thousand Chinese dollars a month feeding people five ounces of rice a day in the Jacquinot Safety Zone. On the faces of the people as they queue up for their five ounces there is not a smile to be seen. The queue lasts for about four hours, going quickly past the distributors. People who have returned to the gutted city outside the zone are much more cheerful. They enjoy piling the loose bricks that are lying everywhere three feet deep so as to replace a wrecked wall or fill in a door-less doorway. I was introduced to two "celebrities". One, the woman who first scraped away the bricks from in front of her door and planted seeds, cleared a vegetable bed from under the three-foot layer of bricks, transplanted the seeds, and brought forth a fine crop of vegetables. Now many others have followed her example. The second, an old man who was digging in the garden beside his wrecked house yet seemed so happy we thought he was taking heroin until, when we asked him, he drew himself up and pointed to his god on the shelf and his long tobacco pipe as his two comforts. "I was here ten years before your fine mission building," he said. "Now this is all I have left."

Twenty-nine December 1938:

These letters should reach you as you return all brown and glowing with health from sunny Switzerland, and with grandparental pride in your progeny. I missed two or three boats out of absentmindedness and not having any stamps, had a guilty conscience, but gained much relief to think that you wouldn't much expect any letters while you were on holiday.

I just finished the four articles on Yan'an, and sent them off to an agent with recommendation from Mrs Millican, who is a friend of his. I finished copying them at four in the morning the day the boat sailed. Maybe I'll get rich on them; I don't know.

Speaking of riches, there is the little matter of £10 which came on "Chrissimus Day in the morning". All fears about the after-effects of paratyphoid may be dismissed, as I am enormously fit and eat magnificently. How about the £10? I was so proud of myself for paying my own doctor's and hospital bills, but of course pride might be sacrificed in an emergency!

I heard a good story about some people escaping from Hankou up river in a boat. The boat had an office staff and equipment, soldiers, a newspaper press and staff, eighty people all together plus a number of refugee women and children who swarmed on the boat or stowed away. The first morning out it was bombed, an incendiary bomb landing right in the middle of it. Most of the staff was on shore, but non-swimming soldiers and refugees were many of them still on the boat. The soldiers assisted the people to save themselves by jumping into the river with tables and chairs and so on. About thirty were killed. Those on shore, my friends included, lay on one side of an embankment as the planes passed down machine gunning people on the other side. One of them said, "As the planes circle, they will machine gun this side on the way back", so they all got up and ran over to the other side, which had already been gunned, and sure enough the plane strafed where they had been lying.

Seven January 1939:

Next Thursday I leave for Japan to stay with Tommy for a bit, on my way to Beijing. I am very much looking forward to seeing him and Japan again. Christmas reigns in Shanghai again today! It is the Russian Christmas today. Shanghai-Landers have two Christmases and three New Yearses! Last weekend I went to stay with Dr and Mrs Lacy who picked me up in Texas and took me all the way to San Francisco. They are very good people, and it was nice to recall the trip.

I am thinking vaguely of coming home sometime maybe next year, and maybe I'll get off at Marseilles and hitchhike across Europe. One gets very "provincial" staying in the East, and I am frightened of becoming one of those people who keeps saying "when I was in the East"! I feel that it is time I really did something. If something turns up, I'd give up the idea of coming home for a bit.

I am suddenly filthy rich. I have enough cash for the journey and maybe a month's stay in Beijing; also £10 and US$100 in travellers' cheques. I wonder where it has all come from. One thing was that Tommy sent me US$52, which he says he owes me.

This may be perhaps the last uncensored letter I can get through. So listen. After a couple of months or so, I may not be able to get any letters through at all, for a long time. I don't know. Anyway I will be safe as houses and having a whale of a time somewhere between Beijing and Xi'an I hope. The last letter before I leave Beijing I will try to remember to put in some perfectly senseless sentence, so that you will know.

Eleven January 1939:

Off to Japan tomorrow! Enclosed are some stocks, or shares rather, worth ten Chinese dollars each; probably worth nothing at all; charity donation to the funds of the Chinese government that operates independent of all Japanese interference in Japanese territory in the Northeast. That's where I'm heading for. These shares are supposed to pay six percent, but don't bear interest until the end of the war. And that means when Japan is out, because these people wouldn't admit it was the end of the war until then.

How about selling them as a joke, say ten shillings each, or more, and give the proceeds to China? I paid fifty dollars for them. They are issued by the Regional Government of Shanxi, Hebei and Chahar, which is according to reports of foreign travellers doing a wonderful and economic job, in this so-called Japanese territory. The government officials are young and efficient, they are going in extensively for popular education. The fact that the people are behind them is illustrated by the yield of taxes, which is higher than ever before the war in this district. They are concentrating especially on making themselves self-sufficient so that they won't have to help the Japanese trade; also they forbid the people to grow crops for export outside the Region because this also would help the Japanese; for example, cotton is much in demand, but should the Japanese make an expedition to this district formerly rich in cotton, they would find that the people were only growing small amounts for their own use. Distribution is through co-ops. The Region supports the army, paid for out of revenue thus ensuring nonfriction between people and soldiers trying to make them give food and so on. The capital is portable, so that if the Japanese make a drive for extermination, they would find nothing there of importance. The regional government keeps in close touch with the national government in Chongqing by radio. Its personnel are largely Eighth Route Army men, and students, from the First Special Region (Shaanxi, Ningxia, and Gansu) on the other side of the Yellow River. The government is of the democratic-communist type peculiar to China; namely, communist idealism, sacrifice, and democratic principles for which China has long been famous in the everyday affairs of the people. Chinese communists are apparently no longer aiming at revolution sudden and violent, but at the growth of a democratic nation as a result of new political consciousness in the people. Education is the first essential. There are many groups and associations, study groups and so on for adults. Men in each locality meet frequently for drill, singing, and talking. These are the local peasants and suchlike. They are not expected to fight except in the last resort, if then. But meeting together gives them a spirit of unity and cooperation that is a precondition of passive resistance to exploitation.

Do you think this is enough to convince the future shareholders? Someone will be sending you a pamphlet about the Chinese Industrial Cooperatives soon. If you can raise any money for that, I think it is one of the most promising things in China right now.

In an article for the *Manchester Guardian* entitled "Japan Tired of the War", Aylwin wrote of his new impressions of Japan, a year after last leaving it:

Coming back to Japan after a year in China it seems that in the interval the country had really settled down to the war. Inevitable groups of "patriotic women" idled away the hours with paper flags at each railway station. Droves of convalescent soldiers, dressed in white kimonos with a red cross, caused no surprise in the public parks, where they rested and played. Mass funerals and new war memorials were common and accepted features of all the big cities. There was no longer any attempt to hide a war in an *incident*.

But whereas in all parts of China war enthusiasm is on the up-grade and constantly receives new fillip, in isolated Japan one gets the impression that morale is going stale. The women are getting as tired of spending the day on draughty railway platforms as their husbands are of cold meals. Enormously swollen takings in the pleasure sections and geisha quarters give the lie to the national campaign for equal sacrifice and the simple life. Widespread corruption in the distribution of ration tickets for an increasing number of commodities furthers the rot. From abroad the Japanese people have just been let into the secret that even the United States is against them. Like Jiang Jieshi's retreat westward, this is considered most unfair. But it hurts terribly.

Certainly the men at the top, not only of the government but the older Army men, are now for the first time worried about the financial situation, anxious for peace, bewildered that they do not get it. But *military* mind has become synonymous for *one track* even in Japan. The pathetic sincerity of these men, which is vouched for by many foreign observers, still deceives them into thinking that Wang Jingwei, Wu Peifu, and even Jiang Jieshi himself must bring the *Japanese way* to poor suffering China. Actually, anti-Japanese feeling in China grows every day, even in pacified northern cities. "The Chinese in Chongqing don't know what it's like to be anti-Japanese until they've worked for them, as we have," confided one Chinese puppet official in Beijing.

The fully conscious intellectuals in Japan are still hibernating. "Since there is no tradition of martyrdom anywhere in the country, there is no admiration for it, no proselytising power to it, so no point in making a sacrifice. Not even one of my friends had the slightest sympathy for me on my return from prison; 'How foolish you are!' was all they could say," is the testimony of one intellectual. As for the lower-calibre intellects which had not the strength to resist propaganda in the first place, they are now more unnaturally frantic than ever to justify Japan, as fear for its fate renews old conflicts within themselves.

The common people can be relied upon to remain *behind the guns*, as the slogan of the day goes, so long as they have enough to eat. In the cities labour is at present in comfortable circumstances. Reliable sources report a shortage of one hundred thousand men in the essential industries, and the wages of armament workers have thus in many cases increased anything from threefold to fivefold. Artificial prosperity has by now spread to other industries, so that after a short period of readjustment almost all classes of wage-earners are better off than before the war. Statistics of a cooperative pawn-shop and savings bank in a representative industrial district of Tokyo showed an increase of 33.3% in savings deposits for 1938 over the figures for 1937, with an increase of only 1.6% in pawnings and of 13.3% in membership over the same period.

In the country districts, however, everything works against the peasant farmer. Not only is the incidence of military conscription greater here, but a previous tendency for the young men to immigrate to the cities has been greatly accentuated. Students are drafted for work in the fields, ostensibly to help those families whose men-folk have gone to the war. Boys from a certain agricultural school spent almost the whole of last year in the fields, and this year student labour is to be organised on an even greater scale. Even during the winter off-season, travellers on the more countrified railway lines could see students working with the women on the land. Although the rice crop was announced almost up to par, official quarters admit privately that the crop was the worst in many years, owing to rains, floods, and shortage of man-power. Meanwhile the price which the farmer gets for his rice is strictly controlled, and prices of things he needs to buy have risen considerably; cotton cloth, rubber-soled boots for working in the rice-paddies, and other things which he had come to regard as necessities are almost unprocurable. Substitute cloth made from wood fibre goes straight into holes and shrinks out of all recognition; boots, whether made from whale or chicken skin can hardly be satisfactory. Each chicken is said to yield seven tenths of a square foot of "leather"! In the country labour shortage means harder work for less profit.

Many have hoped that the return of wounded soldiers would cause general disillusionment in Japan. This has happened to some extent. The authorities were at first stupid in the contacts allowed between people and soldiers. For instance, a famous girl's school was required to send a group of singers to a military hospital. On being ushered in they found themselves confronted with all the inhuman monstrosities of modern war. Limb-less trunks hung in hammocks, men lay without form or face. Two girls began to giggle as Japanese girls are nervous at the best of times. The strained, anguished soldiers became infuriated; "Throw them out! Kill them! Wring their necks!" they shouted. There were many other cases where families heard that their son or father was in a certain hospital, travelled there, pleaded to be shown him, were at last allowed and then came out half-demented with what they saw. A student told me that on their routine visits to military hospitals the common topic is that of atrocities such as at Nanjing. The men boast, the students laugh, but it must have its effect on some of them. There is no denying that the people as a whole disbelieve entirely in the official casualty figures and are far more sceptical about the high-sounding motives of the war than they were a year ago.

Japan is too much divided, horizontally and vertically, for generalisation. In conclusion one can only list some of the influences working for and against support of the war policy. Thus, *For*: national pride; the unbroken record of military success; resentment against a hypocritical big stick from the west; desire for four hundred million customers; high wages in industry and almost no unemployment; unintelligent idealism. And *Against*: fear at the top for financial stability; real poverty among farmers and white-collar salary men; a sneaking regard for the opinion of England and the United States, which often comes out in the newspapers or in conversation; bureaucratic corruption and booming popular vice in spite of the Government purity campaign; scepticism. The *ayes* still have it. But they no longer have confidence and their cards are all played. The dynamic elements are all with the *nays*.

A further article which appeared in the *Manchester Guardian*, entitled "Modern Pilgrimage" described a journey he took to the heart of the ancient Japanese culture:

It is half past ten in the evening on Tokyo station. The platform for the Tokyo-Yamada train is crowded with passengers, and the usual patient group of white-robed *Patriotic Women* waits to meet soldiers off the incoming train. As the long line of electric coaches rocks swiftly into the station an urgent monotone from the loudspeaker director mingles with the hiss of hydraulic brakes, and behind is the clop-clop of hurrying wooden *geta* on the platform.

This is the setting for a modern pilgrimage. Every night this train sets out from Tokyo, stopping here and there to add to its load of pilgrims, for Yamada, the first place of worship in Japan. Probably two hundred years before Christ this was the shrine for neighbouring Yamato, cradle of Japanese civilisation. While the capital of Japan has often changed, the religious continuity of the country has been held here in sacred *Ise*, where dwell the spirits of an unbroken Imperial line. Today it is still to *Ise* that the Imperial messengers must hurry to report on important affairs of State.

In early days the rich pilgrim rode on horseback down the weary road, and the poor man could hardly afford to go at all. Nowadays it is steel and electricity, and the only difference between rich and poor is First and Third class travel. Instead of the thirty-two stations for horsemen, with hotels, feeding places and relays of mounts there is now a swift train, whose uniformed attendants dispense uniform boxed meals.

A cheery, homely, hail-fellow-well-met atmosphere prevails in the sleeper coach after *Mr Boy* has shown us to our bunks. People stand about eating goodnight *mikans* [a citrus fruit], offing their collars and ties, telling each other comfortable and chatty bedtime stories. Then the green cushion, the swirling jumpety motion, and the soothing regularity of steel wheel on steel rail that put you to sleep in a trice.

This train is a *Kaisokudo*, or *Pleasurable-Speed-Train*. Fast, but not too fast, stopping not too often, it rolls through the rich mountain-bordered plain of *Ise* by early morning. A light snowfall has given white caps to the dwarf rice-stacks that people the winter fields. Green tea plants wave frostily in the wind. The straggling stalks of each mulberry bush are tied into a top-knot of rats' tails. In June, these bare fields will be thick with green leaves ready for the silkworms, whose arrival the peasant times to suit the maturing leaves. Frozen rice paddies are broken here and there by the green of a bamboo clump, where parallel stems are gracefully inclined in the direction of the prevailing wind.

At about half past eight the train pulls into Matsuzaka. Even the station buildings here are constructed from clear, knot-free wood, such as is used for the shrines; for it is the birth-place of Motoori Noringa, poet and classical compiler of folk-lore.

> Isle of blest Japan,
> Should the spirit of the land
> Stranger seek to learn,
> Say it's where the cherry fair
> Scents the morning air.

So wrote 18th century Motoori Noringa. The Samurai knight was beautiful in life, and even in his death, like the falling blossom he glorified his land. New-old Japan still echoes his words today.

At Matsuzaka we are already in sanctified country. Hills on either side of the train are dotted with shrines both big and small. Marathon runners, mixing religion with asceticism, run races of endurance from shrine to shrine.

Reaching Yamada, we take the *Inner Shrine* first. The reed thatching of the shrine portals is richly moulded as a cake, while in the garden around, the roofs of the smaller buildings made from flaky cedar shingle give the more delicate appearance of fine pastry. In one such building an old Imperial horse munches out his last days in sacred solitude. A party of school children is purifying hands and mouths in the sacred stream. We watch them file silently between the giant spruce trees that rise infinite, absolute, until their dark, un-lessened trunks are hidden from view. Having doffed coats, scarves and hats, the children range themselves round the outer gateway, over which hangs a white silken curtain. Ordinary folk are not allowed beyond this. In unison they bow low, softly clap their hands, as they have so often rehearsed at school. The white curtain blows softly aside to reveal the closed inner gate to the holy of holies, on which portentous dragon clouds are painted. The court between inner and outer gates is deep in pebbles carried up from the stream by women, after a special purification ceremony. Every twenty years the rite is repeated, and the Shrine is shifted to its alternative site. Over the hand-borne shingle scrunches a party of high government officials, coat-less, in sombre blue uniform; they are led from one place of obeisance to the next by a high priest in flowing white robe and black gauze cap.

Passing back we have better opportunity to see the garden of the shrine. Layered, umbrella-shaped trees fall in to rounded lines in the middle distance. Hill contours mix grandeur with delicacy. Close at hand are the greys of stone paths and of shapely wooden bridges, the burnished green of copper-knobbed balustrades. What infinite care has been invested in the scene! The trees for miles around have been treated and pruned so that each will lend its individual beauty to the harmony of the whole.

The *Outer Shrine* is within the city itself. Watch the ever-changing congregation! A young mother goes gently down on one knee; the white foot bends up sharply from the toe on the wooden *geta*, and the baby in white knitted cloak and cap bobs up and down on her back. An old grandmother kneels quietly and long remains, intensely reverent, in one corner. A commercial school, in yellowish cotton uniforms, lines up ready. Perhaps these boys have spent the last twenty-four hours in a crowded train; now their hardship will be rewarded by half a minute of silent ceremony; two little girls, un-shy, un-giggling, walk simply up carrying the tag which makes them the representatives of their class. In all, nine hundred and sixty thousand such people visited *Ise* during the first month of the year.

Why do they come? What do they think about silently there? We put these questions to a friendly guard. He seemed surprised, as if it were the first time he had thought of such a thing. "Before the war," he answered after a while, "it was generally to pray for the success of some new venture - a business, a baby, a new wife, or a new husband - and to render thanks afterwards; but now it is to pray for the war or for a son or husband at the front"; meanwhile, as a background to this place of worship there is the portentous roar of diving, strifing aeroplanes. The sound suited. To me, in this place of ancient trees, running water, peeping sky, deified nature, it seemed like the sound of distant thunder or a waterfall. To the Japanese who come here it must unconsciously have the same effect; consciously it reminds them of the power and might of their country.

Chapter 9

Kathleen Hall

Aylwin's stay in Japan, during which time he didn't spare himself physically, proved that he had made an excellent recovery from his illness thanks to the careful nursing and feeding by the Millicans in Shanghai. What he really wanted to do was to return to China, to live amongst the ordinary people and see what the war was doing to their daily lives, and to see what new forms of society were developing under guerrilla government and what new industrial revolution was taking place in the hidden villages. He wondered what was happening to the refugees he had seen leaving Wuhan and Hankou. He was interested in the function of the Chinese Industrial Cooperatives, the CIC. He had been the first journalist to visit the earliest CIC Promotion Office when they opened in August 1938, in the New Life Movement Building in Hankou, for a story. He had met Rewi Alley there and had been offered work in the northwest. That was worth thinking about.

He had decided the first thing to do was to get into guerrilla country and somehow get in touch with people he had met in Yan'an. Returning to China through Korea and Manchuria, he made his way to Beijing where he prepared to slip out of the city with Chinese friends, English-speaking students from Yanjing University. He intended to contact his friend General Nie Rongzhen, commander-in-chief of all guerrilla forces in the Shanxi-Chahar-Hebei Border Region:

> As I rolled up in my quilt on the warm *kang* of the inn, while jaunty muleteers supped loudly off millet soup and a crowd of village children swarmed around the doorway to gape at the foreigner in bed, it seemed strange that only a few hours before I had been in the Beijing world of electric buttons, soft sheets, and spring beds. "Is this enjoyable, or is it just one of those things that are going to be nice to look back on?" I wondered, pulling the quilt up over my ears to shut out the mule's goodnight bray.

In the morning, he woke up shivering in high fever and was soon delirious. By chance that day there passed nearby a New Zealand nurse, Kathleen Hall.

Kathleen Hall was born in 1893 in Auckland, New Zealand. After training as a nurse, she came to China in 1922 as a missionary worker with the Society for the Propagation of the Gospel. After some years spent nursing and training nurses at various centres including Anguo in Hebei province and Datong in Shanxi province, she was sent, in 1935, to the small mountain village of Songjiazhuang in the Taihangshan range, on the border of Hebei and Shanxi. There she was to set up a cottage hospital to bring medical aid to the scattered villages in Tangxian County, and in this way bring together the far-flung and isolated Christian communities. In a letter home, dated September 1935, she wrote:

> Songjiazhuang is at most thirty-five miles from the railway and yet it might be hundreds of miles away, there is so little contact with the outside. What am I doing in this place? I have come with two nurses to try to do what we can for the physical ills of these people as well as caring for their spiritual needs. This has been a distressing two months with measles, or rather the complications of measles, carrying off a great many children in the villages all around, and dysentery taking a great many more, while malaria is leaving many very anaemic and too weak to resist other things. There is every kind of disease among the people, but perhaps one of the most distressing things to us is the knowledge that so much of it is so unnecessary; so many of their ills are just the result of their ignorance and utter lack of the simplest rules of hygiene ....
>
> This is a new parish. The first Christian was not young when he was baptised, and he has only recently died. The older Christians are still the keenest. Their simple faith means a great deal to these people. Their farm work is strenuous, their implements are primitive – everything is done by manual labour. There is very little land in the valleys, and most of them are dependent on the hill fields. That means making little terraces all the way up high hillsides wherever there is soil available, scraping out rocks, and building up strong walls to keep the fields from being washed away in the rains. Their fields may be a long way from their homes, and they come back very late for the evening meal. But every evening, when the meal is over, at about half past nine, the Christian men and women come along, or come up or down the hill – for Evensong ....
>
> There are very real difficulties. By far the most important part of our work must be education, and so far with so many seriously ill patients to attend to, we have had very little time for systematic personal hygiene and public health work. It is going to need infinite patience, much tact, and great perseverance ....

In her first five months there, Kathleen made five hundred visits to homes and had three thousand patients. There was as yet no hospital and no dispensary. She and the two nurses camped in a meagre room lent to them by one of the non-Christian families. With her tremendous energy and unwavering support from her two devoted helpers, she made great progress in establishing the mission. Most of the missionaries in China placed great hope in the Kuomintang, an attitude presumably reinforced by the fact that Jiang Jieshi and his wife, Soong Mei Ling, were themselves Christians.

After the Marco Polo Bridge Incident on 7 July 1937, when the Japanese pressed southward from Beijing, the plains of Hebei Province became a gigantic and bloody battleground. Songjiazhuang itself was safe in the hills, but Kathleen was spending a year at Anguo, where she had previously been stationed, as locum for an English nurse on furlough. Anguo was right in the path of military flux. Kathleen's efforts to help the shattered Kuomintang troops have been likened, with no exaggeration, to the efforts of Florence Nightingale at Scutari. During that year, the Songjiazhuang mission was closed down, but in January 1938, Kathleen moved back there to reopen the mission. In that same month at Wutaishan it was decided, and approved by Jiang Jieshi, to set up the Hebei-Chahar-Shanxi Border Region government. This was a United Front administration with the Communists in a leading role. Kathleen wrote of this period:

> The old corrupt county government had gone. So had the worst of the big landlords who had been so grasping and selfish and indifferent to the poverty and suffering of the people. Sections of the Eighth Route Army were gradually infiltrating our area, and with their coming changes began to take place. What a joy it was to have active and enthusiastic men and women with new ideas of cooperation and education for the people, teaching them to elect their own leaders and bringing them hope of better standards of living for all.

Very soon, General Nie Rongzhen, who was commander of the Eighth Route Army in the new Border Region, called upon Kathleen, and during their conversation, Kathleen's worries and doubts about the intentions of the Communists were dispelled. The guerrillas were ensconced in the hills above Songjiazhuang, where they would not themselves be harassed by the Japanese who had established a firmly garrisoned, twenty-mile-wide corridor along the Beijing-Hankou railway line.

At this time, Kathleen realised that, in order to continue her work, it would be necessary to ensure medical supplies as she was no longer able to rely upon her base hospital at Anguo. So she herself started to travel frequently between Beijing and Songjiazhuang, via Anguo, carrying supplies through the Japanese lines. She cashed in heavily on being a foreigner, relying on the fact that the Japanese dared not harm a Westerner for fear of jeopardising their country's support, and she made this journey every second month throughout 1938. In early February 1939, she obtained a good supply and so, armed with her passport and Japanese permit to travel, and as usual on these occasions dressed up to play the part of a "proper" foreign missionary, she took them by train to Dingxian in order to make delivery of part of the consignment to the St Barnabas' Hospital in Anguo. Driving her donkey cart and approaching the village of Gaomen on the Quyang road, after yet again having successfully negotiated the Japanese lines, she was stopped by a group of frantic children.

Kathleen took charge of the sick foreigner. After quick examination it was apparent that she had a typhus patient on her hands. Aylwin was bundled up in blankets and deposited in the back of Kathleen's cart. Later he wrote:

> I remember her scampering like a rabbit over the fields all day to find the best roads, while I sat churlishly in my blankets. Later, when the mountains became too steep for the cart, I remember an almost insurmountable problem of how to keep my balance on top of a donkey's packsaddle piled with bedding.

It took three days to reach their destination, the other side of Quyang County, an ancient centre of marble sculpture, an area dominated by a huge sixth-century temple which was built before Beijing even existed. Finally they reached the little hill village of Songjiazhuang, and Aylwin was installed in the simple cottage hospital. He wrote of his time there:

> Old men on doors, babies and children in their mothers' arms, ashen faced young soldiers on crutches, waited patiently all day in front of the consulting room. Often at night there would be a call at the door, and the nurse would take her hurricane lamp and her big yellow dog, Shimao, to hurry over the mountains, returning at dawn to make ready for another long day's work. The people seemed to trust her as a friend; but not all of them trusted her medicines, so it often happened that she was called in only after all other methods had failed. After the local midwife had done her best with dirty fingers, rusty hooks and scissors, after the local physician had tried pummelling, bloodletting and opium, after the family had wasted long hours and precious coppers in the temple, the nurse would be sent for at some midnight zero hour, and this would be made the test of her skill and of her faith.

His fellow patients were two peasant folk – an old man and a boy – both with infected wounds. One night the local schoolmaster was brought in mortally wounded – teacher by day, guerrilla by night. Kathleen did not expect Aylwin to pull through. Westerners normally had little resistance to typhus and usually succumbed. She had not asked anything about her typhus patient. In the Resistance, it was not *done* to ask people who they were and where they came from. Only when he was going through a particularly bad spell did she open his wallet and check letters for names and whereabouts of relations. He had picked up typhus in Beijing at about the same time as he had received typhus inoculations and so had a fighting chance. After three weeks of very high fever, he was on the road to recovery but needed a lot of rest and feeding up again. "There was no plethora of seafood and other luxuries such as the Millicans fed me up on," he wrote on 6 April 1939, "but there are two goats, together have done very well indeed." During his convalescence, lasting another three weeks, he was able to observe the goings on in the village, the daily life in this border region and the way the people organised themselves in resistance against the Japanese the Self Defence Corps, the Farmers', the Workers', the Women's and the Young Men's Associations, the Children's Corps, all forming a democratic system of their own and having direct access to the government authorities at all stages up to the Central Guerrilla Government of that region.

He talked with the Border Region workers, many of whom had been students and could speak English. At the same time his knowledge of Chinese took tremendous leaps forward. Kathleen told him a lot about the old society, and he lapped it all up. He saw in the lives and hopes of these people that the border government meant everything to them. Despite their abject poverty and lack of food, they would give everything they had, including their lives, for it. What he learned of these people filled him with amazement and respect. Until now, Aylwin had been the fresh Oxford graduate, keen for adventure and desire to shine in journalism, and with perhaps a certain ingrained feeling of superiority. In this village of a hundred or so families, linked by rough footpaths to other similar villages on the hills and in the valleys, a great change came over him. Aylwin had always loved singing. On his travels through Europe and America he collected folk songs. Now he keenly learned guerrilla songs, and songs of the countryside. Kathleen remembers that, as he became well enough to explore the pathways outside the village, the valley would be filled by his rich, deep singing voice: first by "Old McDonald Had a Farm", and then later "Nothing to eat, nothing to wear, only with the arms we capture from our enemy". In later years this song would always bring tears to his eyes with the memories of Songjiazhuang. Normally this song was sung at a galloping tempo, but Aylwin always drew out the notes with emotion, giving the last line the full power of his baritone voice.

Aylwin wrote the following story in Songjiazhuang, in April 1939. Kathleen smuggled it out to Beijing, and finally it was published in the *Manchester Guardian* on 9 February 1940:

> To Sung Kuoxing it seemed hopeless. Soon they would reach a fork in the mountain path. One way led to a point above the village where the Chinese soldiers were quartered; that way meant freedom for him, perhaps money. The other way went up into the mountains, to nowhere in particular. If he misled the band of Japanese soldiers who had captured him they might wander bewildered for days and be trapped before they could reach any friendly base. But he, Sung Kuoxing, would die like a dog with a bullet blasted through his brain.
>
> To Kuoxing the donkey-man, things had always seemed hopeless. For days and years he had plodded the mountain paths of North China behind his beast loaded with wool for the railway, country produce for town markets, or perhaps with some *taitai* (housewife) riding cross legged on the pack saddle to visit a relation. Now and then he emitted an encouraging "Da!" or falsetto "Urrri!" but perfunctorily, not as though he really cared. "Kuoxing thinks too much," said the other donkey-men as they swaggered carefree and laughing alongside their animals, long pipes with tiny metal bowls slung jauntily over their shoulders or tucked down their necks.
>
> It was true; Kuoxing did think too much, and his thoughts were not often of contentment. The others were happy if they could make a few extra cents from their fares. They talked of nothing but how much this man and how much that man had got, for what, and when. But Kuoxing didn't see life in terms of coppers, and he hated the sight of his stubborn, dainty little ass, all woolly black on top and downy white underneath. His secret ambition was to go to a big city and drive a truck! There was the life for a man! No more plodding, no more prodding, but a nice noisy lorry with a horn. And maybe in his spare time he could study and find out other things. Especially he wanted to find out why the little *Ocean Devils* should have come to his village last year and senselessly killed his family and his friends, senselessly burned terrace upon terrace of houses, and scattered meagre stores of grain.
>
> But that was only day-dreaming. Man and beast together ate through all their earnings; nothing could be saved. So Kuoxing brooded and plodded, and learned the lie of the country like the back of his hand. That was why the Japanese had taken him.

They had come to his village a second time and demanded a guide. Kuoxing, whose moroseness had won him no sympathy, was pushed forward. "All right," said the Japanese officer, "you lead us to Chinese soldiers, or ..." and he tapped his revolver with a grin. That *Chinese Army*! So far he had found nothing more dangerous than peasants working in the fields, women with water-cans slung on a pole across one shoulder, stumping along on the butts of their bound feet. He must get results before he could think about going back.

So now Kuoxing's decision was drawing near. Maybe he did have hopeless ambitions, maybe he was discontented, but Kuoxing didn't want to die. He had never told anyone, for all I know not even himself, but he loved lots of things about life; the terraced foothills leading up from the sandy river valley to the great fluted mountains that rose square like cathedrals of perfectly proportioned brown earth, the sky in the hours before dawn, the moon shining on the white bark of poplars by the river, and at last the sunrise, reddening brown earth and mountains; the pride in picking the best path, the sense of achievement at the top of some high stony pass; the jolly, murky bustle of the inn while animals were being watered, the millet soup and the warm brick *kang* at the end of a hard day.

A year ago there would have been no hesitation. All soldiers were fools, anyway; whose they were made no difference at all. Then his village had been wrecked without reason, and closely following it had come soldiers who talked in his own language of a new and unified China. "Japanese militarists and imperialists have sent their soldiers to rob China," they had said; "all we Chinese must stand together to resist. We, your soldiers, will fight; you must help us with our wounded, with food, and with information about enemy movements." That had seemed sense. And then when the Chinese soldiers came back and set up a Government over the district, that was good too. The peasants knew just how much they would have to give in taxes for the Army, and it was paid through the Government, not, as before, to any blustering warlord's *officer* who happened along with a pack of soldiers at his heels. Then there was the drilling in the Self-Defence Corps. Kuoxing knew that he and his fellow muleteers and peasants and shopkeepers weren't very good at drilling, and that they couldn't really stop the Japanese with wooden broad-swords and home-made spears; but, all the same, it gave one a fine sense of being a part of something big, this drilling did, especially when you realised that in towns and villages for miles and miles, much further even than Kuoxing had ever been with his donkey, men were drilling in just the same way.

All this occurred to Kuoxing in the hour of his decision. Suddenly he knew, and his heart was very light as he led his band up into the mountains where it could do no harm.

That night Kuoxing leapt thirty feet down into a dry river bed, and ran crouching away. Rifle bullets whined past him and splintered rocks by his side, but he ran on. Later, the moon came out and shone softly on the bark of the poplar trees, and the mountains down one side of the valley were washed with silvery sheen. Kuoxing walked swiftly all night beside the trickle of the shrunken river; he saw the red dawn light the crags of his mountain and silhouette his crenulated sky-line. And his body seemed possessed of a wild joy as he jumped from stone to stone.

When he reached a certain village he was taken before the Japanese officers in charge. "You must be lying," they said, when he had finished his story; "a body of our soldiers was surprised and destroyed not far from here. It is you who must have led the way to them." An hour later Kuoxing died with a bullet through his brain, but his soul was untroubled.

One day a group of horsemen clattered through Songjiazhuang village and pulled up at the hospital. "We've come for the foreigner," they explained, producing an invitation from General Nie to visit him further west. A few hours later they had left their horses and were climbing past a pair of sentries corseted in hand grenades to Nie's encampment in a temple, just thirty miles away in Fuping.

Chapter 10

Guerrilla Interlude

Aged about forty years old, General Nie Rongzhen was commander-in-chief for all the guerrilla forces in the Border Region of Shanxi-Chahar-Hebei. He was born near Chongqing, in Sichuan, of a rich peasant family. He went to France in 1920 with a work-study group. Whilst doing factory work there he met Zhou Enlai, studied Marxism, and joined the Chinese Communist Party. After that he studied sciences for a time in a workers' college in Belgium and then went to Moscow for two years to study at the Red Army Military Academy there. He returned to China to complete his military training at Jiang Jieshi's Whampoa Military Academy near Guangzhou. After graduation, he stayed on at the academy to take up a position as instructor. Later, at the time of the Kuomintang-Communist split, he joined the First Red Army of Lin Biao, making the Long March with it from Jiangxi to Shaanxi. In 1937, it was he, together with the Border Region's chairman, Sung Sao Wen, who first conceived the idea of setting up an organised government for the countryside after the Japanese had advanced along the railways and the old officials had fled. "This Border Region is only carrying on until it can be linked with the rear and sink its identity into that of Free China," General Nie explained. Aylwin stayed a week at the headquarters. He spent the bulk of each day talking with army and government people who came to see the general.

Aylwin described the start of his journey thus: "Then we packed up and set off on horseback up a winding grey valley of sand, through which the water trickled over a string of boat-shaped gardens. On either side along the lower slopes, cherry or pear trees were in bloom. Brown hills lay behind, and purple razor-edged peaks stood up like stage scenery in the distance. This was the second day of my life on horseback." They were on their way to Wutaishan (Five-Terrace Mountain), the seat of Red Government in that Region. The Eighth Route Army gathered there when the new Border Region was set up, and it was from there that General Nie scored the first, and most important, victory for the Chinese against the Japanese. As the Japanese started to advance south from Beijing, General Nie allowed them to take strategic centres in Shanxi without opposition, but then struck from the rear in the area around Pingxin where the Japanese were put to route.

That evening in conversation over supper, the travellers were discussing the Japanese national character. One of their company, who was a graduate of Tokyo Imperial University, commented of the Japanese, "They are very polite about entering each other's houses, so for a long time after the first railways were built, each train pulling out of the station left many wooden *geta* neatly lined along the edge of the platform." The following day showed them the complete opposite of such consideration for their fellow men. For mile upon mile along the valley, whole villages stood charred and roofless; an area once dominated by a huge Buddhist temple was now reduced to rubble by point-blank gunfire. The villagers had fled to the hills, but a few were to be seen sifting and salvaging through the wreckage. This was how the Japanese taught the people not to play guerrillas: no houses meant no crops, and no crops meant no guerrillas. So the invader could rule supreme over a black and blistered land, generating more hatred than Cromwell and the English kings managed to create in Ireland.

On the approach to Wutaishan, they were met by Chairman Sung. He and other government men had come to discuss with General Nie the subject of army-people cooperation: how the collection of grain, cloth, and manpower was to be controlled. The army needed provisions, and the people wanted to supply. However, the army should not deal directly with the people, unless absolutely unavoidable, in order to keep friction to a minimum.

The Border Region boasted three hot springs. One had been captured by the Japanese, but one of the other two was close by to Wutaishan. Off they went on horseback for a hot bath. Through clouds of steam, sitting in and around the two-foot-deep big stone pool into which spouted the hot water, General Nie, Chairman Sung, the commissioner for commerce and industry, and various other dignitaries described for Aylwin their postwar plans for the area: "Horses, hot springs, and mountain beauty spots, all within easy reach of Beijing when we get a few motor roads through!" The commissioner was very enthusiastic in his plans for a luxury hotel on that spot with special suites for Western friends: for Evans Carlson and for Associated Press correspondent Haldore Hanson, two of the earliest visitors to the Region.

Striking off northwards once more, they soon came across the Regional Government ensconced in an old temple. Here, as in many places around the region, monks and guerrillas lived alongside each other. Aylwin described the scene thus:

> While the busy life of the student groups, the delegations, the telephone messages and telegrams went on all round them, and the offices hummed with the job of keeping hundreds of government units close on the heels of enemy troops, the monks kept up their peaceful rituals. Three or four times each day they shut themselves into a room filled with gold-leafed gods and percussion instruments, and the sound of their wailing prayers came creeping out from behind the closed doors. One of their little bells struck the same note as that of my typewriter, and I could imagine them turning over the pages each time it rang.

Reiterating what he had already commented about what he had seen in Yan'an, Aylwin wrote of the Red Army: "It isn't *red* and it isn't an *army* in our use of the words, and it certainly isn't *communist* in the Soviet-Marxist sense." Much of the time, energy and man-power of the army, he found, was devoted to education, not only of the Chinese people in the countryside but of the enemy troops. In fact the education directed at the Japanese was regarded, in his view, as maybe of more importance than the education of the Chinese:

Each company must learn one new Japanese song each month, and anti-war songs are sung in Japanese across the lines at night; slogans are shouted in unison while going into battle, or written up on walls where the enemy troops are likely to see them; leaflets written by prisoners are scattered along the highways where marching troops or truck drivers will pick them up.

In the same village where he was staying was the headquarters of the Women's Association, which had been founded just two years previously. There was a full-time staff of a thousand who were paid in food and clothing, nothing more. They claimed a membership, in the Region, of several hundred thousand. One of the workers told Aylwin:

> The aim of our association is to mobilise the women for national salvation and reconstruction, to better their living conditions, and get them used to equal political status. Every day there are two thousand classes for adult women, led by the village schoolteachers with our textbooks, besides many other character-recognising, or literacy, and newspaper-reading groups. In the thirty counties where our work is best established, there have already been sixteen women elected as village heads, and 1,431 elected to other committees on the village governments.

This same worker, a mere girl, later told Aylwin her own story:

> When my college friends rushed away from Beijing at the beginning of the war, I thought I would stay on for at least another year, until after I'd graduate. But our student life soon became intolerable. It wasn't so much the jaunty little men in the streets and the way they tried to *inflict peace* on our city, as the thought of my classmates out there beyond the walls. I showed their letters, smuggled in from the hills, to my mother, but she was more afraid of dirt and poverty than she was of the Japanese. To go out and live with rough peasants seemed to her like putting the clock back. "Wait a little! Wait a little!" she kept telling me, "and when you have finished your education you can go to join your father in Chongqing." One night I couldn't bear it any longer, and slipped out of the city by ways a friend had shown me.

City shoes were exchanged for rope sandals, and Fragrant Grass, as she was called, walked for days over the stony mountains of West Hebei. Once, the mere thought of lice struck her with horror but inevitably the time came when she had to share, in country fashion, a peasant *kang*. There, her sleeping companions were sure to be lousy. Her table companions, some of whom she knew to be consumptive, dipped their chopsticks into the same common bowl. She had brought her own enamelled washing bowl with her to avoid trachoma, but it had soon been claimed as common property. After noticing a soldier using her bowl to feed a sick donkey one day, she relinquished all claim to it. She told more of her experiences:

The countrywomen were much stranger to me than the foreign professors at college, and it was a long time before I could make them understand what I was after. Then we got groups competing with each other in making shoes and uniforms for the soldiers. Evening classes became quite popular with the help of the local teachers. Leaders grew up from the women themselves, who could carry on meetings and classes with the help of our pamphlets. The best districts formed women's self-defence corps, drilled themselves twice a week, and began to take over sentry duty, freeing men for work in the fields. Women who had lost face by being unable to bear boy children were taught how to regain status in the family by bringing in a side income from some kind of domestic industry.

Later I was sent to one of the Japanese Railway-Loving Villages on the Beijing-Hankou line. The Japanese at this time were trying out a new policy of kindness with the people, bowing low out of respect to the elders, offering sugar to the children, and buying paper temple money for the peasants to burn over their dead. I tried secretly to organise small patriotic groups, and show the people what kind of false peace it was that the Japanese were really offering them. When they burned the paper money, I reminded them of the burned homes and slaughtered people at other times in their village. After several months passed like this, the guerrillas raided our village to arrest the leading traitors, and I was allowed to come back here with them.

A year later, Struggle (she had changed her name) no longer shuddered at the unwomanliness of the gawky peasant wives; she had learned the trick of keeping her own way of life while respecting what was beneath the surface in theirs. She would get up early and go out to find a tree to sit under or a rock by the river. Then she could come back and talk to them in their own language about the war, its relation to women's emancipation, or the more ancient problems of mothers-in-law and babies. Gradually she became to love them for their ingrown family troubles, their unending labour, and their kindliness.

Back at college, the dainty Fragrant Grass had been in the habit of mild affairs with the men. Now her complexion was gone, and she was apt to have boils on her neck, but she didn't want affairs anyway. At headquarters there was a young southerner called Zhou Weiming. They used to delve into each other's pasts, comparing colleges and families, but more often they talked about the future, when the Eighth Route Army would enter Beijing and the Border District would sink itself into a new democratic country.

One night they walked scrunching through the valley sand past where the women sat stripping leaves for pickling to where the shrunken river curled swiftly round some rocks and a deserted temple looked down from the top of a small hill. Sitting on the rocks, he took her hand in his, felt its quiet yielding. Her head was turned away, but he drew her to him and kissed her face tenderly, then rapturously, striving to awaken its calm sculptured beauty. The poplar leaves rustled on as though nothing had happened; mountains came down dark and friendly in the dusk and a row of trees climbed a jagged ridge against the white sky.

The wedding guests were lighthearted as they sat round the preliminary whetting of tea and peanuts; busy silence came with the dishes. There was chicken, chopped pork, spinach, scrambled eggs, shredded turnips, and sweet potatoes. At each place a bowl of noodles, at each corner a pile of steamed bread. A quarter of an hour later, chopsticks were plying more choosily, poising like divining rods above the chosen spot, deftly picking some dainty morsel from under the leavings. Weiming's department chief rose to his feet and began to speak abruptly. "Comrades," he said, "these two have been rash enough to get married." Everybody cheered and clapped and stamped their feet. "But see how the old bashful love of lace and peach blossoms adjusts itself to the matter-of-fact circumstances! The bride is no blushing rose with cherry lips, almond eyes, lily-small feet, and limbs softly peeking through silken split skirts. Our Struggle in uniform won't have a house and servants or even a honeymoon bed. She's got to keep her mobility, just as a guerrilla soldier has. Marriage in this age and place is a kind of personal united front, which helps each party to give more to their work. China in the making is a third party, who instead of being a snake in the grass holds the other two together. Am I right or not?"

"Right!" cried the guests.

That night, lying on the *kang* in line with his department men, Weiming thought back to a certain Sunday in the Resist Japan Academy in Yan'an. Sunday was a day of change. He had put on his shorts and an old coloured relic of student days in Guangzhou, and had gone down to the river to wash his uniform; then, at midday, to the cooperative's restaurant with some friends. Six planes came over the mountains while they were eating, bombed the city, and raked the straggling hillsides with prongs of death. He had pulled comrades out from the rubble of wood and plaster, and straightened twisted corpses on the streets. One of them was the body of a girl who had marched the roads with him all the way from the south. Sordid-souled and listless, only one thought had comforted him – soon he would be going north to help build resistance within the Japanese rear. Now, Weiming smiled to himself before falling asleep.

Struggle was sent to live in the railway zone. Playing the part of a visiting relation, she was busy organising cells of loyalist women and sending out information. She discovered a heroin agent, and the Chinese soldiers came in to arrest him during the night. Soon after this she found she was pregnant. Proud as a wife, sad as a mother because she knew she would not be able to keep the child by her. As a worker, she felt ashamed in spite of herself.

When she got back, she and Weiming went to see a friendly peasant couple about looking after the child, and came away reassured. A month before her time, she stayed miserably away from her work; a month after a son had been born to her she was back again, driving herself to dull the pain of bereavement. Weiming was away. The war went on. For a time she was able to see her baby after work, then the situation became dangerous, and her whole department had to move away. "You look after your work, and we'll look after your son," the peasant woman said as she bade her goodbye. "If the things you tell us are right, his day will come."

Chairman Sung suggested an extended tour of the Region, so General Nie provided a Yanjing University graduate from his staff, with four guards and six horses. They moved through the Region from garrison to garrison, and Aylwin learned more about guerrilla tactics. They joined company along the way with the Northwest Front Service Group: a band of twenty-four singers, actors, and ex-movie stars who were graduates of the Lu Xun Arts School in Yan'an and were involved in propaganda work with the country people. Filing through the mountains, snatches of songs would filter back and forth along the line; then at each village, word from the front would bring them into strict order and they would pass through in disciplined military fashion, silent as a guerrilla army unit. "We get our food, uniforms, and two dollars a month," Aylwin was told by one of the girls. "That's plenty. All we need to buy is peanuts to munch along the road." On arrival at a chosen village, they would set up their stage in the market place, find a suitable building for accommodation, light a fire, cook their food, and then get down to discussing drama technique and how to adapt old and popular plays for their modern purpose.

A message arrived from the southernmost base informing them that an escort would meet them to cross the Chengtai Railway, and so Aylwin lumbered southward astride a mountainous Japanese carthorse. Its back was so broad that he found when he spread out his bedroll upon it, he could rest very comfortably. For the hazardous crossing of the railway, his party was joined by a hundred or so graduates of the Resist-Japan Academy from Yan'an who were on their way to southeast Shaanxi to start work there. Aylwin asked the same question of many of them: "What made you leave home and go to Yan'an in the first place?" The answers were simple: everything from "dissatisfaction with a comfortable life" to "bombed out by the Japanese". But what it all boiled down to for the majority was a search for comradeship and equality in a national cause. Everything was ready for the night crossing when the plan had to be abandoned. The Japanese had launched a new attack on the railway, and they were forced to march north again. Aylwin wrote "The gunfire continued all next morning, and we moved farther into the mountains, arriving at a tiny hamlet just as the peasant families were squatting round on their haunches to suck their evening noodles. From the rooftops, we could see Japanese planes dive-bombing over the village we had just left." They had to bide time, waiting for the attack to ease up, and then they would attempt the crossing as originally planned. Aylwin continued "One night I was awakened very late by shouts of 'Self-Defence Corps out to carry stretchers!' and peals of the temple gong. In the morning a friendly old man in our nether household told me that over a thousand men had gone from the villages in the neighbourhood." This was yet another illustration of the tremendously well-organised guerrilla structure. The telephone system, evident from the precariously propped lines straddling the countryside, and the postal service, airmail markers being chicken feathers under the envelopes' flaps, which sped the letters from hand to hand by night and day, yielded further evidence.

The Japanese kept striking the area for a week. When they finally withdrew, a twenty-four-hour march brought their guerrilla party down from the mountains. Their approach to the banks of the river, on the other side of which lay the railway embankment, was made by night, and they could see in the moonlight, not far away, the city of Niangziquan. The Japanese flag flew from the top of a tall mast in a Railway-Loving Village just ahead: this was a signal to the sentries on the city wall that all was well. Aylwin continued his narrative:

> The men of the village were out to meet us with gifts of Japanese sugar. After swift consultation they led us across the rails and silently off into the mountains on the far

side. Everything was as quiet as church before the minister appears in the pulpit; frogs
and crickets played vibrant chords, and once a mule brayed from our column in front,
as though the organist had suddenly expired across the keys. The sound was cut abruptly
by the lashing of a whip and the muffled cursing of soldiers. Looking back, I could see
the Japanese flag still floating palely in the moonlight.

They were safely across and were once more melting into the countryside.

Shortly they were to be held up by unusually heavy rains in a village beside the river that
they had understood they should cross in order to reach the present headquarters of General
Zhu De, commander-in-chief of the whole Eighth Route Army. Aylwin continues:

> The summer rains made clean streaks down the backs of the children and over
> their bellies, swollen with the eating of husks and tree bark. The peasants sat grinning
> happily in their doorways. The officers sat in the local mess – a large barn decorated
> with pictures of Mao Zedong, Zhu De, Carl Marx, and Jiang Jieshi – took time off to
> shave their heads, play chess, drink tea, spit on the floor, and read pamphlets to each
> other in loud voices. The soldiers placed bowls of uniforms outside to soak. At intervals,
> someone would remark hopefully, "It will be cooler after the rain."

In the second week of waiting, a storm blew up, and the already-swollen river rose further,
washing right into the village. Aylwin wrote, "A family of camels tethered outside screeched
thinly as the water rose up to their knees, and our soldiers shouted to each other as they packed
everything in preparation for flight by the light of fluttering candles." This was the highest the
river had risen in seventy years. The next day the weather cleared, and the river receded slightly,
but they could still hear the destructive grinding of rocks carried along by the torrent.

By the time they could wade across the river, Zhu De's headquarters had moved away.
Nobody knew exactly where he had gone. The party moved out westward and had to cross
another Japanese-held road. Here, the area was less well organised, lines of communication were
sketchy, and there was greater uncertainty as to which villages were under enemy occupation. At
night and without guides, they crossed fields of mud, made a dash across the road, and forded
a river to reach the foothills on the far side where they found a village to sleep in just as it was
getting light. Aylwin continued:

> An hour later, we were awakened by rifle shots. "It is probably some traitors," said
> a guard as we hurried away from the village. "They are given rifles instead of pay, and
> collect their own food. They fire like that to frighten the people away, and then go in
> for chickens and pigs." After the commotion had calmed down and the intruders had
> left, some villagers appeared and confirmed the explanation. We all joined in pouring
> unmentionable epithets on the mothers of traitors.

After a few more days travelling, they passed into the territory controlled by a military unit
known as the Shanxi Sacrifice Union, which had been formed some three years previously.

The Japanese had invaded the province of Suiyuan, now part of Inner Mongolia, to the north, and the Red Army had ended their Long March by taking occupation of Shaanxi to the west. The governor of Shanxi, Yan Xishan, felt threatened by these two forces. He had his own loyal feudal troops, but they would be quite unable to resist any encroachment from the north and west. Out of this opportunity, a new force rose as a popular mobilisation to resist Japan, and on 8 September 1936, five years after the Mukden Incident, the Sacrifice Union was formed with Yan Xishan as nominal head. At first the union was allowed no real power, but when war broke out in 1937, followed by the swift collapse of Yan's government and army, the increasing activity of the Eighth Route Army and Central Government forces on his borders convinced Yen that he must promote the Sacrifice Union, which formed its own army – the Dare-to-Die Corps. There were five brigades with fifteen thousand men in all, under Po Yi-o. Because funds were short, five brigades being supported on money given for three, they became known as the Seventh and a Half Route Army. Just over half of Shanxi still remained under Yan's control, being governed by Sacrifice Union magistrates. Chairman Sung Sao Wen of the Shanxi-Chahar-Hebei Border Region was himself a Sacrifice Union man, one of Yan's former super-magistrates.

Aylwin and his companions came across the political headquarters of the Sacrifice Union, set up in a temple near Gaoping. Here, Jung Wushen, one of the top five officials informed them, "In North China today, the mass movement is growing and strong, but that does not mean that North China is Communist. The people are being mobilised for resistance and reconstruction, and not strictly for political purposes."

Aylwin saw similar mass education schemes and ideas on propaganda among the enemy troops being carried out here as there were in the Eighth Route Army areas. But in the adjoining village he saw something new. A school had been set up for four hundred little devils. These children had been collected from the Dare-to-Die fighting forces and were receiving concentrated education for the first time in their lives. There was one weedy little boy of ten. At the age of eight his parents had sold him to a traitor for seven dollars. He had been used to carrying messages until some soldiers discovered him and brought him to the school for a different kind of education.

After receiving information that Japanese prisoners were immediately shot by their officers on return to their units, the Dare-to-Die Corps decided not to return prisoners any more. Aylwin wrote:

> When I arrived first at the prison loft there was nobody at home. A few minutes later they appeared up the ladder, looking very refreshed after a swim in the river, and each with a capful of apples in his hand. The jailer himself was ex-captive Japanese, now a Sacrifice Union member. Of the two prisoners recently taken from a marauding party by the villagers, Nishimura had been a Tokyo Industrial High School student until coming to China a year previously. The other, Kawai, was a grocer in Kyoto. Nishimura's head was still bandaged where a farmer had struck him with a pole.

Sitting around on a mat in Japanese style with their shoes off, they conversed through interpreters about the war. It was a very diplomatic conversation that told nothing except perhaps confusion on the part of the Japanese people as to their own government's intentions. Later:

> We went off to show ourselves to a mass meeting. Nishimura made a speech on the subject of a united front against fascism. From the platform I could see how his hands quivered, clasped behind his back, but his bandaged head was held well back as he faced the crowd of curious peasants who two weeks before had almost killed him. Kawai sang a squeaky song which everybody kindly encored.

At last, Zhu De's headquarters were located somewhere to the east with promise of a four-day journey and only one more Japanese line to cross. This line ran right across southeastern Shanxi, from the Taoqing Railway to the Tungpu Railway. The road was heavily garrisoned, lined with fortified villages, and bordered by a wide belt of scorched earth where nothing could possibly live. This line was a road by which the Japanese both drained the countryside of its raw materials and maintained a blockade separating the coal and iron areas in the south from the grain producing areas in the north. Aylwin continues:

> We stopped late one evening on the edge of this belt to squat round in the dusk for a pep talk explaining a complicated system of passwords in case of trouble, then walked on, stubbing our feet in stony river beds, shuffling silently through gutted villages, filing swiftly along narrow paths cut out of sheer cliff sides. Once every half hour we were allowed a breathing spell for the pack animals to catch up. "Tell the mule man he mustn't light his pipe!" the whispered command was passed down the line. "Don't cough!" And repeatedly, "Tell the animals not to make so much noise!" Each time this order came back, the man with the horse behind me swore bitterly, "How can they help it if they've got hooves!" He and his horse were the two most experienced members of the party: one had been a Red Guerrilla in the Shanxi Civil War days, and the other was an old Long Marcher from Jiangxi.
>
> In front ran a squad of soldiers; behind them forty students, an engineer, the Red Guerrilla and his Long Marching horse, the nonsmoking mule man and his mule with my typewriter and bedding. The whole thing constituted a perambulating concertina that in turn strung itself out or dashed in on itself from the rear. The old horse took it all like a circus, scrambling up steep banks, spanking over the open stretches, or pulling up dead at a split second's notice, and all without so much as a snort. But my mule was quite unable to stand the pace, or maybe its master stopped for a pull of baccy. "Where's the mule?" The officer counted us over as we scuttled down the Japanese highway for fifty yards before striking out into country on the far side. Nobody knew. It was more than a question of my things; if the mule blundered into a Japanese sentry post a party might be sent out to investigate and posts ahead of us would be informed. A squad was sent back to find the straggler and returned half an hour later with not only the mule but a roll of Japanese telephone wire.

Two days later they arrived at Zhu De's illusive headquarters, and there Aylwin found his old friend whom he had met at the Eighth Route Army office in Xi'an, on his way to Yan'an in June 1938, just over a year ago. Now it was 8 September 1939, the eighth anniversary of the Mukden Incident, and there was a meeting in celebration. Aylwin continues:

> As we sat listening to the speeches, he held my hand closely for three hours, much as a father holds the hand of his smallest son, so that I was hard put to it to find a way of blowing my nose. His eyes turned upwards into crinkles at the corners, and without his speaking I felt somehow that he was glad to see me.

To the meeting were invited Eighth Route Army personnel, scholars and teachers, landlords and peasants. Shrewd-eyed, lantern-jawed Peng Dehuai, Zhu De's second in command, addressed the meeting: "There are two sets of the Three Principles of the People in China today," he said. "One is that of Dr Sun Yat-sen and our Generalissimo Jiang Jieshi; Nationalism, Democracy and People's Livelihood. The other is that of Wang Jingwei and like-minded traitors; anti-Communist, anti-United Front, and pro-National Slavery." Observing this meeting of extremes, Reds and landlords, Aylwin was reminded of a captured Japanese document that he had seen a few weeks previously, which was the text of a speech given by the commander of the Tenth Division to his officers concerning army-people relations. It read:

> The economic might of our Empire has been flouted by China and by the world. The success or failure of the war is, in the last resort, more or less determined by economic factors, and the main policy of our Government is on the one hand to control domestic economy in the homeland and on the other to obtain the resources of the occupied areas. Thus, alongside the war of military force we must be engaged in a war of economics and of thought .... The Chinese Communist policy is an excellent example. They systematically build up the mass movements. They arm the people and win their confidence. We must do the same. We must win the hearts of the people ....

Aylwin's intention in setting out from Shanghai almost nine months earlier had been to find out what new forms of society were developing under guerrilla government and then to investigate the new industrial revolution taking place in the hinterland. By now he considered the first part of his mission accomplished, and Zhu De urged him on to the second stage by encouraging him in the idea to find Rewi Alley, whose centre of operations was now based in Baoji, west of Xi'an, and asked him to write about all he saw, honestly and clearly, to tell the world what was going on inside China.

Chapter 11

Journey to Baoji

A few days after his arrival at Zhu De's headquarters, two English professors from Yanjing University, Ralph Lapwood and Michael Lindsay (later Lord Lindsay of Birker) turned up from Beijing. These were the first foreigners, except for Japanese, that Aylwin had seen for a long time, and he began to realise how he had come to identify himself with the Chinese people whom he was beginning to really understand: "I borrowed their mirror and gazed into it with misgivings. Could it be that I didn't have a nice yellow face and black hair? Could that gargoyle be my nose, those two protruding glassy spheres, that revoltingly pink and spotty expanse be my eyes and face?"

It was time to make a move, and get on the way to Baoji via Xi'an. The three Englishmen packed up in readiness to leave and awaited word of enemy troop movements in order to make a safe crossing of the blockade line. Aylwin wrote of the trip:

> In the village an old man sat on the ground with a pile of yellow coloured books spread in a circle around him. He looked very sage, his beard being of the same hue as his timeworn parchments, but he admitted in a burst of confidence that he was unable to recognise any more than the titles of his books. He persuaded us to buy a kind of sooth-saying calendar, and Ralph, our scholar, looked up the day. But the evil portended for anyone who dare move on this particular date must have applied to the Japanese, for we were told on our return to headquarters that "the Japanese became confused in the dark and spent last night firing across the valley at themselves with heavy casualties on both sides! The road was clear!"

So they set off south towards the Yellow River. They made very slow headway as Aylwin describes:

> Our average of twenty-three miles a day may not sound much from an armchair perspective, but as a matter of fact they were painful miles, in the covering of which pointed pebbles, rocky river beds and the soft soles of our cloth sandals drove everything else but boils, constipation, lice, sleep, and distance from our minds. We became more and more incredibly British. We were frigidly polite with each other as we folded up our

bedding and put down our morning noodles; along the way we remarked unfeelingly on the weather or the view; and in the evenings we loosened up no end, addressing each other as "old boy".

Their tiredness and discomfort caused them to be aggravated by the smallest things: "We could not understand why it was that at one forwarding station there should be three packsaddles but no riding saddle, while at the next there were four riding saddles but no packsaddle." Later, Aylwin wrote of his companions:

> Ralph is quiet and inexpressibly sound, with a mathematician's attention to detail and a missionary's sense for the something that ought to be done. Michael is tall, slightly bald, with the makings of a fine professorial air. He draws some very pretty comparisons between the present Sino-Japanese struggle and certain aspects of the Hellenic Wars. Over little things he worried, but whenever anything really foul happened he bucked up no end. Michael pronounced most of the food along the way as simply inedible, but was very fortunately fond of roasted flour, and could be seen breathing frostily from his nose after taking a quiet tuck-in of this. He needed all the extra nourishment he could get, for while Ralph and I raced our donkeys together like children at the seaside, Michael strode away in front like a don on a walking tour.

On occasion they would ask a peasant the way, the best route or the distance to the next village. The answer would usually only lead to confusion, or maybe would provide a subject for lengthy discussion. The answer to an enquiry about the distance to the next village might be "You'll be there by the time you've finished supper" or perhaps "Go up the mountain and down the mountain and you're there". Naturally, they would ask about the height of the mountain to be climbed, and the reply could be "three big cakes and twice-drink-water high" or alternatively "ears cold high". Actual figures are an incomprehensible concept for a totally uneducated peasant, and when pressed for a more exact expression of distance his face would invariably take on a pained countenance, and he would give an altogether fantastic number of *li* (1 li = 0.31 miles). Then it would be necessary to ask whether those are "big li" or "small li", to which the answer would be characteristically non-committal: "The li are not big" or "the li are not small".

Their approach to Yuanqu, the intended place for crossing the Yellow River, was down a valley whose precipitous sides towered above them. Here they came across war-torn Kuomintang troops for the first time, which Aylwin described:

> [The sides of the valley] seemed to press down over the men who were creeping along zigzag paths cut out from their flanks. Down in a stony ravine a blind man in uniform asked us to lead him along. Ralph guided him carefully along by one end of his stick, crossing and re-crossing the river by stepping stones every few hundred yards. A fevered soldier started out from some rags as we rounded a corner, asking us to help him move into the shade. Stretcher parties were moving slowly southward, with limbs like sticks, caked in blood and dirt, lying uncovered and pressing directly onto criss-cross ropes of

the homemade stretchers. There were no nurses, and no food or water for the whole day's travel in sun and dust. I sat down by the road to watch a party of sick soldiers deemed fit to walk back to hospital. As they came opposite me they could see for the first time a false crest in the road, with a further long hill ahead of them. Some sank down with a look of infinitely aged exhaustion on their faces; others had the energy to search for lice in their coat edges, the blood spreading slowly up their thumbnails.

There was tremendous traffic along this valley to and from the ferry crossing at Yuanqu. Aylwin continued:

> Teams of sturdy mules, each fitted with a metal tray to carry four thousand rounds of ammunition, pushed everything else out of the way. Long lines of strong coolies, paid one cent a mile, swung along with a hundred pounds on either end of their carrying poles. Donkeys and men staggered and snorted up and down the hills with top-heavy loads of padded winter uniforms.

They were disappointed at the unimposing sight of the narrow strip of water that had halted the Japanese advance from Kaifeng to Mongolia. At that time of the year, the Yellow River is just a fraction of what it often is in the spring when the silt-laden torrents can break its banks and change its course bringing flood and famine to millions of the people who farm the fertile plain. Now, the narrow stream cut deep into the thick, mustard-coloured silt deposit, and the dry wind whipped up clouds of dust off the vast expanse of loess. Aylwin continued his narrative:

> The ferry here at Yuanqu only runs after air raid hours, and the loess cliffs were already turning red with the sunset as our craft cast off from the northern bank. It was a flat-bottomed barge built of thick boards clamped together with massive iron staples. A huge patchwork sail flapped aloft, and from either side projected several oars; these were thirty feet long and had to be manned by three men each, but the blades dipped only three feet into the water. For'ard, a fan-shaped thicket of ropes ran out to a clump of chanting pullers who walked, half doubled-up, along the shore or knee-deep in the water. Broad ledges along either of the ship's sides served as runways for the crew of pole-pushers. A great rudder oar hung over the stern and was manned by the captain.

The pullers and the punters hauled the barge slowly upstream through sluggish shallows, then at the right point where they could catch the current, the pullers let go their ropes, and the oarsmen dipped feverishly to a breathless chant. The barge swung out diagonally where they pulled, suddenly and incredibly, into still water. Here on the south bank was a thriving town, though heavily bombed, providing every amenity for the Kuomintang soldiers and supply trains which crossed the river at this point. The milling streets were decoratively adorned with paper lanterns and the first prostitutes seen since Beijing.

On their way to the base hospital, they overtook line upon line of oxcarts which bore the wounded soldiers who had made it this far and across the river, a week's journey from the nearest fighting. Aylwin's story continues:

> Heavy beams pressed against the solid wheels as the carts wound downhill, making a symphony of clear rolling vibration through the crisp autumn atmosphere. At every jolt of the rigid wooden chassis the men would gasp and grip the sides to prevent themselves from being thrown out.

Aylwin, Ralph, and Michael reached the hospital that night and found the doctor in charge, whose room was ostentatiously decorated with an officer's sword amongst a plethora of elaborate charts. It was Ralph, with his hunger for statistics, who asked about survival rates under treatment and on the operating table. The answer came with grim confidence: "Oh, we're not bothered about that. If a man's going to die, he'll do it before he gets here."

The following day the three Englishmen set out for the railway, where they hoped to find a train to take them to Xi'an. They joined once more the steady trickle of wounded soldiers who were struggling along the road. A fleet of empty army trucks approached, giving the walking wounded a wide berth. They passed Ralph, who was wearing the top half of an old uniform. They passed Aylwin in his altogether worn-out appearance and sadly soiled homemade pants. But on the sight of the distinguished looking Michael with his professorial bald back view, his grey flannel bags, and almost-white linen Oxford-cut coat, one truck pulled up, and all three of the travellers got a luxurious ride to the railway at Lianqi.

After some rest in a mud-and-reed shelter where they fed on persimmons and mutton pasties, evening brought the train which they had longed for. It was only a short journey, however, to Tongguan where everyone was ushered out onto the track. Here, where the railway comes down close to the river, Japanese guns were visible on the north bank only half a mile away. All the occupants of the train must make their way through the hills for twenty miles or so to another train awaiting them further up the line. Aylwin describes the transit between trains as follows:

> From the cliffs above Tongguan we looked across the half-deserted city to where Japanese motor trucks were going to and fro on the far side of the river. In full view of the Japanese, thousands of donkeys, rickshaws and wheelbarrows shuttled passengers from one train to the other. Some sat sidesaddle, with crossed legs and a studied air of nonchalance; others straddled their beasts, railing and kicking for more speed. Some were surrounded by multiform belongings; others carried nothing more than a pot of pickle in one hand and an umbrella in the other. Beasts and men tugged and sweated through thick yellow dust and became locked in cursing heaps where the road was narrow.

The railway to Xi'an ran through an ancient corroded landscape where whole villages modelled in mud were scarcely distinguishable from the crumbling loess cliffs around them. Donkeys ploughed the terraces that rose over the hills, halfway up into the mountains beyond.

The great city walls of Xi'an loomed above them some time after midnight. Aylwin described the comforts that awaited them on arrival in Xi'an:

> Overawed by such luxuries as running water and spring beds in the hotel bedroom, we stacked our dirty clothes in a corner hoping that whatever was inside would not jump out, and crept between white sheets dreaming of hot, buttered toast and coffee in the morning.

The almost-forgotten comfort of a spring bed was short lived, as after only three hours of slumber, they awoke to an air raid siren. They joined the tens of thousands of people sheltering in the catacombs beneath the 1,500-year-old city: the damp and draughty chambers far below the wind-eroded battlements of the city fortress. Aylwin continued:

> As our eyes became accustomed to the darkness we could make out the sides of a corridor about five feet wide, lined with narrow earthen ledges on which people were already sitting, and with smoky oil lamps in recesses. "Pass along to the end please. Make room for those coming in behind," a soldier called out. A soothsayer with a roving eye, a wild lock of hair, and cheekbones gleaming in the flickering light was creating a pleasantly spooky atmosphere of unreality. Suddenly he was silent, pointing upwards with his finger. We sat tense, nerves in tune to the softly beating vibrations, wondering if the huge pile of earth above us could withstand the shock of a direct hit. Then an apologetic voice broke silence. "It's all right," it said, "it's only our cat purring. I bring her down here because she's frightened when we leave her at home."

There followed a week of frequent air raids which prompted everyone who could do so to leave Xi'an. Ralph and Michael went on their own way to Chongqing, and Aylwin took an evacuation train westward to Baoji, the terminus of the Lunghai Railway, a distance of about a 140 miles. He was reminded of his journey from Hankou nearly eighteen months earlier: the passengers sprawling higgledy-piggledy over bag and baggage, and all the useless multitude of odds and ends that scared people take up when the moment to leave home suddenly comes upon them; spending torporous days on end in those cramped compartments, their clothes stinking and sweaty, fleas and lice rampant. This train, like hundreds before it in recent months, came to the end of the line, further progress as yet prevented by the massive barrier of the Qin Ling Mountains. The refugees were disgorged into this mushrooming community which had changed Baoji beyond recognition. A new colony was forming on the east side of the old walled city. The newcomers hastily erected mud huts or excavated caves out of the soft loess hillsides. It was six o'clock in the bitterly cold late autumn morning, but already the streets were ringing with the sound of hammers and saws, and the builders grunted cheerfully as they rammed down new mud into the wall frames. This new East Suburb would soon be bigger than the city itself, the buildings taller and better built, the streets broader and better surfaced. Aylwin had briefly visited Baoji nearly eighteen months earlier, when he was awaiting passage to Yan'an. Then, the East Suburb had been a shanty: long lines of mud and reed shacks along either side of the railway track, lit up in the evening by campfires, and only occasionally was anyone visible, crouching low to pass through a mat doorway. There were no sanitary arrangements, and no one came to bury the casual dead. The only drinking water came from ponds and the muddy Wei River. Families who were so spent by their journey, with no energy left to start again, would sit around for days in the yellow dust beside the railway. The city had just about managed to clear up the shanty and rehouse the Hankou refugees by the time the new wave from Xi'an arrived. The population shot way over fifty thousand, and new shanties sprouted on all sides of the city.

In the autumn of 1938, the Japanese were boasting that the war was at an end. Since the Marco Polo Bridge Incident on 7 July 1937, they had destroyed all but 5 per cent of all China's pre-war modern industry. Now the blockade around the coast was tightened, and Hong Kong was outflanked. Guangzhou and Hankou had fallen. The Annam-Yunnan Railway from Vietnam into China was under Japanese control. The British had been persuaded to withhold use of the Burma Road. The desert trails to the west through Xinjiang into Russia could, in theory, be used for trade, but were difficult because of the immense distances involved, and anyway, Russia herself needed most of what she could produce. It was necessary for inland China to create its own industry, and it was out of this need that CIC was born.

During the first year of the war, Rewi Alley, who had been working for some years for the Shanghai Municipal Council as a factory inspector, initiated the idea of an industrial cooperatives movement, along with Edgar Snow, Peg Snow, Agnes Smedley, and others: a way to organise the manpower of the thirty million refugees into production in support of the war efforts. In August 1938, the minister of finance, Kong Xiangxi (Dr H. H. Kung), asked Rewi Alley to put his ideas into action, and so the Association for the Advancement of Chinese Industrial Cooperatives was set up in Hankou, which was still the centre of the National Government at that time. The guerrilla magistrates in the Shanxi-Chahar-Hebei Border Region were among the first to catch onto the idea of country industry on a cooperatives basis, but the first centre of development on a large scale was in Baoji. In September 1938, Baoji's first cooperative was launched with nine blacksmiths. Here, with the massive influx of refugees, there was certainly plenty of manpower and a multitude of skills. The CIC aimed to bring those skills together, offer organisation to small groups of craftsmen, provide starting funds and affordable loans, arrange supply of materials, and provide marketing channels. There was huge demand for goods, caused by new armies and by whole new populations in the hinterland. There was a glut of raw materials that could no longer be carried to the coast for processing. Cooperatives were formed daily all over the country as the imagination of the people and of the organisers was caught by the idea. There were, of course, failures, due sometimes to shaky organisation, sometimes to political sabotage, but by April 1940 there were about three thousand industrial cooperatives spread throughout eight of China's provinces, making a range of five hundred kinds of goods.

In January 1939, The International Committee for Promotion of CIC was formed in Hong Kong, headed by the Anglican bishop of Hong Kong and South China, Bishop Ronald Hall. Through the work of this committee, more than ten million US dollars came into the organisation from the United States, Britain, Canada, Australia, New Zealand, the Philippines, Singapore, and other countries.

With the fall of Hankou in October 1938, the CIC headquarters were moved to Chongqing, and Rewi Alley moved his own base to Baoji. By that time there were already some ten or fifteen co-ops in Baoji. It was the county magistrate Wang Feng Jei, and a fellow Manchurian Lu Guangmian (K. M. Lu), the director of the Northwest Industrial Cooperatives, who were the organizational powerhouse in and around Baoji. Director Lu would walk around the refugee colonies talking, arguing, and explaining. As soon as he found a group of refugees willing to work together in a cooperative, the new group would be brought to be registered in Wang's *yamen* – the county government office. Groups from Henan, Shanxi, Hebei, Shandong, and Manchuria were put to work, and as far as possible arranged in streets according to their places of origin. When Aylwin arrived with the crowds from Xi'an, there were 104 industrial co-ops with 1,280 members. Using a total loan capital of $173,000, the monthly production was worth about $130,000. Magistrate Wang backed up the CIC with social services, the first of which was a water supply. Finding that his servant drew water from the same pond where refugees washed their clothes, Wang himself searched in the mountains nearby and located springs. Because it was felt that the war would be over before wooden pipes would be worn out and ripe for replacement with robust iron pipes which at the time were out of the question, the spring water was brought bubbling into Baoji at the rate of fifty-seven thousand gallons per day, which soon had to be increased to ninety-three thousand gallons. The first county maternity home was started with US$5 with two penniless refugee nurses in charge. As soon as the doors opened, thirty cases were admitted.

About two thousand prostitutes had come to Baoji with the innkeepers to whom they belonged from cities along the railway. The rapidly expanding town was found to be most congenial for business. Wang realised the necessity for a cleanup operation. Taxation was abandoned in the face of a storm of opposition, so he organised the girls into an Amazon Phalanx by giving them classes in literacy, natural history, and first aid. He insisted that they attend public meetings once a month, dress in black uniforms, and keep their faces washed clean.

The first rainy season brought Magistrate Wang an army of irate truck drivers who demanded that he find them mules to haul their trucks out of the potholes in the roads. This was no small matter. Baoji was at the junction of major routes from the west, east, and the south. Householders were persuaded to knock down walls and rebuild further away from the roads. The roads were rebuilt, widened, and surfaced. The truck drivers were plagued in return with new parking regulations. Pedestrians were urged to stay on the left-hand side of the roads, and beggars were ruthlessly relegated to the back streets. At specific times of the day, boys with white arm bands and hand bells would parade the streets, at which signal citizens would emerge from every doorway to sprinkle clean water in the way of the band of road sweepers.

Wang's daily tour of the streets never failed to bring excitement. Offending features would catch his eye – someone emptying litter into the gutter, a scabrous dog that should be shot, badly parked trucks, an untidy shop front, or a dangerously hung sign. Wang would dash over to the focus of his agitation, leaving his hastily dismounted bicycle to be caught by one of his entourage. Equally dramatically, ideas might come into his head for a park here or an elevated highway there. In his second year as magistrate, his minions had unbound hundreds of girls' feet and sheared off thousands of men's pigtails. There was near revolt. A delegation of superstitious peasants explained: "Pigtails are forests, and forests are rain. No pigtails, no rain!" In answer to the protest, Wang undertook a tour of the countryside. The peasants were amazed, but Wang too was astonished by what he saw. "I'll have to fix that countryside the same as I fixed those streets," he remarked on his return. Sadly, he was too good at his duties, and as the result of political intrigue, he was returned to his previous job as traffic manager, this time on the Lunghai Railway. But by then, Baoji was one of the biggest cities in the northwest. Before coming to Baoji, Wang Feng Jei had lived in Taiyuan, Shanxi, where he was traffic manager on the Chengtai Railway. He had left there just two days before the Japanese arrived. The last bridge across the Fenn River, behind the city, was bombed to pieces minutes after he had used it to make his escape. He had no clear idea of the future. He had no idea where his journey would lead him. All he knew was that he had to build where others destroyed; not to build edifices, but to build human values. Months later he found himself in Baoji's East Suburb, lying on a camp bed in one of those mud hovels, insects falling off the walls and ceiling, prostitutes entertaining their clients on the other side of a thin screen wall.

Chapter 12

Ocean Secretary

Aylwin came to the CIC in Baoji in October 1939 when the organisation was only just a year old. The International Committee in Hong Kong needed a publicity man in the field. In November, he wrote home:

> They're a grand lot of leaders. They've offered me a job – expenses found but no salary. I'm going to Chongqing to make contacts, write up some stuff, finish off my diary, and get letters. Then back here. As I predicted from Tokyo, that was a dividing line – now it's me for China, for a good time anyway. This job will be grand. Officially it is foreign publicity expert. Actually it will be much more practical, leaving the door open for plenty of travelling and plenty of contact with the real people of China.
>
> The other day there was an air raid; luckily I was outside the city and saw the whole thing at a safe distance. Two flights of beautiful silver birds and the hum of the bass stop of the organ in church. Then spurts of flame from in amongst the houses, a fountain line of dirt and smoke shooting upwards, and then a terrific roar. When we got back, the place was wailing. Two bombs had landed right at the entrance to two caves in the hillsides where the poor people live. They can't afford houses, but they thought at least they were lucky in one respect: they were glad to shelter their neighbours during air raids. When we looked in, we could see where the shrapnel made a jagged gash all round the mud walls inside the cave. The jagged line was about head height. On the floor lay the remains of ten people. Two children were already coffined up in a small crater outside, and another man was having his corpse washed and dressed while the women moaned and wailed mechanically around.

Aylwin was given a Gung Ho badge with "No. 114" on it, and was given the monicker "Ocean Secretary". "Gung Ho", meaning "work together", was the motto of the CIC, coined by Rewi Alley, and became the everyday name for the organisation. The name crept into the English language and took on another meaning – "bold and enthusiastic" – through the American armed forces in the Pacific War. Evans Carlson, China veteran and wholehearted supporter of the CIC, was withdrawn from China to form a crack battalion of commandos within the American Marines. The Carlson's Raiders adopted "Gung Ho" as a battle cry, which was later used as the title of a film depicting the commandos' heroic escapades at a time when success for America was otherwise lacking in the Pacific. "Ocean devil" is the traditional name in Chinese for a foreigner: East Ocean Devils are Japanese. "Ocean donkeys" are bicycles, and "ocean carts" are rickshaws, which were introduced from Japan to replace the Chinese wheelbarrows when the roads were improved and became smoother; hence Aylwin's title of Ocean Secretary. Aylwin continued to tell of his new situation:

I purchased a necktie, a teapot, a bedspread of co-op cloth and pinned some photos up on the wall of my twelve-by-six-foot room. A berth was found for my typewriter in the office for a few days, but the noise it made was so much louder than all the abaci in the place, that I was politely asked to take it back to my bedroom.

Tomorrow I shall be at Lanzhou, also a very interesting place just now being the northwest back door to Soviet Russia. We'll stay a couple of days and then back. This is a tour with the leaders in their truck. I've bought a new camera – £8 paid – owing the balance of whatever it costs the friend to buy a new one when he gets to Hong Kong. That leaves me broke, so I hope I find things OK in Chongqing. Today I bought a pair of camel hair home-knitted socks for nine pence and a pair of fur gloves for a shilling! It's cold here, especially on top of a lorry. Also sheepskin enough for a big long coat: total cost about six shillings!

On his return from Chongqing in late December 1939 where he picked up a sheaf of letters, he wrote home again:

Very gratifying after about eleven months without any letters at all. The rest of your letters should be rolling along from Aimee Millican soon too, and then I can have an historical review of the year's events, I hope.

This is a very good job. It combines the best of going into industry and being a social worker, and gives good opportunities for writing too; and travelling. I've been to quite a lot of places in the last two months: Lanzhou in the northwest, and Hanzhong to the south. Later on there will be even more interesting trips. Further south we have a Living Buddha Tibetan in charge of a wool district. Muslims are the star cooperators in Lanzhou. Then there are True Church of Jesus refugees from Hankou – old friends of mine. They are a peculiar Chinese sect and consider themselves as *the only* Christians in the world. But they have their points. Brave. During all the air raids on Hankou and Wuhan they would never move away from their houses, just sit quite still. And only one of them was ever injured. And why was he injured? "Because he was smoking," said the bewhiskered prophet to me with an admonishing shake of his head. Their founder fasted for thirty-nine days; he could have gone on longer, but he thought it would be rather a bad show to beat the Founder's forty.

Did I ever tell you how we eat? It's rice gruel with bread and peanuts for breakfast, a good lunch and not a bad supper. If anybody feels like extra dishes there is a sort of lottery performed by throwing out a certain number of fingers and then counting the total round the table to see who will pay for it. The food probably costs about fifteen to twenty dollars a month per head. But it is paid for on basis of salary. That is, the regional chief engineer pays about sixty dollars and the office boy four dollars for the same food.

I have quite a nice little room. Anything in which one can spread a bit and arrange one's own things would seem nice. It has a camp bed, a desk, and a little cupboard. At present the disadvantage is no stove or fire. If you like, you can have a platter of charcoal which is quite warm but deadly: carbon monoxide guaranteed to produce a splitting headache within half an hour. Some people can stand it okay. I prefer the cold.

These were the first letters he had written since staying with Kathleen Hall, recovering from typhus in March and April 1939, about nine months earlier. All the time he had been with the guerrillas, there had been no safe means of communication, but he wrote at length about those months in his book, *I See a New China*, which has been the main source of information for the previous few chapters of this book. Once he had set down his roots in Baoji, however, letters came quite regularly, but he had to be very careful what he wrote. He should not be at all critical of the Kuomintang. The popularity of the Popular Front was beginning to wear thin after its initial strength during the first two years of the war. Now a rift was appearing between the Kuomintang and the communist forces, but pretence of solidarity continued. Veterans of the original Fourth Army, five thousand of them, had re-formed in mid-1938, and recruited twenty thousand peasants in the southeast. The reaction to their activities was that the Kuomintang started to talk of the front line Eighth Route Army as being enemy number one.

On 12 January 1940, Aylwin's letter home told:

> The other day brought two nice things; one, the good New Zealand nurse who brought me through typhus in Hebei, at her mission hospital. She got burned out by the Japanese, who evidently heard she was bringing in medical supplies for the Chinese. Her mission said they couldn't send her back there because it was too dangerous for other people in the mission. So she went all the way around by Hong Kong and joined the Chinese Red Cross, and now she's on her way back by the road I came down! Plucky woman if ever there was one.

Just a few months after Aylwin had left Kathleen Hall's mission, another foreigner appeared in the area. Dr Norman Bethune, a Canadian medical man fresh from the conflicts in Spain, had come via Yan'an to provide a much-awaited military medical service to Nie Rongzhen's troops. At the age of 48, he was to become within two years a legend. Bethune persuaded Kathleen Hall to step up the medical supply smuggling so that his medical unit might work satisfactorily. She went beyond this by also developing an underground route for students, nurses, doctors, and experts of all kinds to reach the Border Region from the other side of the Japanese lines.

In July 1939, returning from Beijing with a shipment of supplies and personnel, they were met with the news that the mission at Songjiazhuang had been burnt down by the Japanese. It was apparent that a Japanese spy had earlier installed himself in a restaurant to observe her movements and had found out the truth about her smuggling activities. She herself could not return to Songjiazhuang to continue her work as it would endanger everyone she would make contact with. She returned instead to Beijing where the British Embassy informed her that the Japanese authorities had requested them to send her home to New Zealand. She jumped ship at Hong Kong, joined the Red Cross, and returned to China by the back door, by way of Haiphong and Hanoi in French Indo-China. It was slow going in the convoy of Red Cross supply trucks, but at last they got into China and reached Guiyang, Guizhou Province, where the Indo-China route into China meets up with the Burma Road. In Guiyang she received a heavy blow. Norman Bethune had died. He had operated without gloves, which was often unavoidable. A tiny cut on one finger had become infected, and the poisoning spread. In a final note he wrote to General Nie, he asked for this message be sent: "My warmest thanks to Kathleen for her help."

Kathleen was badly shaken, but resolved to return to Shanxi to carry on with her work. She called in at Baoji to find Aylwin. She was thrilled by what Gung Ho was doing there. The cooperative idea was close to her heart, as some of CIC's first followers and successes were in her own Border Region. Soon she was off to Xi'an, and then Luoyang with a medical team led by Dr Jean Chiang. Two months had passed since Kathleen had left Hong Kong. She ached to get back to her beloved mountain villages. She managed to get across the Yellow River into the Border Region, but before she reached her goal, she fell ill with beriberi, and not wishing to be a burden to others, she decided to give up her work and return to New Zealand.

Aylwin's letter continued:

> The other nice thing was the pictures of mine which I sent further west to get decently developed. They are the ones I took all the way along, and I hadn't seen before, so was very glad to find that they turned out pretty well for the most part, and should be a factor in favour of getting my book published.
>
> I dedicated my book to Aimee and Frank Millican, in Shanghai's Seventh Heaven, and to my un-auntly aunt, Muriel Lester, so if the book isn't published they must take the wish for the deed. You ought to have received three quarters of the book in typewritten form from Aimee, and one quarter from me via Hong Kong by now.
>
> I shall be going back the way I came some time this spring, maybe for a few months, maybe longer. CIC has started a few centres there, and I am to go up and report on them, and maybe help in other ways.
>
> We were all asked our New Year's wishes. I said jokingly that I would like to be married; but what is a joke in Europe, and anyway is one's own business, in China is a matter of immediate concern to everyone, so within a few hours many of my friends were calling on me offering their services to help me find a wife!

The book referred to did not find a publisher but formed part of *I See a New China*, which was published in 1944 in the United States by Little, Brown & Co and in Britain by Victor Gollancz.

As soon as he arrived in Baoji, Aylwin became a great favourite of the Gung Ho Women's Department. This department was under the leadership of a Miss Ren, whom everyone called "Da Ren" (Elder Ren), a returned student from England who had studied at the Quaker Study

Centre at Woodbrooke Hall near Birmingham, and then at the London School of Economics. The members of the department were mostly girls who had been on their way to Yan'an but had been prevented from getting there by the Kuomintang blockade, and so had stayed in the northwest, in Baoji. They were a dynamic group around Baoji, organising, teaching, spinning and weaving, in orphanages and co-ops. Da Ren's niece, Ren Li Zhi, known as "Xiao Ren", was among this group. She and Aylwin fell in love. Just two years younger than Aylwin, she was a bright and able girl with a radiant smile and sparkling eyes; the same smile and eyes that I met in Beijing almost fifty years later. I could understand the attraction. Fu Bin, known as Xiao Fu, another member of the group, aged 19 at the time and about the same age as Xiao Ren, told me how the group cherished the relationship and indeed they would have been married after Liberation; but fate held a different path.

As the Kuomintang's hunt for communists systematically swept through every organisation it could infiltrate, so the Gung Ho Women's Department was affected. Da Ren was eased out, and eighteen of the older members were imprisoned in a Kuomintang concentration camp. Xiao Ren managed to escape arrest, and when the folly of her staying any longer around Baoji was realised, it was arranged for her to carry on with her resistance work in Luoyang. Here she could be offered more protection by the Gung Ho office than in Baoji. Xiao Ren left Baoji in September 1940, about a year after meeting Aylwin, but during the next few years Aylwin's work often took him to Luoyang where they were able to meet. Whenever a letter would arrive from Xiao Ren, Aylwin would brighten up, shrugging off the cares of the moment, and the letter would accompany him wherever he went, in his shirt pocket, being taken out, read and re-read, until it would disintegrate into illegible tatters.

Zhu De front right and Nie Rongzhen back right
with Peng Dehuai middle back, Luo Ruiqing
back left and Lu Zhengcao front left at the
Eighth Route Army Headquarters in Xian, 1940

Michael Lindsay, George Aylwin Hogg
and Ernest-Ralph Lapwood

George Aylwin Hogg,
Ocean Secretary,
Baoji 1939

Lu Guangmian
(K. M. Lu) director of
Northwest Region CIC

Refugee shanty, Baoji

Ocean Secretary meeting the people, 1940

Chapter 13

China from a Bus Top

During the next two years, Aylwin travelled a great deal, inspecting cooperatives, organising, making reports to Regional Headquarters, and writing propaganda material for the CIC International Committee. Starting out on a trip, he wrote home on 20 January 1940:

> I am on my way to a place called Ankang, where we are doing things to put refugees to work with fifty thousand dollars of the Lord Mayor of London's Fund money. All along the way are other CIC stations, so it is an interesting trip. I have to go a long way round because, if I went straight, there would be mountains and bandits. There is some way of going straight, but you have to get a passport from the chief bandit before starting out. Anyway it would be too cold by now.

A hundred and sixty miles south of Baoji, there was a small co-op depot at Mianxian, near Hanzhong. Where the Han River ran out of the mountains, a man stood lonely as a fishing bird in shallow water, blue smock opened at the chest and pants rolled up to the knees, with his rough sieve and a shallow pan beside him. The mountains rose gaunt, rocky, and treeless on either side. But the man's loneliness and the barrenness of his surroundings were only skin deep. Behind the mountain's bare sides was gold, and behind the man were thousands of others working in co-ops federated with his own. At the federation office in Mianxian, where the gold from fifty co-ops was collected for sale to the banks, Aylwin saw a member from one of the co-ops far away in the mountains bring out a precious package of little gold nuggets from the lining of his coat. The gold was weighed, the transaction carefully entered up in the books under everyone's close scrutiny, and the member went away to the granary in a back room where he drew some of the three thousand bushels of wheat stored by the federation for distribution to members' families during the hard winter months.

Two hundred miles further down the Han River, another seventy-one co-ops with two thousand members, many of them refugees from Hebei and Henan, were in a sixty-mile radius of Ankang. One of the gold-washing co-ops there had just found a fine site. They were too busy to notice the temple with its carved tablet commemorating the place as a fishing ground of Emperor Xia Yü some four thousand years ago. Chinese peasants, hard hit by the drought and forced to leave the land, were now washing gold in the prized fishing grounds of one of the early emperors, helped along with funds from an English lord mayor.

By joining together, co-ops could hire a group of specialist prospectors to guide the panners to the best sites. Some of the sites needed twenty to thirty days' preparation, and without a co-op the panners did not have sufficient funds to tide them over such a period. Working individually, gold-washers on good sites had to give at least 20 per cent of their gold to the landlords. With the CIC as intermediary, this term could usually be lowered to even 5 per cent. A peasant starting up with no capital would beg $30 or $50 from the landlord who, instead of charging interest, would make the condition that the gold would be sold solely through him. He would pay, however, only two-thirds of the market price. The federation, on the other hand, paid the full price to the washer, keeping only the bank's sales commission to cover its own expenses. With massive inflation prevailing, local gentry and agents from further afield had been buying gold for illegal hoarding. The black market price for gold in Ankang had risen twenty-two times the regular price paid by the banks. Through the organisation of co-ops, black market trading could be checked and at the same time a fair wage assured to the workers themselves.

Here is part of an article that Aylwin wrote based on his return journey from Ankang, entitled "China from the Bus Top":

> It was dark, and the dust blew in gustily, unseen, through the door. The rickshaw puller was huddled in his chariot outside. He rose quickly to light his flickering brass lamp and swung the vehicle silently alongside. Bedding and bundles were piled in, and we fell in behind, walking … cold: the moon came out for a moment, only to disappear again.
>
> "Who's there?" echoed the challenge of the sentry from above the city gate; "Us!" (Only us) we shouted in reply. He seemed satisfied and grunted knowingly as we passed through.
>
> There was a crowd outside the great wooden door of the bus station. It stood dumb as a flock of cold sheep, as though there were something sub-humanly primeval about waiting for the dawn. The paper lanterns on the booths faintly lit men's faces as they merged, and emerged with yellow bowls of peanut gravy. Babies cried sleepily and were fed. Soldiers, hampered by belongings, stood aside, firm and erect. Country people anxiously counted their hampers.
>
> Suddenly a chain clanked, a heavy bolt shot back, and a tiny gap in the door opened. We headed in for it like a football wedge. "Where's 2177?" "Where's 2466?" We ran to and fro searching for our clues. A moment lost in finding the right bus might mean clinging round the edge of a swaying, hurtling mass for the rest of the day. How much more pleasant to be one of the first to dive in over the side, always supposing you didn't meet someone else doing the same thing from the opposite side, and to wedge between a medley of babies, old gentlemen, peasant produce, camp beds, spare hats, oranges, pickles, and if you were lucky enough, pretty girls with eyes as big as pumpkin seeds!

So we all champed around, jockeying for a good position from which to jump aboard at the sound of the starter's whistle. The starter was a soldier who stood on the bus, arranging the boxes, bales and baskets as they were handed up to him. A few of the braver or less scrupulous tried to edge their way on in spite of him, but were roughly pushed back. After a time, a father got permission for his wife and child to advance beyond the handicap line. Some of the others, outraged at this, made bold moves. The starter was seen to be wavering, and a swift all-consuming invasion was loosed.

"Just another inch for my foot please, comrade?"

"Yes, but if you would just put your case *so*, comrade, then we could both sit on it."

The plush upholstered, high-backed monster that booms its way across a continent may exude exclusiveness, but the war-time bus of China at once puts its passengers on an equal footing and anyone who waits for an introduction before speaking his mind may find himself disappearing unnoticed beneath mountains of stuff and nonsense. When everyone is cemented into position, and the out-clingers have arranged for people to hang onto them while going round corners, the conversation begins by which every Chinese tries out new acquaintances and forms a background to his first impressions. Where is your home? What province's food is best? What province's dialect is most difficult to understand? These are the first essentials.

Tickets had already been collected and the motor warmed up, when in walked a latecomer, a cocky little peasant woman with a nice clean towel round her head and the inevitable baby. She passed the baby up to the friendly hands of a soldier, and balanced her bundle on the edge of the truck. Not an inch of room, but she clambered over the wheel and up beside it, then fell in on top of the others trying to make it look as though she had overbalanced. Mother of three who had arrived virtuously early piped up like a chick-proud hen that sees her menaced: "Take your feet off my boy ... you ought to be ashamed of yourself. And *now* look what you're doing, them's my oranges you're sitting on!" she expostulated. Her husband said not a word, but poked at the woman's bundle from the other side of the truck with his walking stick. Smiling and un-perturbed, the latecomer was evidently quite un-vanquished and determined that the whole thing was a good joke. Besides, she had her own ally in the soldier, who by this time had made great friends with the baby. He helped her to clear a little place to sit. "After all, she's a mother too," he apologised to the others, "and we're all Chinese ...."

Exquisitely dressed, eyes flashing, small oval face fringed with the dark blue of a tie-under knitted bonnet, and also with a baby, the second latecomer had the attendant place a ladder up against the side of the bus for her, and stood surveying the scene from the top of it. Her cheeks were flushed and she was breathing quickly from her hurrying. Every eye was fixed on her admiringly; long curving black eyelashes, and a smooth crescent of soft black hair that fell out of the bonnet and down one side of her face.

"Please move a little and make room for me," she says, queen-like. Everybody looks at her, embarrassed, silent, and friendly. A few make polite heaves. But it's really no good, we can't move.

"Please move a little!" she stamps her foot and puckers her brow. We regard her pleasantly. Such a pretty face, such a little baby, we are sorry, but really .... Her cheeks flame with vexation. She calls the bus man, who had retired apprehensive into the background after putting the ladder up for her. "Seven o'clock is really our scheduled starting time," he falters, "and now it's nearly eight. You should really have come earlier you know."

"That's nothing to do with it. I registered many days ago, and bought my ticket yesterday," she replies.

In the end, the bus man agrees to look over our tickets again, and it turns out that there is actually a man aboard who hasn't got a ticket at all. On being discovered he blandly requires the bus man to issue him one. The girl is speechless with rage. "You!" she says, pointing a daintily gloved finger at him, "You! Please be polite a little and make room."

The bus man is quite adamant too. "It's no good," he tells the man, "we won't start until you get off." But the stowaway still has one card up his sleeve. "My bedding roll," he says, "the yellow one, where is it?" Consternation! Everyone, frustrated, tries to get a look at what he's sitting on, and all he can see is a leg or a gown or a shoe. There are more heaves all over the truck, as though a big sea-monster were swirling about close to the surface. But we are really in a hopeless jam and it looks like a *fait accompli* for the ticket-less one. But in the hour of his victory he is not without conscience. "I'll sit on the roof of the cab, in front," he offers, "then the lady can have my place here."

"That's right comrade," says the soldier next to him, as he makes a place beside himself for the pretty girl, well pleased, and begins overtures with the baby.

Our bus is a swan among geese. That is to say that we run on petrol while the others are covered with ugly stove-pipes and charcoal burners. They do a kilometre per *catty* [about ½kg] of charcoal, costing about seven dollars, and we do a hundred kilometres on ten gallons of petrol, whatever that may cost these days. But that is not the only price we have to pay for our superiority; before we are allowed to start, we have to tow each goose along the road, until it is limbered up. The swan must do its bit in these days.

There was snow in the sky and the wind whistled by uncomfortably, lifting up the corners of coats and blankets as fast as the passengers tucked them back again. The only thing to do was to exercise the art of conversation, an art in which all Chinese excel, to make their own surroundings more congenial.

Perched precariously round the edge of the truck were some soldiers going home on leave from the Shanxi front. They hadn't been home for two years, and were picking out old landmarks excitedly to each other. Admiring civilians asked them questions about their exploits at the front, and were answered in a soldierly off-hand way.

Some county government officials on their way to Sichuan for a training course occupied a central position, worthy of their dignity, but with a most undignified mass of people sitting on their toes. Freed for the time being from their responsibilities, they were taking the trip after the manner of schoolboys on an excursion. No doubt it was the *headmaster* of their county who was coming in for a lot of nasty epithets, but they were careful to keep his identity veiled under an affectionate nickname.

Miscellaneously dotted here and there were small merchants and their wares, country people on their way to show off the latest baby in the next town; and up in the front off-side corner was a theatrical singer who must surely have been a *prima donna*. Her music case was clasped against her as lovingly as ever a peasant woman clasped her baby, and she was humming snatches of *Carmen* from under her blanket. She was on her way from Chongqing to Lanzhou, she told the woman next to her, to fulfil an engagement there. If only she wouldn't so provokingly hide her head under a blanket!

The man next to me wore the badge of the Chinese Industrial Cooperatives on his coat. "You know the trucks running on this road are mostly using our charcoal," he said, "and those that don't, use seventy percent of our alcohol mixed with their American petrol. We distil it from Chinese wine, *kaoliang*, and corn." He pointed out other things; things belonging to the passengers and things along the way. The mysterious *prima donna's* blanket, (perish its warp!) had been made in a co-op some way west of Baoji. The gown of a merchant, it seemed, was also made from co-op cloth. A fibre suit-case had a CIC emblem woven into it ... from Hanzhong. "Look at me," he laughed, "I'm a walking advertisement for Cooperation ... uniform, sweater, scarf, stockings, shoes, shirt, brief-case ... everything!"

In many small villages as we rustled through, he pointed out the signboards with the *Gung Ho* emblem, and a guide to the local co-op underneath; carpentering, charcoal-burning, wood-cutting, and sometimes a flour-mill making use of some mountain streams. "This is the China that is rebuilding," he said. "Many of the people in these co-ops were penniless refugees a year ago. Now they are settling down as part of their new community, and making a valuable contribution to the country's economy as well as being once more in a position to support themselves and their families."

Later, the bus stopped at a village somewhat larger than the rest. "You might almost say that this is our village," said the man from the CIC, boastfully - but with a right to boast. The main street of the little place was called *Co-op Street* and scattered through the village and out in the countryside were about twenty cooperatives, turning out everything from paper to boots, leather tanning with local hides to woollen knitted sweaters, uniforms to coal, bricks and fire-bricks to textile machinery and truck repairs, tea-cups, carpentry, house-building, lumbering, soap. There was a joint cooperative store, a night school, an experimental laboratory for the chemical industry cooperatives, a CIC Primary School, a CIC Hospital, and a training school for organisers.

"Our units are all scattered like this," said the man of the moment, who had the whole bus listening to him by now as though he were an official guide with a megaphone. "The Japanese can't find them with their planes, and if they did, it would be a thousand-to-one chance on their making a hit. Look at Lanzhou – some of the heaviest and most concentrated bombing since the war, and our programs there continue almost unaffected; central buying and central selling for de-centralised producer units ... that's our aim."

All along the road were fleets of carts ... handcarts and mule carts, private carts and government carts, carrying flour and cotton southward and bringing back black tea, rice, tobacco and paper money from Sichuan. Towards evening, winding down the well-engineered mountain road into the Han River valley, we passed a whole fleet of handcarts flying a cooperative pennant. The men were leaning right back into the shafts so that the runners at the back dug into the road to brake them. "That's our Baoji Transport Cooperative out on the road," said the CIC man. "They work this stretch from Baoji to Guanyuan with loads of cotton and rice." And as it grew dark, there was a long line of camels on their way back to Lanzhou with wood oil and tea that would make its way right up through the neck of Gansu, across the sandy deserts, over the barren mountain passes and up the verdant sea-level valleys of Xinjiang, into Soviet Russia. The CIC man didn't claim the camels, curiously enough, "But we do have a Muslim co-op in Lanzhou," he said, "tanning good leather. So maybe we could get these camel men into one too." He seemed quite struck with the idea. "We've got all kinds of sects," he went on, "True Church of Jesus refugees from Hankou, American Baptists from Changzhou, Muslims in Lanzhou, a *Living Buddha* up in Sanpan, and we're thinking of getting a co-op formed among the Japanese prisoners near Baoji too." He glanced back at the camels, who were flinching, duck-eyed and panicky under the headlights, "so why not one of these?" As he spoke, one of them got out of hand and leapt over the cliff side, nearly dragging the others with it. "Maybe you'd better leave the camels out for a bit?" we all suggested.

Just before we got into Hanzhong, we saw a very old man, who must have been stone deaf as well as blind. He waddled along in the middle of the road with a great load of firewood piled up over the back of his head. We hooted along for a while within six feet of his tail, in bottom gear, but it was no good. The assistant driver leapt down and angrily cuffed the old man, who fell over into the ditch, either with surprise or the force of the blow. Old China, with the camel and the wood carrier, must give way to the new; but we wished that the new could find a way of being more polite about it!

Hanzhong was twinkling proudly under its new electric lighting system, and there were lots of good things to eat on the streets. The old women sitting beside the booths of Sichuan oranges, fat dried persimmon and beefcake sandwiches, were comfortable in the fashion of the place, with little baskets of charcoal sending a draught of warm air up their skirts, and others on their laps to warm their hands.

Aylwin broke his journey in Hanzhong, situated in the centre of the rich basin that extends for sixty miles along the Han River in the heart of the Qin Ling Mountains. In the time of the Three Kingdoms (AD 220–265), Hanzhong was the central battleground for triangular contests between north, south, and east. It lies at the crossing of the Han River by the road from Chongqing to Lanzhou, and the west. This was the main route to Russia and was therefore a vital link in the struggle that the north and south were engaged in against the east. This also was a rich area. In the mountains could be found iron, copper, lead, coal, gold, quartz, asbestos, and wood oil nuts while in the valley there was cotton, hemp, silk, bamboo, palm fibre, lacquer, and tea. The task that the CIC had in hand here was to supply organisation to the myriad of small producing units, to provide running capital, to standardise production, to regroup workers into economic units instead of families, to arrange joint supply of raw materials and joint sale of products. The old handcrafts were being killed by wartime uncertainty and rising costs. This is how Aylwin portrayed the Hanzhong Oilcloth Cooperative, an example of what was being done by the CIC:

> The nine members of this co-op were all former workers in a small factory under private management. They had been badly exploited by their owner, who was a long-nailed petty official with an exceedingly vicious temper. His second wife, whom he had married hoping to get an unpaid manager of the factory, had been constantly beaten and humiliated, until at last she had cast in her lot with the workmen and left with them to set up a new factory.
>
> But they could not find capital until some members of a canvas co-op came in to talk, leaving behind them two small CIC pamphlets. The group met daily to listen to these being read aloud by the wife of their old master. Discussion followed, and then the thing was finally settled – they would form a co-op, and the woman Qing Wenshiu would be its chairperson.
>
> The CIC office, approached for a loan, was out of funds, but by writing in the members' looms as share capital it was discovered that an immediate advance of cotton yarn could be secured on this backing from the Federation Supply and Marketing Department. The profits on the first batch of plain cloth would buy wood oil, which would be used for oiling part of the second batch, and so on, gradually shifting right over to oilcloth.
>
> During the first three months, $9,040 worth of cotton yarn had been advanced from the federation. In this time, fifty-four bales of broadcloth and six of oiled cloth had been delivered for sale, which exceeded the amount of raw material loaned by $1,020. Qing Wenshiu and her fellows worked hard and slept soundly.
>
> But the looms were not always busy; for the Supply and Marketing Department itself was often short of running capital. Once when Wenshiu took in her cloth, she was told there was no money to pay for it and no more cotton yarn in stock either.
>
> "We've sent our traveller to Baoji with all our spare funds to buy more yarn," said the man behind the receiving counter. "He'll be back in a few days."
>
> "What can we do meanwhile?" she asked anxiously. Her cloth would fetch a good price out on the street right then. "Food costs us seven hundred dollars every month, and if we can't keep working we will starve."
>
> "Suppose we give you rice in exchange for your cloth?" suggested the salesman. "As for vegetables, perhaps you'll be able to find a way of your own."
>
> So Wenshiu ran home, well pleased, and after telling the others about it she fixed her headcloth and went right out to borrow some vegetables from a friendly stall keeper

down the road. I happened to meet her on her way back, and we walked up to the co-op together.

"He never really thought we'd do it," she said later, about her husband, "not run our own business and be able to support ourselves, I mean. At first he just laughed and said I'd come back when I got hungry. Then, when he heard how we were getting on, he must have become very angry. First he went to the CIC office people and tried to use his influence to have the co-op closed down. But they told him we were working well, and had done nothing against the law. Then he went to the magistrate and told him that our men and women members were living sinfully together. He ..." Her smooth rounded features were all screwed up; she spoke hoarsely, faster and faster, fighting to keep back tears.

Then suddenly, with a toss of her head, she became a strong working woman again. Putting finger and thumb to her nose she shot the mucus harshly out, in mock fastidious contempt, and went on, "Just because we've made a success of our own factory instead of his, he had to insult us with such vile words! Don't his four gentle sons all live in a mixed college for men and women? And why should we uneducated people be any different from them?"

The night after this conversation, Qing Wenshiu went back to try once more at making a success of her old home. Next morning her mother found her hanging unconscious by a rope around her waist from the ceiling, her hands tied behind her back, her body black and bruised. She called in CIC, who called in the police. The husband and his eldest son were arrested, and Wenshiu went to the hospital.

A few days later she was back at the co-op. They had received a contract from the Public Highways Administration, placed through the Federation Supply and Marketing Department. As Wenshiu herself told me of this on my next visit, I could see that she regarded it as a fit reply to her husband. Homeless, she was bringing all the dynamic force of an illiterate, embittered and intensely sympathetic woman to the job of making a successful family out of her co-op.

Continuing to write about the bus journey:

Early to bed and early to rise is the rule of the road, providing you want a good place on the truck. Long before dusk, people were up and about calling for "wash face water" and "rinse mouth water" and downing their breakfast bowls of rice. While it was still dark they were packing themselves into the truck.

A mile out of the city there was trouble; an inspection station. The inspector put a ladder up against the side of the truck and demanded that we should all get down. "Aiya! But getting down is very troublesome!" vouchsafed someone, after there had been a long awkward silence. "But if you get down now and let me look at your luggage there will be no more trouble for the rest of the day," wheedled the inspector, who had three red rings round his hat. No one was rude enough, in view of the red rings, to ask him why he hadn't come to look at the luggage before we started, but everyone thought it. Some of the people on the outside jumped down, hoping to be able to get a better place in the scramble back again, and a few of those with good seats actually stood up. Just then Red-Stripes caught sight of an old friend in the shape of one of the county government officials on the bus. "You do like to bother people, don't you!" the official joked. "Only my duty, only my duty, you know," replied Red-Stripes, unconsciously raising himself up and down on his toes. The moment had passed. Those in the centre flopped back into their places, and those who had jumped hopefully off the sides sneaked back again. Red-Stripes beamed generously through his spectacles and cheeped on his little whistle.

We were off again and happy. The soldiers, as they neared home, became more and more excited. One of them had found a fellow villager, who knew his family, among the passengers. He was getting all the local gossip out of him beforehand ... who had been married, who had got rich, who had got poor, who had died, whose family had new children. "You must come and see us tomorrow," he insisted to the soldier, "my mother will ask you to take supper with us." The peasant boy smiled happily to have made friends with a hero.

So the bus charged on through this new-old part of China. Chicken feathers flew, pigs scattered like black bullets or chased along head down behind us for the simple reason that they had forgotten to stop running now that we were passed; bright red bales of paprika shone in the sunlight, and tattered rags tied to sacred trees flapped in our wake. Dogs chased us, and birds raced us. Cows lumbered swiftly away with tails flying, little boys ran down to meet us, and little girls tried to look as if they weren't really afraid. Old men shook their heads ever-wonderingly, and old women nudged each other and cackled behind their hands at the comfortless passengers piled in on each other like so many sheep for the market. There were long lines of soldiers on the road carrying their huge iron pots and their converted gasoline tins. Camel trains that had been walking all through the night padded past, too sleepy now to take any notice of us. New and old, women blinded by trachoma and bright-eyed girls treading sturdily on their unbound feet, soldierly men, ignorant men, scholarly men; the whole making a composite picture of the China that was, is, and will be.

In Hanzhong, Aylwin had been so pleased by the shaving brushes being turned out by one co-op that he bought one for himself. It caused quite a stir when he contracted anthrax by using the brush. A small point about sterilisation of the bristles had to be immediately put right at the co-op to prevent further contamination. Anthrax is a particularly nasty disease, but luckily the Gung Ho hospital in Baoji recognised it in time, and so the cure was made relatively easy.

Chapter 14

Old Number Six

On his return to Baoji, Aylwin wrote a letter home on 3 March 1940:

I am afraid it is quite a long time since I wrote to you, as I have been away for several weeks. It was a good trip in spite of various inconveniences such as lice and Japanese aeroplanes. One of the better moments was after spending a long day pulling a cart with a machine on it over a muddy mountain track in the rain, for forty miles, and then finding some Norwegian missionaries at the end of it, who turned out their best ladies' bedroom to put me in, all dirty and mud covered as I was! Their homes had just been gobbled up, and England and France had just pulled out, but still they were awfully nice. They had a round telegram saying that the families of all Norwegian missionaries are safe, but that they must economise, as money is going to be difficult.

Another good day was on a nice level road, with our handcart on bicycle wheels just big enough to carry the machine and one man lying on it. I had stayed the night with some American missionaries, and was dashed if I was going to leave very early and so miss the chance of a foreign breakfast, so we didn't get off till eight o'clock, and forty miles to do before dark. I pulled the puller ten miles and he pulled me thirty. When I pulled, he rested on the cart and *vice versa*. That's how I got lice. He was very embarrassed to be seen resting while his fare pulled between the shafts, so he covered his face with his hat. The day we left one place, thirty-four aeroplanes flew over our heads and bombed it terribly, and the next day we saw the same planes again, and arrived in the evening to find our destination still burning, women crying, and coffins everywhere. Next day the Japanese got very close with their armies, and people had to start refugeeing even before they had picked out the remains of their dead and belongings from the burning rubble. I went with the refugee stream in the night, through the hobbling bound-foot women, and the kids, and the men carrying enormous bundles on either end of poles over their shoulders.

We've had some quite interesting visitors here in Baoji lately, including an American schoolteacher who came specially to investigate CIC, and a group of patriotic overseas Chinese youths from the Philippines and Singapore. They were jolly fellows, but were rushed around far too quickly so that they learned practically nothing. The other visitor was a YWCA worker from Chongqing. She tells me of a place where I can probably stay in Chongqing when I go, where they have ice cream every day, and lots of pie. I haven't tasted an ice cream, or a pie, or chocolate for about eighteen months now, which must beat even your rationing for sheer privation!

The other night I had a dream that my rugger team was playing out on the field and everybody was clapping and yelling *schoo-oo-ool* like mad, while I was being given a jaw in the headmaster's study; which shows that my subconscious wants to be back in Europe!

Despite the subconscious desire, he was obviously enjoying everything he was doing as the following letter, written on 12 June 1940, clearly indicates:

It is difficult to think of you all having such a foul time when life is pretty swimming here on the whole. Of course I often feel that there's something wrong, and I shouldn't enjoy life so much; but I can't help it. The other day I got a letter from our big boss in Chongqing, Rewi Alley by name (a tough but very bright New Zealander), congratulating me on a report I put in. I also gave a forty-minute talk in Chinese about my trip, and later on put in a quarter of an hour of quite involved theoretical stuff about the co-op movement, which people said was in quite understandable language, so I am really feeling that I have some grip on my work. This is what Chinese would call "inflating an ox-skin"; that is to say, "blowing my own trumpet". But I thought from your letter which arrived today that you would like to know that Old Number Six is getting on okay, even if Numbers One to Five and the two preconditions are in a tough spot. Not to mention Aunt Doris walking up and down Bow Road like a perambulating ray of sunshine. It must be an extraordinarily interesting situation though, from what the *New Statesman* tells me. That's the funny thing. What is almost unendurable to the people in half of the world gives spice to the intellectual cakes over which we sit at tea.

I have now trained my restaurant to serve quite good scrambled eggs that aren't swimming in more than half a pint of oil. Recently a thing called "ocean white vegetable" came into season; it is very like the best cabbage. Together with bean curd, and freshly baked crisp flour cakes (two with sugar inside and one ordinary) it makes a meal worthy of the *New Statesman*.

There's a wife beater just beside my favourite restaurant where I read; too bad. The man, who is about thirty-five, comes into a dark little windowless room where he keeps his wife, aged fifteen, and family far away, and beats her with a slipper. It doesn't hurt very much, but she naturally resents the indignity and struggles against him, biting his shoulder. You can see it all, if you want to, from my once-exclusive and quiet restaurant. Then she goes back to bed and cries, and he goes away for a few hours before coming back for more. Maybe I shall go and see if my friend the magistrate can't do something about it.

I have copied out all the important bits of two months' *New Statesmen* and am going to make a talk from them sometime. The magazines are going to a German refugee friend of mine in Xi'an and to the heroine of *Unfinished Story* – Fragrant Grass a.k.a. Struggle. So you see they are being well used.

On 24 August 1940:

> Nasty bombing here – more caves collapsing and burying people; it's their own fault in a way. Anyone could have seen that the cave was a weak one. I got some startling pictures of people un-burying their relations, which I won't inflict on you. I suppose it happens in London too. One old boy dug away for half an hour, expecting to jab the spade into his wife any moment, and then gave up exhausted. Then he found that his wife had been one of the first to be pulled out, dead, only he hadn't recognised her.

On a visit to Chongqing, the Kuomintang Capital since the fall of Hankou, in September 1939, Aylwin wrote the following:

> Today being Friday and about eleven o'clock at night, old Hitler-man may at this very moment be launching his death attack on Britain. And there my thought ends. As I walk about the wreckage of what was once a beautiful city and imagine that London may very soon be worse than this, plus every other city in that incredibly small place, much smaller than one province of China, called England ....

There was, through 1940, proceeding all over the country a campaign of rightist propaganda, emphasised in some places by arrests of progressive men and women. Pressure was brought to bear on all organisations relying financially on government support to enrol their members in the Kuomintang Party. A Three People's Principles Youth Corps, which acted as a strictly party organisation and refused admission to non-Kuomintang elements, set to work along the same lines among high school and university students. Anyone refusing to join was branded red; student arrests became frequent, and many were forced to flee without graduating. High government officials publicly denounced the reds as traitors, who were storing arms, ammunition, and men for the coming anti-Kuomintang struggle. Rumours of burnings and burying alive were thought up and spread around, often in pamphlet form at the government or army expense. The concentration camps in Xi'an, Luoyang, and Lanzhou, which held hundreds of young students caught on their way to or from the Eighth Route Army areas, were enlarged and came out into the open; no secret was made of the fact that the inmates were there, or that they were being held purely on account of their political beliefs. The military blockade of the Eighth Route Army special districts north of Xi'an increased in severity, and communications with its southeast Shanxi area became virtually impossible after reinforced Kuomintang Army units had forced the communists deep into the mountains. Along with the suppression of communism went a reactionary movement that spoiled all constructive effort. Suspected bodies found that the best way to clear themselves of all suspicion was to wear expensive clothes, knock off work for a month, and be seen constantly in public restaurants and tea shops. There was a widespread feeling among Chinese youth that real service to their country was too dangerous, and too likely to be misconstrued, so that the best way was to return to abstract studies, since almost every career then offered possibilities only to the intriguers and politicians.

The past record of the Chinese communists proved that, left to themselves, they were the most patriotic, self-sacrificing, and democratic force in China. They alone had been able to mobilise the people, and youth, over vast areas giving unstinted service without thought of personal comfort or advancement. Their courage and determination had been, for years, the secret admiration of youth all over the country, and more recently the model for much of the democratic advances in Kuomintang China. To millions of Chinese, the suppression of sympathy for the Eighth Route Army meant suppression of democracy, forcing them to choose between one of the two political extremes and so driving many into the bog of political disinterestedness.

It was about this time, in the autumn of 1940, that Xiao Ren was forced to leave Baoji. Aylwin escorted her to Luoyang where she continued working for Gung Ho. On his return to Baoji he was, understandably, in a very low mood, and Rewi Alley asked him to use his connections in the Eighth Route Army to get a young girl, Wei Wei, into the Third Drama Troupe, which was operating in South Shanxi, in the Border Region north of Luoyang. Wei Wei was 14 years old, daughter of Widow Zhang, a peppery Hebei woman who was an old revolutionary and now worked in the Baoji Gung Ho. Everyone loved Wei Wei. Rewi's concern was to get her out of harm's way, out of the present intrigue and finger pointing in Baoji. It would also be an immediate therapy for Aylwin to concentrate on someone else.

Aylwin did his best for Wei Wei. He used his influence in the Border Region and then asked a CIC inspector, who was going into north Shaanxi, to take Wei Wei with him so that she might get to Yan'an for training. The inspector must have talked, for Wei Wei was arrested on the journey and returned to Baoji.

All this on top of the mass arrests in the Women's Department made Aylwin extremely angry. He knew who the Kuomintang agents were in the Baoji Gung Ho office. He made it quite clear who was to blame and consequently made it very difficult for himself. These people were powerful. A big factor for his safety, for the time being anyway, was that he was a foreigner. The Kuomintang was very careful when it came to dealing with the citizens of countries that showed them support. Wei Wei did, however, finally manage to get to Yan'an.

Aylwin's letter from Chongqing goes on despondently about all that he had written so far about progress within war, warlordism to democracy, the power of youthful energy. He wondered whether it was worth carrying on because of increasing evidence that the old corrupt ways that had seemingly been on the decline were now showing up in increasing strength, tearing at the fragile fabric of the new democratic movement. But he continued in a more encouraged mood:

> Of course there are some good things left in the world, aren't there? One of them is CIC, or rather its potentialities. Another is my friends in the southern United States. You should read the Left Book Club's *Let My People Go*. Reading that book, which I found in a missionary's house here, really gave me a lot of pep to go back to my own work, which is sometimes discouraging.
>
> Today, Ralph Lapwood and I beat the missionary and his son at tennis. It is only about the twelfth time I have played organised games of any kind since September 1st 1937. After it, I really feel that lack of organised sport is one of the causes of world wars!

They ought to be compulsory for parliamentarians and dictators. You remember Ralph Lapwood, who made the last part of my trip with me last year. He is now working for CIC, loaned by his mission university. The other one on the trip, Michael Lindsay, is now acting as press attaché here. It was amusing all meeting again and reminiscing about the trip.

Things may get exciting in the northwest soon, for which reason I have just got a part-time job as a correspondent with the American Associated Press Agency. If nothing happens, however, I am scheduled to make a tour of all CIC work in the country, for writing and inspection! Sounds good, eh? It's amazing how healthy I am. The temperature here has been well over 100°F on several occasions, and for two weeks didn't drop much below 90°F even at night; also about 99 per cent moisture! But after a few days acclimatisation, I was able to eat quite heartily and put in a lot of work. Now nearly everybody, including Chinese, is feeling pretty bad – but me; I'm physically fine.

A month later, in October:

When I first came to China I had a firmly instilled idea that everybody is as good as everybody else, white, yellow, brown, black, or whatever. After a while, I was terribly disillusioned and began to think that the white man had a burden, and the yellow was a terror after all! Now I think I can see things in their proper perspective, and understand a little just why people act the way they do, and the relationship of society to the individual's actions. Chinese society is one of the most complicated things in the world, and when people do things that in England would make a man a pariah, he may still be a thoroughly good-hearted person, because different conditions call for different kinds of action. It is also sometimes difficult to live right in amongst the forest and still see the publicity angle of its trees. One tends to see only the unprintable prickles, snakes, toadies, and hyenas in the undergrowth.

At the end of 1940, Aylwin left Baoji on a trip into the Qin Ling Mountains.

To Shuangshipu, one of the most amazing little villages in China. It includes a Bailie Training School, a million-dollar electric power plant, an up-to-date chemical laboratory, and a hospital; all in a place practically unheard of four years ago.

Here the people are terribly poor; though untroubled by wars and refugees, they are naturally too poor to buy salt resulting in grotesque goitre in a large percentage of the people, and children under the age of fifteen often go right through a winter without a single pair of trousers! There is good wool produced locally, and people have done much to raise their standard of living through cooperatives, which give them new techniques besides new organisation and joint salesmanship. Hundreds of thousands of woollen blankets are woven here for the Chinese soldiers.

How is Rosemary? Funny thing about our family, the way it doesn't write to itself. The other day a man in the train looked at my eyebrows and said, "Your eyebrows are too much spread out. That means that your relationships with your brothers are too far apart, and that they will desert you when you need them." It was with some dignity and cold English reserve in my voice, I hope, that I answered him saying that, however it might be with people whose eyebrows were spread out in China, this was not necessarily the case in England, my country, and that my three brothers were all very big and very reliable. Then he asked how old my father was. Fortunately, I could remember to within the nearest five years, and the statement which I was able to give him silenced all aspersions cast upon our name.

Rewi Alley is here. He is the so-called pioneer of our CIC and much played up in American magazines to that effect. He is a very tough New Zealander. His chief merit so far as I am concerned just at present is that he can make plum puddings out of persimmon. He has got some Chinese sons, and specialises in washing scabies off any old boy he meets along the road, in his spare time.

Did I tell you, I've got a couple of sons in school here? They were a bit weedy at first and needed a rubber sheet in their bed more than anything else. However, they are growing up to be very tough now and will no doubt be a credit to my old age. Needless to say, in case with your well-known restraint you go spreading this around Harpenden or elsewhere, they are not my sons by blood.

"The book" as it stands is no good. Since writing it, I have got a lot of new stuff, and I am sure that I will sometime be able to write a good book from the best of the old plus new material.

Chapter 15

Lanzhou

At the end of December 1940, Aylwin again wrote home telling of interesting characters he had met on his travels:

> I spent Christmas with some missionaries in Xi'an. Nice people. The best Christmas pudding was made by a Chinese girl, educated in America, based on a Yorkshire recipe using entirely local products.
>
> Odd folk, missionaries; they live in great houses behind high walls and thick gates, which ruins their prospects of doing much good from the start, but mostly they mean well. There's a new one who played rugger against me at school and afterwards went to Oxford, recently come out with his wife. He has breakfast at about nine every morning in dressing gown and slippers, spotless tablecloth and cutlery, months-old newspaper propped against the toast rack, just like Oxford. So jolly. "This could never happen in England" is his chief remark.
>
> After Christmas I set out with my bicycle to a place beside the Yellow River. The Japanese and a lot of friends of mine are somewhere over the other side. I can see the mountains they are in, but no hope of going over there – till after the war. Met an odd, but better-than-most, Swedish missionary who roams about the countryside with an expensive accordion presented to him by his aunt in London, and a dog he named Trotsky for some reason. He lives quite close to the people. His life has been as full of adventure as well as heartbreaking emotion and so on as mine has been stolid. You would love him at sight because he's all enthusiasm and keenness. He was converted to religion at seventeen and read the Bible through by flashlight under the pillow because his firmly conventional church-going father and mother would have laughed at him. He was very rich and very happy; delivered his first sermon impromptu at his sister's society wedding in a harangue against champagne drinking and shallow frolicking. Afterwards, Father apparently came up with a hoarse voice saying, "Thank you my boy", and his sister cried and cried. It all started when he jumped down from a twenty-foot rock in bare feet onto a broken bottle as a boy. His life has gone along in that strain ever since. I think mine must have started when Soney banged my front tooth out on the chamber pot. But I haven't had such a bad time, taking it all in all, have I?

The next month was spent on a trip into Gansu province. On a mountain road on the way to Lanzhou, he stopped off in a tiny village "somewhere very small, with snow in the mountains and camels in the main street" to celebrate the New Year, 1941, with some missionaries there. He wrote in a flippant mood:

> This job I do continues to be good fun. I board trucks here and there, and meet all sorts of strange blokes, some of whom are too good to be true, and some of whom are positively medieval in their malignity; cunning blokes in plenty but always a good many really trying to make things work. And as things work, they mean quite a lot to this country both in economic support and in the growth of democracy.
>
> There are some good missionaries here, who invited me to dinner and gave me a bath. It was a very small tub, but very welcome. There are some Americans, some Canadians, and some English. Pronunciation causes difficulties, especially at milking time. The Americans say "caf" for "calf", and somebody thought that the "cat" was being milked or that the "calf" wanted a saucer of it. So now they all call calf "poddy" which is apparently Australian. A doctor from further north was very blasé about lepers. He says it is practically impossible to catch it from them if you keep normally clean and are not otherwise in bad health. They have about seventy lepers, some legless, some handless, in a compound outside his hospital. By the time you get this letter I shall probably have seen them.

Continuing on his way, he sat in a truck going further north to Lanzhou, where the camels came down to the frozen Yellow River and, padded over the ice for a little way to crane their necks down for an iced swig.

> The truck journey was exciting. Petrol is short; therefore, drivers are given only enough petrol to carry them to their destination if they free-wheel down all the hills. So the motor gets switched off, but the foot brake isn't very good either, so one hand has to go on the hand brake. But sometimes the horn has to be blown, going round a Swiss hairpin bend, so that leaves no hands at all. Only the ingenuity of the Chinese overcomes such handicaps.

I might mention here that, fifty years on when I was there, petrol was still tightly rationed in the northwest, and driving technique had little changed. However, luckily nowadays the brakes usually seem to be more efficient.

Gansu was the "problem province" of the northwest. With one end in Shaanxi and Sichuan, it thrust out like a great dumbbell into Qinghai, Mongolia, and Turkestan. From the north came Russian trucks, planes, petrol, ammunition, guns, and Russian advisers. Six counties in the southeast of the province were controlled by the Chinese communists. The province was simmering, as it had done for hundreds of years, with racial overtones of feeling between Han and Muslim boiling over, on occasion into bloody massacre. Turkic, Tibetan, and Mongolian formed appreciable minority groups, each of which had its own issues. Here, communications were vital. Across Gansu, as today, ran the Yellow River from west to east, and the international highway ran from northwest to southeast, following the ancient silk trade route.

Little attention had been drawn by the Chinese to this northwest highway, which ran through Gansu and Xinjiang to a branch of the Trans-Siberia Railway, within sixty miles of the border. There were no news flashes as there were about the Burma Road in the south. There were so many hundreds of trucks dashing across the desert from Hami and Ürümqi to Lanzhou, and the government's intention was to keep it open. From Lanzhou to Chongqing, the massive Russian six- and eight-wheeled trucks were a common sight on the roads until the Chinese were able to take over that section of the supply line. The trucks were carrying mostly arms and ammunition. The less-important supplies like aeroplane spare parts and petrol were carried on thousands of mule carts and tens of thousands of camels. Their return loads were made up of wool, fur pelts, tea, and wood oil, which were the main items from the Chinese side of the barter agreement. The major part of this activity was during the period 1938–39, which was about the time of maximum Russian influence in China proper.

Up to the end of 1939, there were in Lanzhou a good number of Russian airmen and military advisers as well as commercial attachés to manage the barter agreement. The city blossomed with watches, silk stockings, and clothing. Hundreds of people attended the night schools to learn the Russian language. During 1940, Russia decided to cut aid to China, and the flow of goods steadily fell off so that, by the time Aylwin got there at the start of 1941, there was no sign of the Russians. He could walk the streets without seeing anything more than the ordinary merchandise that had been going to and fro along that route since the days of Marco Polo.

Aylwin met other sorts of "foreigners" in plenty:

> Up on the hill lives a Mongolian prince. The YMCA secretary would feel very much at home in Nashville, Tennessee, while he has an assistant from the Philippines. There is an American missionary with a Frigidaire who invites one to eat ice cream. There is a home of lepers from Tibet and the northern part of Gansu. It was started by an English missionary who invited one leprous beggar to stay on his compound, and then another, and another. Up to now, scores have wandered in from the northern wastes to spend their last days peacefully chatting in husky whispers, grinding their own flour and beans for their milk, listening to Bible stories, and looking down at the eternal waters of the Yellow River swirling away into the distance. Uygur women with long veils of bright-coloured stuff round their faces bring a touch of India to one quarter of the city. There are bargemen who have come down on inflated sheepskins from Qinghai Hu (Kokonor), and camelmen from the gravelly Gobi wastes of Mongolia. There is a Cantonese restaurant serving tropical dainties.
>
> I met a German Jew who was for four years in Dachau concentration camp but escaped on the eve of war into Italy, from where he miraculously got a visa to cross the Balkans and Russia, found his way through Xinjiang into China. The British and French refused transit visas across India and Indo-China; China was the only country in the world willing to take him. I also met two young Polish-Americans who ran away

from America to Russia just about the time I was leaving Oxford, and have been on their way ever since.

They started off in Eskimo walrus-skin boats from Alaska, were jailed on reaching Russia as they had no passports, later escaped to Xinjiang, were jailed again for twenty-seven months, and finally escaped to China proper, still a haven apparently to almost anyone who likes to come. Also met an American sheep that guerrilla'd it for a thousand miles or so from Shanxi and was about to give birth to the first Eurasian lamb. Also, in the same experimental station, some castrated Japanese horses. The man in charge, native of Nanjing, seemed to think that it would be a good way to deal with all Japanese, but his view must not be taken as typical.

To be a bit more precise about the sheep, ten years ago, Mr R. T. Moyer, of Oberlin College in Shanxi, brought some Rambouillet sheep with him from the States back to Shanxi. At the outbreak of hostilities with Japan, he was holidaying on the coast. What would happen to his precious flock, grazing the hillsides around Taiku? As Moyer anxiously scanned the daily papers for news of the Shanxi campaign, his shepherd, having no desire to be fleeced himself or see his good sheep made into mutton, was scanning the horizon for the Japanese as he took off with his flock into the mountains. By Christmas morning they had crossed the Yellow River and were bleating into the 420th mile when they happened upon the good missionary Bryan of Sanyuan, Shaanxi, who, as he put it later, "felt it was nice to meet a shepherd watching his flock and asking for the mission on Christmas morning." Touched, Bryan gave them royal winter quarters and put them onto a bus for Lanzhou as soon as the warm weather came. The experts at the experimental station got busy crossing the American rams with fifty Chinese sheep. Though they and the rams were considerably stymied by the short stature and very thick tails of the ewes, their efforts were finally rewarded.

Not only sheep have settled down and begotten families in Lanzhou. There have been eighteen cooperative weddings in the Lanzhou depot in the last year. I was invited to one wedding. The bridegroom had once been a refugee from the war areas in Shandong, while his bride was a local girl. The wedding carpet was part of the ten thousand yards of army blanket turned out that winter by the joint efforts of bride, bridegroom, and other members of their cooperative.

Co-op blanket making in Lanzhou is the concern not only of eleven weaving co-ops, all of whom are on their way to financial independence, but of a widespread organisation that embraces four hundred and fifty members of women's spinning co-ops, and about ten thousand domestic women wool spinners. One day I went for a twenty-mile walk up the frozen Yellow River and found a little village which missionaries said would have starved but for our co-ops and the extra work afforded by them to thousands of wool spinners. The five co-ops in this village had all moved out of Lanzhou after serious bombing. Now they are making their own homes in the village, making a new community too. I saw the curious evidence of farmers turned industrialists: spread out over a field to dry in the sun was an acre of wool, and sitting squat in the middle of it was a watchman's hut made of grey army blankets.

Returning to Lanzhou, I took a baby raft of shiny yellow inflated sheepskins across the river. On supple two-inch sticks tied over thirteen sheepskin balloons, we floated off from the hard ice and pushed out into the little tinkling lumps of loose spring ice floating swiftly downstream. The paddler knelt athwart his craft, and gradually, spinning round in every eddy, worked it crosscurrent until we could land a mile downstream on the far side.

Walking up under the shadow of a vast irrigation wheel that in summer lifts the water in little troughs and pours it neatly into a runaway *fifty* feet above the river's level, we came to a Muslim fur co-op that had opened in 1939, after a Lanzhou *ahung* came to CIC and asked that fifteen of his believers then working as private factory hands might be allowed to form a cooperative of their own. Walking through the gate, we saw the co-op practically smothered under the raw material that had just come in for them to fill an order from the military for thirty-five thousand fur coats. Through this order, they paid for their new buildings and made a net profit of over seven thousand dollars for the year. There was next door a leather tanning co-op run by refugees from Henan, Shanxi, Shaanxi, and Hebei as well as some Gansu people. For the first stage of the journey from Lanzhou down Marco Polo's highway to Xi'an, I jumped onto a so-called motorbus which careered over the mountains, this time proudly using Chinese petrol from the Yumen oil wells further north. It is true; we had to stop now and then to clean out the carburettor and petrol lines. Chinese New Year passed on the road. The main items of amusement are dancers on stilts, men dressed up like women, and swings from trees. This is the biggest holiday in Chinese tradition. Everybody who possibly can knocks off for several days, although by government order the *Ocean* New Year is now observed, not the Chinese. In the old days there were holidays for about twenty days, and the peasants still stick to it like grim death.

As early as three and a half to four thousand years ago, the first day of the first moon in the lunar calendar was known as the head of the year. However only two thousand years ago "passing the year" became widely celebrated as a holiday. Widely popular folk dances were performed, walking and performing on stilts, the lion dance, dramas, operas, the land boat dance, the dragon lantern dance, all to the accompaniment of firecrackers. The origin of all this lies in a legend that in ancient China there lived a strange and savage beast called the Nian, which appeared on the last day of the twelfth lunar month. On one of these occasions it appeared at a village where there happened to be two boys competing who could crack a whip the loudest. The Nian fled in fright and never returned. On another occasion it came to a village where two red gowns hung on a door. Again it fled in fright and never returned. On a third occasion, the Nian was frightened away by lights. So it was learnt that the savage Nian was frightened of three things: noise, red, and light. So these three elements became the main ingredients of the Passing the Year celebrations. This was the Chinese New Year which, after the

Republic was formed in 1911 and the introduction of the Gregorian calendar, became known as the Spring Festival.

Aylwin was forced to abandon the fancy motorbus with its sticky petrol and continue the journey bouncing comfortably southward on some of the four hundred tons of wool being sent down to blanket cooperatives in Shaanxi and southern Gansu. It took three days to reach Tianshui:

As our ancient Chevrolet crossed the last pontoon bridge of creaking inflated pigskins before the city, the tyre that had been half flat when we set off in the morning was still half flat. There had been thirty-seven stops for minor repairs, and the petrol tank, which had begun the day modestly under the front seat, was suspended flamboyantly from the roof in order to give the added flip of gravity to the motor's failing powers of suction. But the ancient city seemed to resent even this degree of mechanisation, for we were asked to leave our truck at the new bus station that lies outside the city wall.

Once within the gates, the traveller is taken back a thousand years. A long dusty main street squeezes itself through ten narrow gateways in two miles, and down it pad only lordly camel trains bearing salt from Qinghai, wool from Mongolia, or dried fruits from Xinjiang. Bazaars line the street on either side. A black-bearded "son of Allah" dressed in a sheepskin gown sits toasting his feet on a platter of charcoal, his walls hung thick with skins of tiger, leopard, wolf, and fox smeared with ancient potions of the forests. Next door to the furrier, the sun glints in over the polished tops of lacquer furniture, while further on again sits the herbalist doctor beside his weird potions of mountain roots, crabs, tusks, tortoises, and unmentionable anatomical portions of rare beasts.

But though Tianshui changes slowly in the eyes of an outsider, things are moving swiftly when seen in the perspective of its forty centuries. In the temple commemorating the birthplace of one of the Empire's earliest kings are now housed soldiers who have been crippled in the defence of the Republic, and those of them who can still work have formed themselves into a machine co-op making all sorts of technical equipment.

Another Taoist temple, dedicated to the women's goddess Quanyin, nestles into a hillside beyond the city wall. Expectant mothers hopefully lay images of male babies here, maidens come to pray for the safety of their soldiering sweethearts, dutiful children seek health for their sick mothers, while in a side temple whirs the only printing press for miles around, turning out everything from visiting cards to school books and army field maps. The printers themselves are co-op members, and the printers' devils are probationary members, of whom five were recently promoted to full membership. Partly to keep in good standing with the local population and partly in the form of rent, one co-op member regularly joins the other pilgrims to the temple on the first and fifteenth of the month, contributing the press's pew rent in joss sticks [incense] and coins of silver paper.

The printers get their paper from another co-op down by the river, which makes it by hand from a mixture of shrub bark and old sandals. The chairman of this co-op is a returned student from Tokyo and a refugee from Japanese-occupied Taiyuan. "Why didn't you stay in Taiyuan," I asked, "and run your paper factory there?" "I wouldn't have been allowed to run any paper factory," he replied. "The Japanese keep track of all their old students, and I would have had to become one of their puppet officials for sure!" So the technician left his factory and reverted to a thousand-year-old process – "For the present," as he says hopefully, "until we can get this place mechanised."

Writing home, Aylwin described the process thus:

First dig a hole about six feet deep in the tennis lawn. Then put on your pruning gloves, borrow Daddy's penknife, and start cutting all the old hemp sandals and other bits of rope you can find lying about the place. Cut 'em up fine. Don't worry about time. Then borrow one of Aunt Ger's cows, pretend it is an ox, and make it pull a millstone, which you can borrow from the British Museum, round and round in a stone trough, mashing up the bits of sandal sole into a tasty mess that will remind you somewhat of All-Bran or Daddy's Sunday night supper of shredded wheat. Then go up the common doing deep breathings and bring back with you some of the chalk off the dells. Drop this into Daddy's supper – I mean the sandals. Then put everything into the tank you dug in the tennis lawn and stir with a long pole. Maybe you'd better ask Ellen to help you do this, as it is rather strenuous. Now go upstairs to the wardrobe and take out one of Granny's old dresses of some fine material, spread it over a frame so that it will make a sort of gauze sieve. Put on a pair of Wellington boots and jump into the tank with the sieve. Pass the sieve gently through the murky water and bring out a fine layer of Daddy's supper on the sieve. Instead of giving it to Daddy, or to Karen [the family Samoyed dog], instead of giving it to poor refugee children who haven't had such a good chance in life to dress in, spread it out on a board or a spare piece of wall to dry in the sun. Then you will have paper and can write me a letter on it.

The first step towards mechanisation of Tianshui's industry was taken by a group of flour millers from the lower Changjiang (Yangtze) region. They couldn't reproduce the steel rollers or electric power plant to copy their Changjiang mill, there in Tianshui, but they were able to get hold of a truck motor, which they converted to burn charcoal and used it to drive a couple of old-style grindstones day and night, at three or four times the record speed of a Gansu donkey. Machinery was as rare as diamonds in Gansu.

Taking once more to the road for the relatively short last stage to Baoji, Aylwin mounted a bicycle. Along the journey, a flat tyre brought him into contact with yet another mode of transport:

There was nothing for it but to hail a passing wood puller, put my bicycle on top of the load, and help him pull the cart. Like most coolies seen on this road dressed in half of an old uniform, he was a runaway from the army, and not ashamed of it. "We only got a few dollars a month, and had to buy our own shoes out of that," he said. "There was never enough to eat, either. Moving east to Hunan, the officers were so afraid we'd run away that they locked us into the train even during air raids. The train was bombed, killing a lot of men, and that was when I ran away."

Getting up early to haul his cart up the mountain, stacking it with wood and hauling it back next day, sometimes going twenty-four hours without a meal, he had managed to repay fifty dollars in two months on the hundred and fifty dollars capital lent to him by a friend. This, he said, was infinitely preferable to life in the army. "And now, Brother, if you wouldn't mind helping me push it over this hump, and then stand on the brake while we go downhill, that'll be a help."

Chapter 16

Yellow Wind Cave

After six weeks of being on the move, Aylwin arrived back in Baoji hoping to find news from home. Indeed, a pile of letters had arrived, and dutifully the office staff had forwarded them to somewhere along his route. He had no time to wait for their return, as next day he had to set off to Xi'an to meet Rewi Alley. The two of them got onto a train to go to Luoyang. About mid-journey they arrived at the familiar spot at Tongguan where Japanese gun batteries on the other side of the Yellow River could be seen from the railway, which was within firing range at that point. They weren't firing that day, so the traveller's were spared the twenty-mile walk through the hills. They were shuttled across the exposed section, on a rail trolley, to the train that awaited them out of firing range, in which they resumed their journey to Luoyang. On 16 February 1941, Aylwin wrote a letter home, referring to the outstanding Longmen Grottoes, which date back to the fourth century and are one of the three greatest examples of grotto art in China. Extending for about one kilometre, the Longmen (Dragon Gate) Grottoes are comprised of over 1,300 caves and 750 niches containing over 100,000 sculptures and 3,500 inscriptions and carved stone tablets:

> Luoyang is an ancient capital that is steeped in history, did one but know it. Also sweating in curios did one but understand them. There is one beauty spot that I passed in a bus visiting here last year, where the whole mountainside of rock is carved into Buddhas, *bodhisattvas*, and all the divine guardians. Inside the mountain are caves full of Od's curiosities. I hope to visit it soon.
>
> Tomorrow I am leaving here for a trip back across the Yellow River, into the fringes of the country I came through in 1939. We have some co-ops up there. In spite of periodic Japanese attacks and suchlike annoyances, they are carrying on fine and have their own primary school and public baths. Some of them have been thrown out of work last year by a fresh invasion. They were offered back their jobs with higher pay by Japanese agents, but weren't having any of it.
>
> Then, in about ten days' time, back to Baoji which will be full of things to do and hopefully your letters will have arrived by then. After staying in Baoji for a week or so and writing up the situation there, I hope to get a quiet month in Shuangshipu to finish off my book.

If I had to choose anywhere in particular to stay, I think I would like to stay here. I have many friends, and they are doing good work. What more could you want?

Here in South Shanxi was the border between the Kuomintang and the Eighth Route Army. Here, all the most important and worthwhile civilian jobs were being carried out by the guerrillas. The Kuomintang was trapped between them and the Zhongtiao Shan range of mountains, and the guerrillas were busily organising the resistance for when the Kuomintang would surely soon retreat in the face of the Japanese. Aylwin described his journey across the river, accompanying Xiao Ren into the mountains away from Luoyang, thus:

From Luoyang across the Yellow River and on northward for about fifty miles into the mountains. Here, thirty-three guerrilla co-ops are working and at the same time were literally holding their own *sector* since the Chinese troops had withdrawn temporarily from that district. The Japanese took advantage of this to send small parties of soldiers marauding; one village in which two co-ops are situated was completely destroyed, all grain, furniture, tools and doors being carried away by an army of ruffians following the Japanese soldiers. Fifty women too ill or otherwise unable to leave were raped in two villages here. A co-op member was shot in the leg as he ran, and was bayoneted. A co-op chairman, going back with his son too soon in his anxiety to see what had happened to co-op and family, was bayoneted and thrown down dead into the water of his own mill race. Six other co-op members were carried off, but later escaped.

Under such conditions, it was good to see the way in which other co-ops were carrying on with their work within earshot of the enemy guns; actually often much less than ten miles away. For those co-ops unable to continue work, as their machinery or source of raw material was now a battle-ground, a training course in accountancy and cooperative theory was held. Debates, sing-songs, and lectures are held out of doors, and curious peasants gather to hear and see what it is all about. The sole equipment for this guerrilla training-school is a blackboard for the teacher and a small knee board for each student, on which to take notes squatting cross-legged on the ground. It is really quite inconceivable that any kind of industry but cooperative industry could continue under guerrilla conditions. De-centralisation, individual initiative and loyalty, and consciously working towards an ideal are all essential. Self-discipline is most important of all.

One of the most striking features of this war area was the casualties from under-nourishment and disease. From one-third to a half of the population of village after village and town after town has died within the past few months of typhus, typhoid, relapsing fever, and 'flu.

Under these circumstances it was encouraging to meet, on my return to Luoyang, two representatives of the International and British Red Cross, Messrs Barger and Wright, and to hear that they planned to cross immediately into the Shanxi area with drugs. These two are capable, and determined to do a good job. They have learned an amazing amount of Chinese in seven months by means of gramophone. Someone unkindly remarked that they sound very much like a gramophone running down, but all in all, for seven months it's pretty good.

I also met Jean Chiang, an old friend from my Hankou days, a doctor able to eat bitter [Chinese expression for enduring hardship]. She now runs a maternity home in caves. I was amazed to see her cave full of babies in baskets, reminiscent of our co-op products in the joint warehouse.

Baoji, 10 April 1941:

I haven't heard from you for months, but I suppose you are still alive, because if not someone should have told me. Funny thing the post is these days. I hope you have as last revised your old dictum that "there is no such thing as lost in the post". I think I only get about half the letters that are written to me.

My last few letters have been written to you en route to various places. Now I am back in Baoji, and preparing to go to a nice little country place, Shuangshipu, where I shall rest and read and write for a bit. After that I hope to do some more travelling.

The *New Statesman* and *Nation* are coming through about three or four months late, but fairly regularly, over Siberia. Prices here are terrible owing to inflation; cost of living in some places is nine or ten times higher than at the beginning of the war, and still going up. Hoarding, of course, increases all the time because that's much the easiest way to make money when prices are going up all the time. I went to a large student centre in the country a few weeks ago. The students work nearly all and every day, almost no outdoor exercise or sport; recent medical examination reveals nearly half of them have TB. And they can't even eat enough to avoid hunger, let alone under-nourishment. The school gives them twenty-five dollars per month for food, but food now costs at least thirty dollars, which means that the poorer students are either starving their way through college or quitting. The craving for a university degree and traditional respect for scholarship drives them on. I get tremendous face from having been to Oxford! Every time I make a speech, that is the first thing my introducer mentions. The other day the introducer happened to be a smart London University student, and he told the audience how gentlemanly and well-dressed Oxford students always were. The people glanced over me and were somewhat surprised to see that I was wearing a pair of blue string sandals such as Chinese peasants wear. Too bad, but maybe they put it down to mere gentlemanly eccentricity.

Xi'an, 25 April 1941:

I have just got back from a week's holiday in Shuangshipu, the wonderful little place in the mountains where there is a bungalow to live in, some coffee and other good things to eat and drink, a river to bathe in, and a hot, but not too-hot sun also to bathe in, mountains, and a lot of goitrous, cretinous, but quite amiable village lunatics. For company one Graham Peck, a Yale man, whose book *Through China's Wall* has just been published in England. It is a good book, very picturefully written, and also well illustrated by Graham himself who is a good artist. He is a very sound egg. He can draw all sorts of funny or serious or funny-serious pictures, but is best at drawing heads of people. Maybe I'll get him to do one of me and send it to you. Did you get those snapshots? He helped me write a couple of short stories, and I helped him as interpreter with the village's ancient inhabitants and suchlike. Now I am taking him to Luoyang and handing him over to our people there to look after.

Your war seems to be not quite so good these days. I don't know what to say about ours, except that it continues to receive tremendous influence from the ups and downs of Europe. Meanwhile we rub along, trying to make things a little better, or a little less bad than they would be without us; and at the same time trying to keep alive the goal of better things. I'm very Chinese by now. One just can't help it, living right here amongst them for so long. And I think that some of my peculiarities – rather naïve, rather idealistic, rather laughter loving – have much in common with the non-citified type of young Chinese.

I am rather pleased with myself because the last trip I did was to a place where none of our people had been for a long time, if at all. And I made a report on what I saw there, which immediately resulted in fifty thousand dollars being sent, with more to follow later. It really must be one of the most war-torn, disease-stricken and refugee-ridden places in China, which is saying a lot. Apart from the fact that the Japanese alternatively drive in refugees from other places and then send in raids to destroy food supplies, and apart from the fact that what isn't taken by the Japanese is commandeered by the Kuomintang armies, and apart from the heavy Kuomintang conscription and forced labour, and apart from the bleak mountains which make the district a poor one anyway, various kinds of diseases have killed off one-third of the whole native population in the last few months.

Baoji, 6 May 1941:

As you said in your letter, winter was pretty grim but now spring is more than here, and things are grimmer than ever. I listened to the BBC announcing with all the enthusiasm it could muster, the incredible, devastating, miraculous evacuation of Greece, exactly the same as Dunkirk. Next night there was a lot of stuff about a baby who cut its teeth in a lifeboat. A dear old missionary schoolteacher, commenting on the appallingly bad British propaganda as against the rather clever propaganda of the opposition, said, "It's rather nice that we British are so guileless though, isn't it?" At which Graham Peck nearly went up in smoke!

I am just back here after taking Graham Peck along to Luoyang. I am now rather an expert at travelling, though I say it myself! We had to go through the most difficult place in China to manage without proper passes, and his pass really didn't take him this far, let alone to Luoyang. However, when the police official came to call and inspect, I talked to him for an hour and a half about the weather, the cost of living, CIC, mutual acquaintances, the beauty of spring, the English attitude towards China, whether I liked Chinese food, why I hadn't married yet, and other kindred interesting topics. At the end of all that, he got up to go having forgotten all about asking for our passes! Patience, tact, discretion are all doubtful as virtues but very necessary just now.

In Luoyang there is a good printing co-op working in electrically lit caves fifty feet underground. Air raids no matter at all.

Writing from Baoji, 30 May 1941:

Things are quite exciting here now, as the Japanese are attacking again. We are well in the rear however, and will have plenty of time to move off if anything happens. Meanwhile, with air raid alarms every day, I have written eight chapters out of the nine to finish my book, in about ten days. I think they are okay, but the first part of the book may not be.

The other day our HQ boss, Lu Guangmian, was almost killed, going across the exposed part of the railway at Tongguan. Although it was night-time the Japanese fired a shell right into the carriage, where it burst killing quite a lot of people and wounding his companion.

The place across the river where I went in February is right in the thick of the worst fighting. Goodness knows how our people are. There has been no communication with them for weeks. They have probably got hold of rifles and machineguns and turned themselves into guerrillas for the duration of the attack.

Today is an ancient holiday in Chinese lore. I don't quite know why, but it is something to do with a poet, much beloved by the people, who was wronged and committed suicide in a river. The thing to do is to go out in a boat on the river and throw him nice things to eat today, but as there is no big river here we are eating the nice things instead.

My room is the coolest room in Baoji. It has pink paper venetian blinds held in place by vermilion coloured wool. The walls are whitewashed; the ceiling is of mats which are rather eaten by rats. The windows have green gauze over them. About the best kind of pictures available are maps, so there are three of those. I would like to get some nice scrolls, and maybe I will some day. I wish I had those prints I bought for you and Rosemary in Japan.

His next letter home, written at the end of July 1941, gave a little further information about his own home:

We had a conference for all the leaders in CIC in the northwest a week or so ago. Every morning there was a lecture from an American guy who flew here from Chengdu especially for the purpose, and then the rest of the day was spent in discussions and sing-songs, swimming in the river, and suchlike. It was always about ten in the evening or after when I would thread my lonely way back over the river, up a cliff, past some maize stalks, through somebody's back yard where there is a dog, up onto the mountain where there are wolves, to my little house. I slept up there instead of in the hotel because of the prevalence of tanks, guerrillas, and aeroplanes in the place, which being interpreted means bedbugs, fleas, and mosquitoes. I forgot to mention torpedoes, which are lice.

On Sunday there was an expedition to Yellow Wind Cave. It was here that some thousands or hundreds of years ago (my history, never having advanced beyond the English and European 1750–1815 stage, wouldn't know just which) that a famous monk, sent by the emperor to look for the Sutras, had an unfortunate accident, which came near to being mortal catastrophe. This monk had been reincarnated eight times and hadn't married on any of them, so he was very pure. He had a lamp on his head which glowed with magic holy fire so long as the old boy's thoughts were holy, but went flickering out whenever they weren't. While the lamp burned, no harm could come to him. It was the ambition of all wicked folk to get a bite of his flesh, because this would mean immortality for them, but of course if the lamp burned they hadn't got a chance.

Near the cave of the Yellow Wind lived six wicked fairies, or maybe sirens. Said one wicked fairy, "Sisters, if we do a striptease act as the old boy comes along, and bathe in this 'ere silvery pool, his thoughts won't stay pure a minute. Then we all get a bite, heigh-ho, of immortality."

All went according to plan. The lamp flickered, the flame dropped, and the old monk looked like he was due for a fate worse than marriage. But in the nick of time, just as he was being whisked away to a sharp knife, his faithful bodyguard, who was a monkey by the name of All Is Insubstantial, did a neat somersault of several thousand miles and rescued him. I don't know how long the lamp took to burn up again. But the story, more or less as recounted, is all painted up on the wall of the Yellow Wind Cave, and the silvery pool is still there too.

Maybe you think that your youngest son is doing nothing but looking at such places of ancient beauty, and giving naught for the cares of the world. This is not the case. I am working hard at one thing or another, most of the time. Just recently I have been trying to turn statistician and accountant, which is sadly foreign to my nature.

Apparently our co-ops are going to get a lot of help from America for education, health, and new technical equipment. This makes life very interesting, and gives me a lot of work to do. Because if people want to help a thing, they want to know about it first and afterward too, and this is where the "Ocean Secretary" and Publicity Man comes in.

Today the postman put a letter from you through my window. Luckily the rats refrained from eating it before I returned. Also very luckily it narrowly escaped being bombed to pieces after having taken all the trouble to go from Brampton to Baoji, for on the very evening it arrived the post office yard was wrecked! It can't get lost in the post! Well, well, times do change. This was the first letter in three or four months. And it mentioned having received a letter which I can vaguely remember having sent off nearly a year ago.

Yesterday twenty-seven very beautiful aeroplanes came to Baoji. They looked so nice, and they sounded so nice and it was all quite like Hendon Air Show except that we were in the natives' huts. At least some people were. Others, such as me, had a hole under the city wall to dive into as soon as the good old whistly noise such as cricket balls make when they get old began to swoosh. There were a hundred prostitutes in another such hole, not so stout (the hole's walls I mean), and they all got buried. I went out to look afterwards at the fires and the collapsed mud-and-wood houses, and the piles of wreckage all down one street of our little town, and I thought that this must be about one-hundredth of what it is like in London town and other such places. Only maybe there are a few fire engines there, instead of rather disorganised groups of people throwing wash-basins-full of water into a furnace. In just that one raid, six of the co-op places were hit! Nobody hurt there, luckily.

Chapter 17

Old Mr Three

Following another spell of travelling, Aylwin's next letter was written in Luoyang, dated 12 September 1941:

I've been living out in the real countryside, in a village of one thousand three hundred souls called Shi Hou lying at the foot of the Sung Mountains near the south bank of the Yellow River, about twenty miles southeast of Luoyang where the people haven't really changed for hundreds of years. They all have old-fashioned looms in their homes, and grow cotton; since the war has shut off imports of machine-made cloth from the coast, even these peasant looms in the villages are becoming important. Now the CIC is trying to improve their weaving methods and organise them into domestic co-ops. That means that they don't have to move out of their homes into a workshop even; the loom stays right there in the front parlour, and anyone, from grandma to the daughter-in-law, who has a moment to spare just pops onto the seat and rolls off a few inches of cloth. The advantage of going into a co-op is that you get enough capital so that you can store up your cloth into large amounts and sell it for a good price in bulk where the market is good. Otherwise, the only thing to do is to walk into town, about five miles away, with a bale of cloth on your back, haggle half the day with hard-hearted merchants who gang up to make the peasants sell cheap, and finally exchange your cloth for enough cotton and a little more to weave the next bale.

In the Chinese village home, the old folk eat best because they haven't got many teeth. They get extra oil in their vegetables, and the whitest flour that is available. These titbits they share with the children under eight. Working men from eight to fifty get second class fare: grey flour and cooked vegetables, meat maybe twice a month. Women, even those who are nowadays earning a good income from the loom, get third-class food: grey or black flour and raw vegetables – carrots, turnips, etc. How would you like to housekeep in such a family when everything has to be divided into three classes? And how would you like to housekeep in a poor home which maybe only has enough grain of its own to last half a year, and has to borrow at thirty-six percent for the rest of the year? Common fare is potato skins, dried cornmeal, and a kind of flour made of ground persimmon cores!

The oldest inhabitant, aged seventy-three, of the village was called Mr Three. This is because everybody in the village is called by the same surname, Zhou (imagine a village full of everybody called Hogg!) so that, to avoid confusion, the sons are called Mr Great, Two, Three, Four, and so on according to their seniority in the generation.

The village schoolmaster is a very good man, who has actually been to the city and lived there for several years. He writes out the engagement, or betrothal, contracts, and gave me a specimen which I haven't translated yet. The most important clause is the one at the beginning, perhaps best called the preamble, which makes it quite clear that the proposer of this betrothal considers his family to be far inferior to the other party's. "Heaven and Earth may fade away, but love" (contracted for by the parents, but often just as successful as or more so than "modern" marriages) "is eternal", says the closing sentence. He says that "point belly, make relations" betrothals, that is to say before the prospective bride and groom are born, are occasional between very close friends.

Mr Three was the oldest inhabitant of Shi Hou, Mr Two and Mr Great having died four and ten years ago respectively. Since he had had considerable influence in local history, his name, Honourable Mr Three, was reverently spoken not only in his own village but in those within a ten mile radius. Mr Three had his Boswell – a small humble neighbour whose clay-dyed smock matched the colour of a long drooping moustache. It was he who was the main source of material for the following story:

"It was in the First Year of the Republic (1911), when he was forty-two years old, that Mr Three became famous," said his neighbour. In that year, taking advantage of the confusion, bandits came down from the mountains and began to loot the villages on the edge of the Luo River valley. Mr Three had always been the local champion in swordplay, archery, and rifle shooting; he had actually graduated from the provincial military examinations with the rank of *wu sheng* [a non-commissioned officer] so it was he who now led a band of two hundred villagers armed with swords, spears, and a few rifles, to rout the bandits in a battle some ten miles away from Shi Hou.

Ten years later the bandits were out again in great force. Shi Hou, which always had news of approaching raids before the villages deeper in the valley, delegated Mr Three to go to Kungxian, the county seat, and ask for soldiers to help; but the *xian* magistrate refused. A week later the bandits captured this same magistrate, and it was Mr Three who led a force of villagers to the rescue. Several bandits were captured. They turned out to be all local men who had become bandits in the hopes that this would lead them to an official career or because they had no other work to do.

Again, in the seventeenth year of the Republic (1928), a bandit force of three thousand came from the south. Mr Three led out his force of villagers, realised that the odds were overwhelming, and went back to Kungxian to ask for help. The magistrate, a new one, refused to believe his story. To prove his sincerity, Mr Three laid the fourth finger of his left hand on the magistrate's table and cut it off with his big sword. The severed finger jumped a great way to the other side of the room, which was convincing proof of his sincerity. He was hauled off to hospital while the magistrate called for military aid from the city of Shao-yi. The forces there refused to act without orders, but passed on the request to General Feng Yuxiang, the Christian General. Feng ordered troops to be sent, and the bandits were frightened away without battle, burning several cities in the path of their flight to the south.

For his bandit-suppression expeditions, Mr Three never asked any special help from his family, taking only one nephew to look after him. In return, he had no special concern for his family. "If I am killed, you will have to look after yourselves," he would say as he left the house. They always knew when he was going into danger, for he would take down the ancestral tablets from above the altar and put them in his pack to carry away for the duration of the campaign.

As a commander, he was always a stickler for promptitude and for strict obedience to the demands of collective security. If any village or family failed to send its quota of young men for the expedition, Mr Three would stand up in front of his force and gash himself with his sword until the tardy volunteers arrived. Such was the strength of public opinion aroused in this way that no family was ever known to fail twice in sending off its soldier properly equipped for battle.

After the 1928 bandit incident, General Feng Yuxiang sent for Mr Three and awarded him with a certificate for valour which hangs today beside the family altar. He also invited Mr Three to come to Kaifeng and accept office. As was proper, Mr Three refused twice; but on the third occasion he "thought it best to save Old Feng's face", and so in 1928 he became a military official in Kungxian city.

After 1930, things became quieter; Mr Three was sixty-two and beginning to feel the need for a little peace himself. He returned to his home in Shi Hou.

The dominating ambition of his life now became to open a middle school for the district. "If the people are educated, they can earn their living in peaceful ways and teach others to do so. Bandits in Henan are often only the most spirited and adventurous sons of large families with little land, who can discover no other way of making a place for themselves," he explained.

Another, lesser but still haunting, ambition came later. He wanted to build a temple, with stone tablets commemorating all the local soldiers killed fighting the Japanese and to add to these the names of those killed in the old days while fighting the bandits. Alongside the men's names were to go those of their widows, "so that they will never dare to marry again," explained Mr Three, "and because women must be heroes as well as men. Men have men's work, and women have women's work. When the men were killed, didn't all the work of the home and of bringing up the sons fall on the women?"

When he was still young, Mr Three had already selected the site for the school. It was a small hill in the most strategic position for miles around, commanding the bridge over a deep gully that rifts the yellow loess in a wide circle around this group of villages. When he retired from public life, he set to work to collect money for the land and new buildings. His reputation brought in many promises of support, and Mr Three, quite carried away, began to buy land. The result was saddening. Mr Three had no head for business, and found himself running deeper and deeper into debt, while many of the promised subscriptions failed to materialise.

To pay for what he had already bought, he felt himself bound to sell one after the other of his own few acres, sometimes getting only a part of the land's value, and sometimes throwing in all the year's crops on the land he was selling out of sheer distaste for haggling.

One day Mr Three's two sons and the sons of his two dead brothers came to him. "You are an old man," they said. "What happens to the family lands doesn't matter to you. But why should our future be sacrificed to a school?" Mr Three could see the reason to this, but his creditors were pressing for settlement. If his family preferred land to honour, thought Mr Three, then his simple brain could see only one other way out; he must write a letter to the magistrate asking to be imprisoned as a defaulter. He received a very formal reply, which turned out to say that the magistrate was unable to fall in with Mr Three's suggestion.

Doggedly, he made arrangements to sell more of his family land. His nephews came to him again, very solemnly, just before New Year's Day in 1935. "Honourable Mr Three," they said, "our family has lived and multiplied in one household for eight generations. We have eaten plentifully together when the harvests were good, and together paid the interest to moneylenders when they were bad. When you go to join our ancestors, the eldest son of your eldest brother will be the head of the ninth undivided generation; the household will be honoured by the government, and given a special sign to hang over the courtyard door. As the family has remained undivided, so have the fields. Yet to divide the land is better than to sell it. If there is no other way to keep what remains, then the families of the three sons of our grandfather must split the land between them, so that you can sell only your own share."

Old Mr Three was too mortified to eat or to see anybody for the whole three days of New Year celebrations; but his nephews were adamant, and eventually the household split the remaining land in three separate parts.

Now more than ever, the importance of making his school a success obsessed him. Twice or even three times a day he would go to the site, begging a ride on a farm cart as his wounded foot was hurting him, or limping along with only a stick to help him. He would plod up and down his hill, tap the walls of his half-finished buildings, and put his finger into the damp polished notches left by the axe in the sides of the caves. Once a passing traveller, intrigued by the old man's story, gave him some money to complete the well; old Mr Three was so delighted that he spent half the money putting up a stone tablet to immortalise the traveller's soul.

When at last sufficient promises had been redeemed to complete some of the caves and to open the school on a small scale, the old man's joy knew no bounds. But it was short lived. With no endowment the school had to close down after a few terms, and the cave lay idle.

Leaving the village by moonlight in the early hours one morning, old Mr Three walked southward past the unburied bones of the bandits he had killed years before, to a lonely temple on the Sung Mountain. Here lived a fraudulent and paralytic old Taoist priest, who, in return for cakes, wine, and a few coppers given ostensibly to the spirit of Lao Tzu, made mystic passes with a stick in a sand tray, and interpreted them as being the oracle's handwriting. Peasants with sick family members or insoluble financial problems would come to ask the oracle's advice, and go away comforted by a sense of divine guidance.

Mr Three's request that morning was unusual. "Spirit of Lao Tzu," he said aloud, "if I cannot see my plan for the school to completion, let me die now, and send a younger man who will do the work better." As he was on his knees in bowed position he didn't see what happened next, but he could hear the sound of the stick speeding over the tray, and the voice of the priest intoning the characters that were scrawled there in the sand.

"Old man, be patient! You have many years to live, and your works will prosper." The priest wrote out the message for him afterwards on a sheet of yellow paper so soft that it seemed about to fall apart as he took it in his hand.

Perhaps it was this piece of paper, kept carefully folded in the drawer of the altar table in Mr Three's home, which held the family together even after the land had been split. If the spirit of Lao Tzu had said that Mr Three still had many years to live, and would succeed in his school, who were his nephews to oppose him? So on Mr Three's next birthday, the sixty family members gathered as usual to do him homage. They found him locked up in his room; only after he was quite sure that they were properly represented did he come out to speak with them.

"When I wanted you to help me before, you were angry. Now you come running back with all sorts of presents, but I'll take none of them. You may contribute a hundred and twenty dollars worth of national bonds to the State as my birthday present every year until the day of victory against Japan."

So far, no one has fallen behind in his contribution. It is evident that Mr Three's prestige is as high as ever. Every morning for a week after CIC first opened its office in Shi Hou, old Mr Three dropped in at half past four in the morning to see if the city folk were getting up. *Cooperatives* was a new term to him, and not one that he was going to accept all at once, but finding that the newcomers rose almost as early as he did himself, he went away satisfied. When, later, they lent seven hundred dollars and their handcart to take some accident casualties to hospital, he felt that here indeed was something worthy of his help. And when he heard that cooperatives meant night schools at the very least and possibly technical schools for the village youths, when he understood that the peasants would be able to support themselves through the winter instead of falling back, as many of them had done before, on money-lenders and pawnshops at sixty percent interest, he tacitly became a member of the CIC staff himself.

Every day he dropped in unasked, inspected the cloth to see if anyone had cheated by adding water or chalk to it so as to bring up the weight. If they had, a word from the village's oldest inhabitant was enough to prevent a second occurrence; the practice soon died out. He gave the caves of his school as storehouses and workshops. Better still, he used his enormous prestige with the peasants of Shi Hou and surrounding villages to give them confidence in the CIC organisers. The fact that these organisers are made welcome in the peasant homes is as much the achievement of Mr Three as of anybody else.

One day I walked along with old Mr Three to his hill, and sitting on the ground beside him, heard him tell his story: "Buddha bestows all blessings, Buddha bestows all rank, Buddha bestows long life," he said, ending his story. "The cooperatives provide the chief blessing – work and food. They offer the chance of education, which is the way to achieve rank, and they give the people enough to eat so that they may live to an old age. The co-ops are doing Buddha's work for him."

The one time ancient capital of China, Luoyang, was quite near the front line, protected by the Yellow River. Aylwin visited there before returning to Baoji:

Some months ago there was an attack on in Luoyang and things were dangerous so the co-ops had to evacuate. There was one co-op of girls who had never been outside the city before. Their parents were more afraid of what might happen to them if they left the city than what the Japanese might do to them in the city. Eventually about half were allowed to go off. They settled in a village about ten miles away, taking them three days to get there, and made friends with the peasants. Then they sent messages back to report on their well-being to the parents of those members not allowed to go. They found that the said members had put up such a successful campaign of screaming and non-cooperation and crying and nagging that the parents were only too glad to let them go. Next thing the girls did, getting away from home influence, was to cut their pigtails off. This is rather daring and modern, but the girls considered it essential in their process of emancipation. Now they are all bobbed. Now lots of the village girls want to join the co-op too. All the co-op girls have adopted sisters and godmothers and suchlike among the villagers. Every week or so, one of them goes back to the city with some of their earnings. It is incredible to the parents that the daughter should bring in anything to the family income, and so they are beginning to be pretty keen cooperators themselves. Did I tell you about the girl whose hubby ran away because she was uneducated and awkward and couldn't read? Now she has learned to read and to laugh and be light hearted. She wrote him a letter all about it, and he has promised to come back for the New Year. So our co-ops are both economic and matrimonial agencies, social steam engines and whatnot.

When he got back to Baoji in October, he found to his great joy two parcels containing books and periodicals from home:

I couldn't get over this for a long while. Then I tried to prop all the books up in a row on top of my cupboard, but they wouldn't prop; there were too many of them, and I hadn't got anything heavy to put at the end. Then I thought to myself, "What you need is a bookcase," so I had in a co-op carpenter, and he made a nice little shelf such as I used to make for myself in the workshop, only better. I hadn't arranged books in a bookshelf for so long; it was grand fun putting the right ones next to each other and getting all the backs flush with the edge of the shelf.

When I got the bookcase fixed up, that made the top of the cupboard look so tidy that I hardly knew it and I got out my one and only ornament – a sort of white dog whose front paws are broken off so it's always falling over on its nose – and put that in front of the book case. This was a great success. "Ah!" I say to myself. "You've got to fix this room up proper." Funny thing, I'd lived in it for about a year and never thought to fix it up before. Next thing I did was to get a big corner shelf up, with hooks underneath it; old hats on top and clothes hanging from the hooks, buy a nice bit of cloth to hang down in front. That takes all the conglomeration of things off the back of the door, so that they don't keep dropping down whenever you come into the room in a hurry.

The next step was after I somehow got a nasty shock just looking at the suitcases piled against the wall, kind of musty, with their locks broken, but useful for keeping things in; and you can always tie them up with bits of rope when you want to take them away. "Them suitcases," this new artist inside me remarked, "they don't look too good me, man." So I calls back the carpenter and has him fix up a table to go over the top, fixed to the wall so it won't wobble. Funny thing about a Chinese wall; it's only made of mud, so you can't nail things to it very easily. You just hit the wood plumb into the wall, and hope for the best. Of course it may fall down, which will give the rats a bit of a shock, but you can always restore them their privacy by going outside and mixing a bit of mud and water and daubing that on the wound.

At about the same time as your books arrived, the British Embassy suddenly took it upon itself to send me a mass of illustrated propaganda, pictures of empire outposts and tanks and so on, of Churchill, Eden, and Major So-and-so. Final touch was to pin a postcard of bulldog Churchill over the maps already decorating the wall. Facing him is the cutting of Roger Hunter with the series of very intelligent remarks from Muff and Mrs Hunter beside it. The *New Statesman* and other magazines go on the new table, which is also covered with co-op cloth, like the new wardrobe. Such is civilisation, which I had almost forgotten. Now, reading about all the happenings in England from Penguins [a selection of Penguin paperbacks included in the parcel], no doubt it will all come back to me.

I rode a bicycle halfway down the province of Henan, from Luoyang to a place called Nanyang, west to Zhenping where we have a lot of silk co-ops (I went there last spring too) and back via another co-op place; for company, an artist. While I wrote my notes, investigated business in each co-op, he drew pictures. These he exhibits in China and Hong Kong, as publicity, so in a way our jobs fit together. He is from Shanghai, son of a rich official and an educated mother, but ready and willing to live on nothing these days. Lots of funny things happened on the way, but some of the best times were eating; cabbage fried with chestnuts, fish baked in a sauce made of sugar and vinegar, soft jellyfish, persimmon and crispy pears, moon cakes and tea.

Coming back from Luoyang we had to cross the gap on the railway at Tongguan. We made a terrific detour for safety, on a truck, and caught the train at the other end and got into Xi'an just in time for a bath. In Xi'an I went to see a dentist; I haven't had a filling since leaving Smallbone's tender care. Had one inspection in America, and one last year, all with favourable verdict. This time was favourable too as he couldn't find anything wrong. But evidently he wiggled something loose, for two days later a filling came out. I suppose I shall have to go back to Xi'an and have it put back.

Chapter 18

His Adopted Family

Back in late 1940, Aylwin had been given the responsibility of overseeing the new Bailie Training School in Shuangshipu – Double-Stone Village, a small cross-road village, nowadays called Fengxian, in the Qin Ling Mountains about forty miles south of Baoji.

Since the start of CIC, it was realised that technical training must also proceed hand in hand with the establishment of cooperatives. Various short courses, refresher courses, and advanced courses were tried. Courses in cooperative theory, statistics, and accounting, technical courses of various kinds; they were all tried. Gradually, it was felt that technical schools should be started throughout the Gung Ho organisation, providing an all-round education for youngsters from the cooperatives; teach them to read and write, give them a grounding in business and technical subjects, both in theory and in practice, then send them back into the co-ops to inject a modern outlook and a sound basis for the future. The idea was popular abroad. Using funds subscribed through the CIC International Committee, the Bailie Schools were born.

Joseph Bailie, after whom the schools were named, had been an American missionary. He had come to China in 1891 at the age of 31 and got involved in numerous relief projects around the country, placing Chinese students in American factories, helping apprentices in Shanghai. It was there where he and Rewi Alley met, in Rewi's early days in Shanghai in the 1920s. Enthusiastic and courageous, Joseph Bailie loved the Chinese people. He founded the College of Agriculture and Forestry at Nanjing University and was a great advocate for reforestation of the long-ago denuded mountains and hillsides of North China as a measure to prevent erosion and promote water conservation. From early on in his life as a missionary, he would say that there is no use in teaching religion to people who are starving and have no hope. "You have to improve their livelihood before you can do anything like talk philosophy to them." Many "Bailie Boys", the returned students he had placed to study in America, became the backbone of the Gung Ho movement. The name of Bailie was well known in America – a factor which may help to raise funds for the schools – but also, in Chinese, *pei li* means "train (prepare) for the dawn", which seemed appropriate. In 1936, Bailie was told he had prostate cancer. Hospitalisation in America did not appeal to him and in any case would be, in his opinion, far too expensive. Not wishing to become a burden upon anyone, he took a pistol and shot himself out in his own backyard. Rewi Alley had the idea to make the Bailie Schools a living memorial to his old friend from Shanghai.

The first school was started in 1940 at Ganxian, in Jiangxi Province, closely followed by a short-lived one at Baoji; neither lasted long. Two more were started up, one at Guilin, in Guanxi Province, and the other at Laohekou, in Hebei Province. These were soon abandoned because of disruption caused by Kuomintang officials. Another one was tried in the northwest at Shuangshipu, and it was Aylwin's job initially to help work out projects, make appeals for money, write reports, and get pictures and human-interest stories on the boys at the school.

In the first year of its existence, the Shuangshipu Bailie Technical School had a succession of eight headmasters. Somehow, none of them managed to grasp the reason for the school's existence. The general attitude seemed to be that the school was some sort of badly run foreign charity and that the only thing to be done, short of getting out, was to eat one's rice and live through it the best one might. Mainly for this reason, but also as Aylwin's increasingly outspoken attitude toward the Kuomintang had made him an obvious mark for their agents, Lu Guangmian urged him to take on the headmastership of the school. In that way, he could try to put into practice the ideas about which he had been writing, and in addition he would be out of the immediate sight of the Kuomintang agents and therefore, hopefully, out of their minds. Headmaster number eight had been an intellectual fellow with the benefit of several years of European education behind him. In March 1942, he resigned and Aylwin stepped in.

About that time, Aylwin was taking some time off to write his book, and to do so he was staying in a small house that Rewi had had built for himself as a quiet country retreat. This was in Shuangshipu. On 8 March Aylwin wrote from there, calling it "our place in the country":

> You might all have been dead since last August for all I know to the contrary. A lot of people are dying these days. No doubt some letters will arrive someday soon.
>
> Here in "our place" everything is very calm. No bombing even, as all the Japanese planes are temporarily engaged elsewhere. We have a school here full of oddly humorous boys. They are always dropping round to have a look at the strangely funny foreigner, drink some of his peculiarly funny coffee, bang on his typewriter, play on his gramophone, have a bath in his peculiarly warm room (bath in a basin), and generally have a good time. There is a pane of glass in our paper window, right in front of the desk, so that I can look out over the mountains and do imaginary deep breathings. You would love it.
>
> Several very fortunate circumstances have combined to give me two weeks here in which to write. I feel it in my bones that the great book will really be okay this time, and say what I want it to say, and what nobody has said before. Whether or not anyone will be found to publish the thing is a different matter. It should be finished by the time I leave here in a week, but then I'll have to find time to type it out neatly while in the midst of travelling and doing other reports, which is a sweat.
>
> I've got three adopted sons now. After they'd been out of my tender care for some time, I found seventy-four lice in one of their shirts, and there were a lot more, so I burnt it and bought them two shirts and two pants each. Last time I inspected, they only had three fleas between the lot of them. Proud father beamed. They love taking baths now, too. The fleas have taken root in our room. Such is life.

I told you about my girlfriend who got left on the other side of the Japanese lines, didn't I? Well, I've just had a letter from her – first in a year – and she's okay, so I'm rather happy!

Just over a year earlier, in a letter written on 31 January 1941, Aylwin had mentioned for the first time some adopted sons:

I've got a couple of sons – did I tell you? – in school here. They were a bit weedy at first and needed a rubber sheet in their bed more than anything else. However they are growing up to be very tough now and will no doubt be a credit to my old age.

He mentioned only two, the eldest of four brothers. Now, a year or so later, he had taken the third to live with him temporarily. Later, all four brothers came to Shuangshipu to be with him. I met the Nie brothers, my "cousins", in Beijing in 1988. There was Nie Guang Chun (Lao Da – Number One), just newly retired after a distinguished career as a senior researcher in electrical engineering; Nie Guang Han (Lao Er – Number Two), a senior mining machinery engineer in the Ministry of Mining; Nie Guang Tao (Lao San – Number Three), a senior agro-economist with the Ministry of Agriculture; and Nie Guang Pei (Lao Si – Number Four) the youngest, a geophysicist with the Oil Ministry. There was no doubt about it; they were cetainly a credit to Aylwin's "old age". I was able to piece together some of the gaps that had been left in the story that I already knew.

They were all born in Manchuria, and their father, Nie Zhanglin, a schoolteacher, was a very early member of the Communist Party, becoming rather active in the underground movement around Beijing. At about the time that Aylwin originally arrived in China, the Kuomintang police arrested Nie Zhanglin, and he was imprisoned in Beijing. Mother, with two small boys, a toddler, and a baby, somehow managed to make her way to Beijing to be nearby. The communist underground arranged Zhanglin's escape from prison, but it was necessary for him to get as far away as possible; he was too well known to stay in Beijing or to go back to Manchuria. He made his way to Yan'an and then to Baoji where he was able to work again openly as a teacher, and he sent word for his family to follow. It was there that Aylwin and he became good friends when Nie Zhanglin was made head of the Gung Ho Depot in Baoji. It was only a matter of time before the Kuomintang police took interest in him again. He was tipped off about an imminent raid and made his escape to carry on his work in South Shanxi, but this left his wife with four small children and no means of support.

Some time after his escape, Aylwin, on a trip to Luoyang, met up with Nie Zhanglin. He had taken up activities in the Taihangshan range of mountains that run along the border between Shanxi and Hebei. He was understandably worried, as people generally were afraid to offer any help to families of known communists, even if they were sympathetic to the cause. It was dangerous to be associated. Aylwin left his friend with peace of mind after promising to watch over Mrs Nie and the four boys, and on his return to Baoji called to check out the situation. Soon after Aylwin met his friend, Nie Zhanglin was captured by the Kuomintang, bound, stripped, hung up, beaten, and left for dead. Long after the war was over, it was learnt that other cooperative members cut down the senseless body and took Zhanglin into hiding where he recovered to carry on with Gung Ho work. Eventually, after the war, the father was found in the northeast, having become one of the leading cadres there, and he was reunited with his sons. Aylwin's own words take over the story:

The mother was a pretty worthless creature, so I adopted the two eldest of the four boys and took them to the Bailie School in Shuangshipu, leaving the others, aged five and six, with their mother in a village near Baoji.

Last month [February 1942] school affairs entailed a two-day visit to Baoji, and it happened to coincide with the biggest rains known there for twenty years. It rained without stopping for nine days. Lots of houses, built of stamped mud without foundations, fell down and crushed people to death. Walls fell all over the town, and the road back to Shuangshipu was blocked for two or three weeks. This gave me a good break in Baoji, which I occupied by seeing to the affairs of my adopted family. Guang Chun, the eldest, had come with me, so I sent him off home with a hundred Chinese dollars in his pocket to see how things were going with his mother and small brothers. Next evening, Guang Chun was waiting for me at the guest house. "I've been looking for you all day," he said. "My mother is very ill and is going to die. She is thin with no flesh at all; just bones. She talks all the time about dying. She looks terrible; not like my mother at all."

Next morning we got up early and caught the train to Lo Li Pu, and thence by ferry to Yuichinpu. I found the mother filthy and unkempt with a face of skin and bones, eyes huge and wild, gown torn, legs like sticks and caked with mud, squatting by the fire.

"Aiya, you come only now! Why didn't you come a month ago? Look at me now. I'm finished. No better than a dog. I was better a month ago; I could walk then. Look how thin I am." She tore her gown open, showing a skinny filthy yellow body, no breasts at all, ribs sticking out, and no stomach. "Aiya, I am going to die. You are too late."

Guang Chun squatted down beside her and tried to help. His every movement was greeted with a shower of curses: "Worthless stupid son; crazy turtle's egg!" whenever he opened his mouth. He was tearful, trying to help without crying openly. "Why didn't you come before? You call yourself my son – you never came to see Mamma, nor wrote to her. Now you come and fuss around here when I am going to die. All the villagers here say I am going to die. They say to their children, "She is going to die of an old sickness. Don't go near her or you will catch it too!" I've had to carry all my own water, cook my own food, spin wool as well as look after my child. Often I am hungry, but there are no vegetables. Thirsty, and I have to drink un-boiled water. And now at this time you come! Look at me! Am I any better than a dog?"

The smallest son, stocky, swollen bellied, was standing imperturbable against the door. His hair was very long and full of lice. He seemed to be listening and taking it all in, but also realising the uselessness of words at this point. He seemed to realise that his mother had gone crazy. I tried to stop the flow of talk and swearing, but it seemed impossible, so I gave Mrs Nie a basin of water and told her to wash her head and feet for a start. Then I took the smallest son out into the sunshine and bathed him. He assented tacitly; remarked that he was cold, or that he would like something to eat, but all without any expectation of results. His clothes were full of lice. A year ago I would have burned them all, but now clothes are too expensive.

I still can't bear squashing things, so flipped the lice off on to the garden weeds; parasite unto parasite! I washed a bit and then looked for the lice that had crept out from the seams, washed again, flipped again, and so on. Then I hung the clothes on a haystack to dry. Meanwhile Mrs Nie's flow of talk was coming out from the room where she was washing her head. I dressed Number Four again and sent him off to shave his head. He came back in a few minutes looking a different man. Mrs Nie had now finished washing her head but seemed to be working herself up more and more, and would do nothing but sit and swear. I tried to make her wash her feet and body. "Let me wash outside then. I won't go back to that room – I hate that room, and the *kang* is too hard. My body is all sore – look!" She laid her hips bare. At this moment her sister, Mrs Zhu, came in and was greeted with further curses. Number Three, who had been looked after for the past two months by Mrs Zhu, came too and, seeing his mother, immediately burst out crying. Mrs Nie started swearing at Mrs Zhu for letting him get trachoma and become so thin.

By this time, coolies were waiting with a stretcher brought from the CIC hospital to take her into Baoji. On hearing the stream of swear words they immediately raised their price from two hundred to three hundred dollars. In the end, I had to pull her trousers on myself, wash her feet, button up her gown and pack her into the stretcher. She was swearing now at the neighbours and at the cavity in the stretcher as we started off along the road. I had brought a syringe and camphor shot in case her energy failed with the strain of the journey, but the greatest strain seemed to be on Guang Chun, who had to bear the brunt of the swearing: "Why are you lagging behind? Come up here and let me talk to you, you worthless son of a turtle." And then she swore at the carriers. They began answering back at first, until we managed to convince them that the woman was crazy and was not to be taken seriously.

Mrs Nie had amazing energy and refused to lie for long. She sat up in the stretcher remarking on people and things along the road. Gradually she grew quieter, like a child, and began pointing out various crops and enquiring into the carriers' family history, number of children and suchlike. "Is your baby as big as mine? No? Well, it is good to have four sons even if I am going to die."

Arriving at the hospital, she was amazed at everything, not least at being supplied with clean clothes. She was contented with not having to make her own food, but anxious about all her household belongings. Strict instructions were given to Guang Chun: on no account to pay anything to the landlady, "who was very bad and had cheated her and swore at her and turned the neighbours against her."

Next evening, Mrs Nie was very bad again: "Aiya," she moaned, sitting on the bed cross-legged, "You have white-wasted energy and money bringing me here. I might just as well have died at home. Aiya, what will happen to my sons?" I assured her that everything would be all right, and was sure she would get better if only she wouldn't worry. But if she did die, the sons could just be our sons – Mr Alley and I hadn't got any family so that would be very convenient! She seemed happier then but wouldn't hear of not dying. "*Aiya!* You don't know, and the doctor doesn't know. I'll live five days at most. Maybe I'll die tonight. Will you let my boy stay with me here tonight? I'm afraid I'll die and he won't know." Guang Chun looked very tearful, so I took him outside and explained that she was talking crazy talk and wouldn't die, but that he had better stay with her for the night to make her restful.

Next day the rains had begun. I went out to Yuichinpu to see Aunt Hua (Mrs Zhu) and the two youngest Nies, now both with her. I found her busy making shoes for Number Four, he sitting on the bed all day playing with paper boats made by his uncle. Number Four was quite happy and contented; he had cried only once and stopped when told that he could go and see his mother as soon as his new shoes were ready. New clothes were the next problem. It takes about seven feet outside and seven feet of lining, plus one pound of cotton wool for a padded suit. Aunt Hua suggested that she make his clothes and I buy the cloth, the orphanage supply his food; a good working arrangement!

Number Three came in wearing hugely oversize orphanage clothes, very happy to be with his brothers again. I carried him in to the city on my shoulders, he holding the umbrella. On our way we passed a place where he had seen a beggar without any legs, and somebody giving him a dollar. "Did you give him anything?" I asked.

"No, I didn't give him any money."

"Suppose you had had some money?"

"I never do have any money."

"Suppose I gave you five dollars and we met the beggar. Would you give it to him?" Silent thought. "Yes."

"What? All of it?"

"No, perhaps I'd keep three dollars and give him two. That would be best."

We walked into the hospital, Guang Chun going in first to see if his mother was in a good mood. He called us in. Number Three stood just inside the door at the foot of the bed; his sleeves hung down like a scholar's gown, and his trousers had come unrolled. His newly shaven head, triangular and flat at the back like all northeastern children's heads, stood up like a wall above the back of his neck. His mother looked at him quizzically from the bed; her son looked questioningly back, expecting to be sworn at or hit. There was silence ... then, "Come over here and let Mother have a look at you." He toddled obediently over. "What's this you have got on? You don't look like a man at all. Why doesn't Aunt Hua make clothes for you that fit?"

"Aunt Hua is making clothes for Number Four. I have clothes that fit, but they are being washed."

"Have you got lice?"

"Yes, all the boys in the orphanage have lice."

"How are your bowels?"

"Runny ... we only get rice, and all the boys' stomachs are running."

"How is Number Four? Did you look after him properly?"

The small son was standing quite still at the end of the bed, an imp with shaven triangular head and upturned nose. The eldest son was sitting proudly on the bed opposite, drinking in every word of this family interrogation.

"Number Four's all right. He is laughing a lot, very happy. Uncle Zhu made him paper boats. Aunt Hua wouldn't let him get off the *kang* till she had finished his new shoes. He sat there all day today, playing. "Tomorrow can I go and see my Ma?" he asks everyone who comes in."

"Does he cry?"

"Last night he cried for you a lot. I took him into my bed. I had to lift him up. He soon went to sleep."

Ma nodded approvingly. "Son," she said, "we are all different now. I am not the same here as I was at home ... all clean and getting better. You are not the same either. You are on your own, with fourth baby to look after. You understand?" Grunt of assent.

Afterwards, riding on my shoulders again, "She's different," he declared. "Much better. That day I went home and saw her ill like that, I cried. Today she talked nicely."

I took Number Three back to the guest house, scrubbed him down, rubbed his feet warm, and rolled him up in a quilt, but not before feeding him up on chicken soup and bread. His stomach was swollen by eating un-nutritious food, and he is always craving for more. I put some ointment in his eyes and left him rolled up in the quilt while I flipped five hundred lice off his shirt, wondering how many had fallen down my neck while he rode on my shoulders. For breakfast he ate large quantities of *baozi* and egg soup, and his final remark as his eldest brother took him off to the orphanage was, "I'm still a little hungry."

In spite of his parting remark, Lao San had evidently overeaten. At least that was the explanation given by the orphanage staff for the return of the old malaria next day. "Malaria is afraid of three things – tiredness, cold, and too much food," they said. The theory is that the malaria germs lie next to the skin, so that if the stomach is too full, the skin compresses and the germs come out!

For three days running I went to the orphanage to give him quinine and put drops in his eyes. He was very unhappy; high fever, dizzy head so that he couldn't sit up. The fever came every morning and stayed right on till about midnight. Lao San was careful to point out all the boys who had malaria, and make me give quinine to them as well. He struggled up on his elbow to point them out to me one by one. On the fourth day he didn't seem much better, so I carried him into the city where we could give him more attention. I decided also that we should have to take him back to Shuangshipu afterwards to feed him up, as he would have little chance to recuperate on the orphanage rice. There followed two more days of dosing in the guest house on our wide bed between his brother and me, and constant attention. He was still no better, but getting steadily weaker. At last, after a shot of quinine, he started to sweat, and the fever came down. Then we began to build him up with eggs and noodles; and the dysentery got better too, but on the day before starting for Shuangshipu his legs and feet began to swell.

We had left Lao Si with the Women's Sewing Co-op. He was very happy, and Lao Da brought him down to the hospital to see his mother several times. One day it was too wet to send him home, so Lao Si came back to stay with his two brothers and me, all on one big wide bed. He is fat, chuckling, but apt to become round-eyed and serious on matters of food. Poor Lao San didn't welcome his small brother. "He is too bouncy," he said. We told Four not to bounce, as Three was ill. After leaving them together on the bed for a minute, we found Three crying and Four sitting very solemnly watching him. "I just sat here and he began to cry," said Four, injured. We asked Three what the matter was. "He just talks and talks and talks. You can't stop him," said Three.

Owing to solemnity and fatness, we dubbed Lao Si "Doorway Clay Buddha" and asked him if he would like to spend his life sitting in a doorway shrine looking at the people who came in. "We'd all come and bow to you," we said.

"Seeing people would be all right, but what about meals?" he asked.

"Think of all the cakes and sweetmeats you'd get on festival days," said his brother.

"Festival days are too few; no, I wouldn't be able to stand it."

Before going to bed, Lao Si announced proudly that he never wetted the bed. Unfortunately, this was not quite true. In the middle of the night, the steely silence was broken by an urgent announcement to nobody in particular: "I want to make wee-wee." It was one of those terrifically momentous things, as though he had been lying awake for the past half hour wondering what he was going to give birth to, and now at last had tumbled on a great scientific truth.

"I want to make wee-wee." He staggered over to the pot. After a minute's silence, another terrific announcement rent the stillness: "It's not wee-wee, it's big convenience!" So I had to get up after all.

Next morning, lying in bed, very serious, he was staring up at the ceiling, wondering what he'd get for breakfast. His brother called out, "Hey, Doorway Clay Buddha!"

Lao Si forgot his dignity, or missed the gibe. "What's up, brother?" he answered in broad Shaanxi dialect. "*Kai'sa?*"

This was greeted with peels of brotherly laughter; but Lao Si was still very serious and determined not to jeopardise his chances of a good breakfast.

Later, as Lao Da was taking him back to the Women's Sewing Co-op, Lao Si asked for an oil strip – a piece of fried batter from a stall – to eat.

"Have you any money?" asked his brother.

"No, but I'm hungry. You exchange something with him for an oil strip."

"Good idea!" said his brother. "I'll exchange you and then I'll be able to eat the oil strip myself! Are you still hungry?"

"No, I'm not hungry anymore," Lao Si muttered.

We put Lao San on top of a handcart and set off over the Qin Ling Shan for Shuangshipu at last. Unfortunately, on the first night, high up in the mountains, the only bed available for the three of us was a three-foot plank. I put the two brothers, One and Three, at one end and myself at the other; but it was a mistaken tactic. It should have been them end-to-end and me, being the longer, alongside. As it was, my feet came outside Three's back, and let the draught in. He caught cold again, and malaria returned next day. On arrival in Shuangshipu, Three's temperature was 106°F. I couldn't make him sweat until I remembered some tablets left me by an American. These made him sweat beautifully, and the fever disappeared with some quinine.

Lao San has a toothbrush now and is learning to use it with great seriousness. He is entranced with two white rabbits with pink eyes, brought him by Bailie boys, and he gave a demonstration on how the rabbits washed their faces.

Meanwhile, the mother is in the hospital in Baoji still. I don't know where she will go when she comes out. She wants to come here and live off me, which seems rather hard as I put her through hospital when nobody else would go near her, and fixed up her four sons! But the Chinese idea is still rather that, if you save a man from drowning, you have to support him for the rest of his life. Maybe she thinks that too.

Chapter 19

Home Life in Shuangshipu

Three months later, in May 1942, Aylwin wrote:

My third son is now pretty fit and chases goats all over the mountain. I have made him a magnificent pair of padded cotton trousers, and in a day or two he will be trudging back to Baoji to school.

I heard that the mails were beginning to come through again, but so far I have received no letters from you for many months. Last one dated July 1941 I think! One has to get the trick of being complete within oneself or of fitting easily into one's environment today. It is no use trying to keep up old contacts except by memory. Lucky you always taught us to be self-reliant, ever since the days of school in Switzerland, and before.

I've got a change of jobs, to being schoolmaster for a boys' technical and cooperative training school. I am dean! It is very interesting. Not an ordinary technical school. The idea is to get 'em young, get 'em from tough backgrounds so that they will learn to look on the school and on CIC as their home. Ordinary school qualifications, good handwriting, nice manners and so on, count for nothing. The result is that we have got an interesting bunch of lads, full of character. One of them lost his mother on a crowded ferry while evacuating Shanghai, and never found her or his family again. One is a newspaper vendor, or was. Some are refugees from the province of Henan, which is so overcrowded that most of the poor families have to send one or two of their sons away to fend for themselves. Four or five are refugees from Manchuria since the Mukden Incident of 1931. These sharp-witted ones are mixed up with some native peasant boys. They learn to talk each other's dialects. Big ones, small ones, middle school graduates, and near-illiterates, all mixed up and all learning from each other; and I from them.

In the first year of their history, the school changed heads eight times! Nobody seemed to be quite clear as to what the school was trying to do or how it ought to be done. Meanwhile I was writing propaganda for it to get money from America. In this way I had plenty of contact with it and plenty of opportunity to think out ideas about it. When the eighth man failed they put me in charge to see if I could put any of my own propaganda into effect! Apart from being headmaster, I teach English and geography.

Did I tell you about the pacifist Scotsman who turned up? He is a Friend's Ambulance Unit man. Just before leaving England he spent a day in Harpenden and had a drink of beer in the Silver Cup. He plays the bagpipes very well, much to the delight of the surrounding countryside. For the moment he is staying here and teaching the boys about motor trucks, through an interpreter.

The technical school was not much of a place at first. When Aylwin took over there was a three-roomed school building equipped with one loom and a warp winder, and an extremely bare kitchen standing on an open plot sporting a flag pole with a badly tattered and almost bleached national flag flapping in the wind on a bleak hillside. The listless, undernourished, lice-infested, twelve remaining boys covered with scabies slept on their desktops in one room. The Gung Ho people laughed. "Why bother with such a place? Forget it!"

Aylwin was the only instructor at first, but quickly managed to arrange that Chinese instruction would be provided by Gung Ho staff from the village. Rewi Alley had commissioned the building of a cottage near the school as a retreat for himself. Aylwin took over the nearly complete cottage and made it into a school dormitory and proceeded to have a cave dug out of the hillside behind it. Walls were built around the school and dormitory, and within the walls a basketball pitch and gardens were laid out. As spring turned to summer, cooperatives in Shuangshipu, Baoji and other nearby places started to send in their apprentices.

In June, still having received no letters from home, he wrote with some sound advice as to keeping healthy in a totally foreign environment:

I am fat and robust. It is a noteworthy and memorable fact that only people who try to live like a foreigner find life difficult. It is wearing and exasperating to try and live in your own way when everything around you is setting up friction with this way. In wartime, and under blockade, it is becoming harder and harder. But if you go right over and live according to your environment, all is very simple. Take wet feet for example; wet roads, slushy paths, no taxis or buses, no good shoes, no galoshes, and nowhere to dry your shoes when you get home. What would you do? Try and make the best of these things and worry about "it wouldn't be like this in England?" No. Don't think anything of them. Buy yourself a pair of cloth sandals that grip the mud, don't wear any socks, go out and frankly splash though all the puddles you can see. Cover your feet in lovely squelchy mud. Have a good time. When you get home, take off your sandals and wash your feet. Nothing could be healthier or nicer.

I now have the magnificent official title of CIC Inspector now that a long-awaited little pass has arrived, with the signature of Premier Kong Xiangxi on it.

Just lately no travelling for me, however, as I am too busy being schoolmaster. We are having a lot of fun, producing some otherwise un-producible boys, and incidentally getting me a lot of material to write about. The boys are a bit wary of their foreign dean, and whenever I do anything wrong, or anything they can't understand, this is scathingly dubbed *yang chu'i*, or "Ocean Principle". However, we get along quite well really, and better so now that I am learning their ways. They are just at the age when Chinese kids are most apt to begin to be nationalistic. We had a few stormy sessions about opium wars, foreign concessions, and suchlike, but it all calmed down when they realised that, in spite of the height of the respective bridges of our noses, we really saw more or less eye to eye on these subjects. We've only got about thirty boys so far. They learn all kinds of things – Chinese and arithmetic for the younger and less educated ones, accountancy for the more educated, cooperative theory, economic geography, textiles, current affairs, motor mechanics, elementary mechanics and mechanical drawing, health and first aid, diary and composition, and English. Each day there are five hours of classwork plus three and a half hours practical work in our own workshop or in various co-ops in the neighbourhood. The boys also buy their own food supplies and run their own consumer co-op, at which they spend their small allowances on towels, soap, toothbrushes, straw sandals, pencils, writing brushes, and so on. We organise expeditions for them and have them write their reports or report to the school meeting. Every week there are debates and a self-criticism meeting for training in the workings of democracy. They are divided into three "houses", each with its house captain, and there is also a captain of the school.

I don't teach much – some English, economic geography, current affairs, singing and cooperation – but there is plenty to do putting the school on its feet and organising things in general, giving pep-talks to the boys, and trying to mould a school tradition on which to build for the future.

It is very interesting, and the school is going ahead pretty fast. Now the CIC is planning a similar school in Lanzhou, one near Chongqing, and a third somewhere in Henan, probably at Luoyang. When the money comes, I am supposed to travel around to these places and help with them.

After graduation, the boys are supposed to go into the co-ops and CIC as "middle men" between Western-trained engineers and the co-op members. As it is, the former often have great difficulty in getting their ideas over to the latter. Language is often different, thought processes always so. The boys from our schools will know enough of both worlds to act as go-betweens. They will interpret the engineer's ideas for broad technical improvement to the co-op workers, and at the same time will bring their first-hand knowledge of co-op conditions, native people's difficulties and attitudes to the CIC specialists.

The other day we did some spring cleaning, and I thought that maybe you were doing some too, unless a bomb had done it for you first. Our house is half cave, half house. The house projection part is nearly all window – paper window with a pane of glass two feet by one foot in the middle. First, we covered the brick floor with lime and left it for a day or two. This is to kill the fleas. Then we brushed all the ceilings and walls down. The ceiling still looked a bit grubby so we used some paper to cover it with. Then we tore all the paper out of the window, as it had got kind of grey and opaque, and put new paper in which, though of course not transparent, still lets in a very good white light. The window is divided up into brick-size compartments by slats of wood. In pasting the big sheets of paper over the window, the art is to get the joins in the paper to come exactly over the wooden slats, otherwise the joins show up in the light. The only snag in our spring cleaning was that I put my foot through the *kang*. This is a bed made of mud bricks, with a flue left in it for a little fire, sending hot smoke in circles underneath the *kang* during winter. We have planted cabbages, leeks, paprika, and eggplant in the garden. We have two puppies. "We" is Andy Braid, the Scot who once drank beer in the Silver Cup, his Chinese helper, occasionally Rewi Alley, and me.

The cave house up on the hillside above Shuangshipu was becoming popularly known as Rewi Alley's Cave. Very many visiting foreigners stayed there, some passed through. There were all sorts of rumours flying around. Aylwin wrote about it in the last chapter of his book: "Some speak of it with sentimental affection."

"Very primitive, my dear," they write to their friends back in comparative civilisation. "Of course there's no doorbell or knocker. The dear Chinese just walk in and out as though they owned the place." Certainly other quarters have held it to be a splendid country mansion, built out of squeeze money [corruption money], and hired out at fantastic rentals to rich Americans. The only possible basis for this rumour was Graham Peck, who was at that time almost penniless; Graham filled the cave's then empty bookcase with a row of attractively done wooden blocks entitled *From Blind Alley to Cooperatives*, or *Up Your Alley* and so on, but he certainly paid no rent.

Various well-meaning friends dispatched equally well-meaning emissaries to reform Rewi's household ménage, and restore the man to at least a semi-foreign shadow of his respectable Shanghai Municipal Council days. These people usually go away saddened. Some of them have even stopped coming back to look; instead they walk about the village picking up stories while their truck fills up with petrol. "The people up there live just like the Chinese. Their cook can't even make the simplest semi-foreign dishes." Such stories ripen alarmingly with age, so that in some places "that poor man Alley" is considered to have already degenerated past help into a piece of Oriental "poor white trash."

The main distinctive feature of Rewi's cave in Shuangshipu is exactly the same as that of his former house in Shanghai; that at any time out of school hours it is filled with boys; boys looking at picture magazines and asking millions of questions, boys playing the gramophone and singing out of tune, boys doing gymnastics off Rewi's shoulders or being held upside down, boys being given enemas, or rubbing sulphur ointment into each other's scabies, boys standing in brass washbasins and splashing soapy water about.

Rewi would never admit that the number of fleas on the floor had anything to do with the number of boys who heaped their clothes on it before bathing.

"It's those damn puppies of yours," he insisted. Later on, when the cook had secretly hatched a brood of fifteen chicks and two ducks, and these grew old enough to join the fun in the living room cave, he could always blame it onto them.

The flea era lasted for nearly a year. On coming into the cave, those who were in the know and so wore shorts could immediately slap a dozen off each leg. If we liked the look of a visitor we would warn him to roll up his trouser legs before coming in. If we didn't, he would soon be fidgeting uncomfortably and remarking that it was about time he went down to supper before it got dark and the wolves came out.

We covered the floor in inches of lime, and scrunched through it for days; the fleas were undaunted, and came out thick as ever when we took the lime up thinking they would all have been burned to death. The puppies were bathed and disinfected, the chickens slaughtered and eaten; still the fleas throve. Tins of Keating's Insect Powder were scrounged off friends in distant cities; the fleas simply lapped it up. A university expert, to whom we wrote for advice, said that common salt was the very best thing. We bought up a hundred pounds of it from the market and smashed it in with our heels; the local farmers, calling up to have their skin diseases attended to or listen to the odd noises emitting from the foreigners' cave, were horrified at the waste and spread the story of it all through the neighbourhood. Many of them had to eat hot pepper as a cheap substitute for the rare and expensive salt, and consequently suffered from goitre.

Finally, we invented a steriliser into which the boys could drop their clothes before bathing. At the same time the large *kang*, or mud-brick bed, that had filled half the cave and made a nice breeding ground for rats, was broken up and spread over the garden. The fleas gradually lessened and died out.

Encouraged, we had the walls re-whitewashed, the frontage re-papered, and a new pane of glass that had been brought all the way from Xi'an fitted into the middle of the paper window. Various pictures were pinned up on the wall. New Zealand Maoris fishing from outrigger canoes, Chinese soldiers posing boldly in woodcut, American scenes cut out of a magazine, photos of friends: Ida Pruitt with a group of American-born engineers whom she'd brought out of Hong Kong to work for CIC; exquisite Nym Wales [Helen Foster Snow's pen-name], head and shoulders; Henry Luce and smooth-tailored wife Clare Booth snapped standing in front of a Baoji towel-making cooperative; Mike, one of Rewi's two adopted Chinese sons, looking rather like a whimsical rat.

We bought a tablecloth and scrubbed the bare wood furniture with sand. On the desk against the light of the paper window we stood a large, amply robed Buddha with folded hands, who in the case of extreme need could be conjured into frock-coated butler bringing in tray of drinks. To add a further touch of culture, we dug niches in the walls in the shape of cathedral windows, and filled them with high-nosed, bearded statues of hitherto unsung contemporaries of Marco Polo, unearthed from the new city moat being dug around Luoyang. Shortsighted missionary visitors could hardly believe their eyes! If they were the kind who had rolled up their trousers in the flea-ridden days, we took them over to look; if they were the other kind we let them go away muttering dark things about heathen idolatry.

Rewi Alley spent most of the time travelling from co-op to co-op, from depot to depot, from CIC Headquarters in Chongqing to the various regional bases. He would at intervals return to his cave-house in Shuangshipu to rest up, recuperate, attend to correspondence, and recharge his batteries. On these occasions, Aylwin would arrive home from school to find Rewi sitting comfortably on a piece of cooperative carpet spread over a cooperative armchair, beside a cooperative stove burning cooperative coal, his feet protected from the cold of the cooperative brick floor by a pair of cooperative leather slippers; everything, except the coal, being plainly and individually marked with the Gung Ho trade mark.

On his desk would be a terrific pile of correspondence, which critics swore he addressed to himself, answering himself on his non-stop careering around the countryside; on the stove a pot of coffee which he and Aylwin would work through together while discussing the latest developments in CIC, in the country as a whole and in the Shuangshipu Bailie Training School

Turning to a letter that Aylwin wrote in late June 1942, we can read further of a happy domestic scene:

> The gramophone alternatively played "Ave Maria", Maurice Chevalier, and some piece by HM Coldstream Guards or some such; our hen, now nearing her twenty-first day of sitting on eggs clacking deprecatingly at food placed before her in her corner of the kitchen, a mass of little boys learning to do the highland fling to a Chinese folk song; two puppies rolling and barking at each other's fleas; somebody digging the vegetables. Altogether quite like home. Not very like Wayfarings, but still a home. No women, and so everything in a bit of a mess. Andy Braid has shaved his head, grown a beard, sun-bathed himself bright pink, and sits down to breakfast opposite me without a shirt on. Rather disturbing, that. We sit carefully not exactly opposite each other because the table is narrow and we feel the wind in each other's faces when each of us blows on his porridge. All this only happens on Sundays. On weekdays I usually get up first and do deep breathing, swinging from the hips and so on with my schoolboys. Such is one's hangover from early environment! The other day, two very trying Yorkshire men, at least man and wife, turned up full of zeal to reform us and turn us back into respectable whites. We really think we are quite civilised anyway, and there is an underlying philosophy, as explained in my last letter.
>
> In another few days our school is setting out to walk over the mountains to Baoji to take part in the Northwest CIC celebrations on Cooperative Day, July 4th, and on Lugouqiao (Marco Polo Bridge) Incident Day, July 7th. We have taught them a lot of songs, including one English round and several native Gansu peasant songs we picked up in the mountains. We shall take a cart with us on our trip to carry the small boys when they get tired, and a blanket each. The weather is hot, so we shan't need much.
>
> Our American committee wrote asking for information of a kind that would appeal specially to the American labour movement, which is taking a lot of interest in CIC just now. So I have been trying to work something out. Conditions are so different that it is difficult to link the two countries up in terms of a labour movement. But it is interesting to think that we are appealing to that kind of person. Did you know that Mahatma Gandhi and Jaharawal Nehru had taken special interest in CIC and stated

that it was a thing India must develop for herself? I still want to get to India sometime. My original plan to "stay in China for six months or so and get a deeper knowledge of the country than I would as an ordinary tourist" certainly extended itself, didn't it! I don't think I shall ever be able to leave it permanently any more. My job will be to link up with other countries and peoples or to work inside.

Shuangshipu Bailie School

The cave house at Shuangshipu

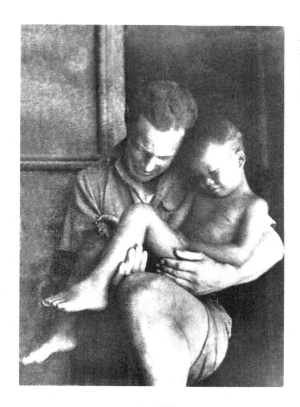

Aylwin
with Lao Si,
Shuangshipu
1942

Aylwin with
Andy Braid and
his interpreter in
Shuangshipu

Lao Si and Lao San
in Shuangshipu

Lao Si and Lao San
in Shandan

Chapter 20

Flood Relief at P'ing Men Xian

In August 1942, Huang He – the great Yellow River – China's Hope, cradle of Chinese civilisation, ancient source of life-giving water and rich silt for the cultivation of food for millions, showed for a moment its other personality – China's Sorrow. A devastating flood was caused in the county of P'ing Men, just upriver from Tongguan. A call for help was received at CIC in Baoji, in answer to which Director Lu Guangmian and Aylwin set out to investigate in order to suggest ways of productive relief. A short account of what Aylwin saw was published that autumn in the *New Statesman* and the *Nation* magazines, but here is a more detailed story:

A hundred or so years ago, the accumulated sediment of mud and sand which the Yellow River carried down from the treeless territory to the north forced the river itself away further east. Though the virgin mud of the old bed promised rich harvests, few native Shaanxi farmers dared settle there, fearing that the river would return suddenly and treacherously to its old course. So it was left to landless famine refugees from the north and east; taller, tougher men, who were willing to gamble if only they could eat and to till the soil of the old riverbed. The local Shaanxi gentry staked out huge portions of the new territory, but remained as landlords, living on the high land and taking rich revenues from the settlers' produce.

In 1929 this strip of reclaimed riverbed, which stretches forty miles north of the bend at Tongguan, received county status for the first time; but still nothing of much importance was done for it, owing to the opposition of the rich landlords, who were now left in Zao I Xian on the high land. These feared that a new *xian* government for the ordinary people would interfere with the collection of their rents.

It was not until ten years later, when war refugees began to cross the river in thousands and Japanese troops were already digging in along the opposite bank, that the Central Government suddenly awoke to the tremendous importance of P'ing Men Xian as a defence area, and decided to push ahead with its reconstruction.

A new and progressive *xian* magistrate ... himself a war refugee from Shandong province ... was sent to take charge. New schools were opened in the villages, good roads were built, and industry was encouraged. Over two hundred thousand trees were planted every year. By 1942, fifty thousand acres of land were bearing good crops of millet, corn, kaoliang, beans and peanuts. A population of twenty-seven thousand had settled in about ninety villages and hamlets.

Besides tilling the soil, members of the six thousand three hundred Ordinary People's households pressed peanut oil, reared an incredible number of pigs on the peanut waste, sold the pig bristles and pork; they dug up several thousand tons of salt every day. They made themselves spinning wheels and looms on patterns brought by memory from the textile areas of Hebei, Henan and Shandong, and so created a market for native Shaanxi cotton. New villages, each with its allowance of saplings from the government, sprang up almost every month; in fact, you could tell the age of each village by the height of its trees.

It was then that the Yellow River took a hand. Following cloudbursts in Qinghai and Gansu provinces, a huge wave of floodwater varying from six to twenty feet high travelled the whole length of the river. There was no question this time of China's Sorrow changing her course. It was merely that there was enough water for two rivers, so that wherever its banks allowed it to do so the river spread out over them. P'ing Men Xian, which ordinarily lies only a few feet above water level, was covered for fifteen hours by water ten to twenty feet deep, travelling with force enough to wrench huge lumps of coal from a Shanxi seam seventy miles further north, and strew hundreds of thousands of tons of them in the mud all the way down the opposite – Shaanxi – shore as far as Tongguan.

When the water subsided, it was found that neither a single bean, ear of grain nor any of the peanut crop remained in the whole of the county of P'ing Men. All the spinning wheels and most of the looms had been carried away. All the oil-pressing equipment had been destroyed. Two out of the three salt mines had been buried irretrievably. The pigs being short of limb and unable to climb trees had nearly all perished. Over a thousand oxen, donkeys and mules had been swept away, so that even the river's gift of good new mud could not be used ... there were no animals to pull the ploughs. Houses, built of earthen bricks, had dissolved into their component particles of Yellow River mud, and the roof poles had floated downstream. Amazingly only a few thousand people were drowned, partly owing to the number of trees and partly to the buoyancy of the thick, muddy water. Very little remained in the old riverbed; an area of a hundred miles by fifteen.

Rumours about the flood soon spread to the rear, but, probably for strategic reasons, were officially denied. Robbed of the relief funds that publicity would have brought, the officials in charge wired Lu Guangmian, of CIC in Baoji, asking him to come and see conditions for himself and then use his good offices to get a grant for constructive relief.

The county magistrate and his staff, dressed in a medley of garments, met us outside the city. "Excuse our appearance," said the magistrate, "but we all lost our clothes in the flood." The city wall has been washed away, and all but a few houses. "We were only a small *xian* to begin with, and poor," he continued, "but we were just beginning to look like something after three years' hard work. Now that's all finished overnight.

Two things are left though. One is the trees we planted; the other you'll see later – the spirit of the people and their desire to rebuild. So these at least remain of our three years' construction and education work! They are the symbols of our past work, and the hope for our future."

As we walked in at the *xian* government gate, Magistrate Wang waved his hand airily towards some mud. "My reception room," he remarked; and over in the other direction, "Here is the Education Department and the Economic Research Department," indicating equally formless piles of mud. A wooden pole had been placed across from the fork of one tree to that of another. "My two secretaries spent the night upon that perch," continued Wang. "The accountants were up in that tree over there, and the Self-Defence Corps soldiers made a platform in the tree outside their barracks. The trees saved everybody."

"How about you yourself?" I asked.

"I was up on the roof of our new office buildings," he replied. "I had a ladder put up against the roof, and pushed women and children up until the roof was full, and the water nearly upon us. Then I went up myself and climbed over to the north side to watch the flood come. There was a terrific roar by that time, and a stench from the muddy water like rain on dry mud, only a hundred times stronger. Then, in the dusk, we saw a white wall rushing towards us. There was a horrible jumble of agonised noises; donkeys and mules braying, oxen bellowing, pigs screeching, dogs barking, women shrieking, children crying, men shouting and trees cracking under the weight of rocks and coal being trundled down from up-stream; and all the time, the roar of the water. Then the Japanese began to open up with their big guns across the river." Later, it was found that they were covering their own retreat into the mountains, thinking that the Chinese might take advantage of a shift in the river to cross; meanwhile the Chinese thought the Japanese were making use of a shift in the river to attack them. Actually, both sides were flooded equally badly but neither side knew that then. "By next morning," Magistrate Wang continued, "the water was only a few feet deep, but still running fast; by eleven o'clock we could come down and wade through the mud. Tomorrow you will see for yourselves the desolation we found everywhere."

The morning after our arrival, the town crier went around with a big gong: "Women who can spin, come to the meeting place to hear Mr Lu speak on productive relief."

Nearly a thousand women, all expert domestic spinners and weavers, turned up. When Lu had finished, one of the older ones stood up to speak, leaning on her neighbour's shoulder to take the weight off her bound feet. "I've cried so much I just can't cry anymore," she said. "The women of our village have had mass cries and individual cries, and now I can't cry because no tears will come. I'm cried dry!" Merry wrinkles reappeared at the corners of her swollen eyes. "So if you'll help us to get spinning wheels and looms to earn our own livings with, we'll be very grateful, I'm sure."

Another old lady had refugeed to P'ing Men after the strategic dike-breaking flood at Kaifeng in 1938. The latest flood swept her off the roof of her house clutching a small grandson; buoyed up in the turbulent muddy water, she had found herself, half an hour later, gently deposited ten miles downstream and still clasping a live grandson. "I've escaped him twice now," she laughed at the Yellow River. "He won't get me!"

Going out on my bicycle after the meeting, I found in the first village I came to that thirty out of a population of one hundred and fifty had been drowned. Not a single house or part of a house was left in the village, which was now a mud flat on which some trees are growing. "What happened when you saw the water coming?" I asked a peasant. "Why didn't you run away?"

"The soldiers ran up to the high land in time, so we could have done that too really," was the reply, "but, you see, we are *the people*. We have our houses, crops and animals. We hoped the flood would not be so big, and we stayed. By the time we could see how big the water would be, it was too late. All we could do was to tie ourselves to the trees and wait."

A peasant in another village, where mules and oxen and two thousand pigs had been swept away, said, "In our village, a man is lucky if he gets one meal of soup a day. Over fifty households have gone away to become beggars in the last three days. If we don't get grain seed within three weeks the district won't recover for five years. If we can only get our grain sown, we'll have hope and stay by it – even if we all almost starve to death before harvest comes."

Then there was Liu Qing De, a twenty-eight-year-old Shandong refugee, who clung to an ox-cart with her whole family and was carried downstream for miles on it. "We tied the cart to a tree before the water came, but as Pei Lu An is a new village the trees are small, and the flood dragged the cart and the tree together. I was holding my baby, but I swallowed so much water that I became unconscious and let him go. My father and husband and two children are all drowned."

"How do you live now?" I asked.

"When we can beg for any scraps to eat there is still great difficulty in cooking it. The whole village has only one or two cooking pots that we dragged out of the mud, so now we have to use these in rotation."

The villagers went through their families, counting up the casualties for me to put down in my notebook. "The Kao family, six out of seven dead; Sung family, four dead out of five; Li family, four dead out of six; Wang family, only one left out of seven"; and so on.

"Someone told me that my ox had been found on the flats about ten miles away when the flood went down," said one old man. "But I haven't been to see it yet. I've lost three children. There's no point looking for your ox when you can't find your children."

Ho Qi Quin, aged six, could speak enough to tell me that his father and mother had been carried away, and he didn't know where they were. Clinging to the tail of an ox all night, this little chap had crossed from Occupied to Free China!

Two brothers Wang told me they had been carried nearly to the far side of the river by the current, and had managed to reach land by swimming. They were pulled out of the water by Japanese soldiers on the east bank, suspected of being spies, and imprisoned. At night they escaped and jumped back into the river, with which they were very familiar, managed to swim across to the bend of the river on the southwest bank in Free China, and walk back to their own village.

The villagers stopped telling of their lost families. "You don't have to write all those figures down," the headman told me. "We've all lost many loved ones. Write down the important things to tell them."

Some women were crying again, and even the children, up to that time very proud of themselves for having survived, looked solemn. I changed the subject.

The only signs of former inhabitation in the next big village where eight hundred people had lived until a week or two ago, was one half-wrecked school building and a clump of trees. The mud flats, now cracking and peeling under the sun, stretched down unbroken, save for the lumps of flood-born coal, to the shore and seemingly to the foot of the Zhongtiao Shan range of mountains on the far side of the river!

A group of people sat under some trees beside a pile of coal, which some of them were loading into wheelbarrows. An old woman was sitting all by herself, crying. "What's she crying about?" I asked.

"She just got back here after walking forty miles back from where the flood dropped her. Now she finds the village like this and her things all under the mud. That's all."

On returning to Ordinary People's City, we found that Magistrate Wang had spread out a terrific meal for us, and I am ashamed to say that I ate a lot. Although I had seen enough concentrated starvation, misery and destruction to last me for weeks, I was exhilarated; thinking of the talks I had had that day. Now I knew it. I knew that these were the real people of China, who would remain and rebuild, whatever complicated muddle the round-cheeked, shiny-eye-lidded bureaucracy got itself into. I felt refreshed. For a long time I had been waiting with the thought in mind, "It isn't really quite like this, but then it very well might have been, and anyway it's no worse propaganda than thousands of other things people write these days." And suddenly today I had woken up to find that it actually was like that: that the people actually were infinitely more heroic, in quite an ordinary sort of way, than I or anyone else could ever make them out to be.

Chapter 21

Developing the School

This is an extract from the diary of Zhen Xi Quei, a pupil at the school at Shuangshipu:

> The sun was setting gently behind the western mountains. A small red cloud, really loveable, was hanging in the warm atmosphere. I walked alone over the mountains in the evening light, and came to a grassy stretch in a lonely uninhabited valley. I was looking around me at the beauty when out from the grass jumped two yellow-grey animals, like dogs. My heart dropped, my courage fell, as the wolves came chasing toward me. I had no weapon. I ran. In front was a ravine, behind were the wolves. My spirit was ready to ascend, but at the most dangerous moment I shouted .... I awoke. In the school dormitory it was just about dawn. Dogs were barking far and near, and these familiar sounds drove away the thoughts of my dream.
>
> It was my turn to go out and buy vegetables. As I left the school and started down the hill toward the village, it was already six o'clock, and by the time I got back they had already finished breakfast. Tomorrow I must get up earlier.
>
> At evening meeting, after the flag-lowering ceremony and a talk on the day's doings from the teacher, we discussed the food-supply problem. We eat only bread, millet, and noodles, and one dish of vegetables for six people, but last month we used all but five cents per head of our allowance; this month things are even more expensive.

Zhen Xi Quei left his home near Nanjing with his mother when the Japanese were almost at the gates of their village, and walked for several weeks across to Hankou. From there he took a refugee train to Xi'an, worked for a while as a factory boy, and then set off for Sichuan. But the mountains and the length of the road were too much for him, and he ended up in Tianshui, Gansu, where he became a CIC office boy.

Here he was busier than ever: first up in the morning, rushing all over the town with messages on a bicycle several sizes too large for him, and last to bed at night. But he was happy and keen at his job. One New Year's Day, when everyone else had gone home, Aylwin, who was on one of his frequent visits to Tianshui, heard Zhen Xi Quei ringing the office bell imperiously, giving himself orders in a deep husky voice, calling up all sorts of imaginary bank officials on the telephone and announcing: "I am Chinese Industrial Cooperatives" in a very loud voice. Then he disappeared for several hours, and came back happier and huskier than ever, having hauled the Ocean Secretary's bicycle up the mountain above the city and coasted all the way back again.

Eighteen months later, Zhen Xi Quei had been elected as head boy at the Shuangshipu Bailie School, and chairman of the student consumers' cooperatives. He was nearly ready to go back to a Tianshui cooperative as accountant.

When Su Qing Ho came to the school from an army-blanket-weaving cooperative in Baoji, he was old enough to become a useful workman within a year or two, but still young enough to absorb the idea of CIC to the full. Without sufficient learning to put ideas into his head about being a scholar or a petty official, he yet had sufficient for grounding, and a great deal of common sense. His family was poor, which had given him the habit of looking after himself, but not so poor and sonless as to depend on Qing Ho for its livelihood. His future was thus a blank page with Chinese Industrial Cooperatives underlined at the top. After six months in the school, he was sent with five other Bailie boys to study new small-unit woollen textile machinery under an American engineer in Chengdu, and to bring the machinery back to the Northwest.

Aylwin writes about a native Shanxi lad who arrived at the school:

> Filthy, illiterate, with the back of his head shaved and the front hair coming down over his eyes. He proved to have an extremely sturdy and independent personality, taking no nonsense from anybody. Today, with his head shaved all over, he is clean even behind the ears, can write letters and do long division. This kind of boy potentially would be worth far more in terms of loyalty and pep to the movement than the cost of their food and clothing in school.

Four years previously, in the heart of Henan lying north of the Yellow River, a small boy on his way home from school was taken off by a Kuomintang regiment to be its "boiled-water pourer". The boy fetched and carried and made tea for the officers at the front for several years, until the regiment was ordered south to help the British in Burma. One day during the second week of marching, the boy found himself drinking from the same spout of a teapot belonging to a fellow Henanese, who was chairman of a cooperative in Fengxian, near Shuangshipu.

"Where are you off to fellow countryman?" inquired the owner of the teapot.

"We're going to England to fight the Japanese."

"To England! But a little dog like you will never get there at all! The rains will come and still you won't be there. Why don't you come and work in our cooperative instead? We could do with a lad like you."

So Zhang Seng I buttoned up all the buttons he could find, and painted ink marks around the holes of those he couldn't, and went off to ask leave from his officers.

"Sure, you stay with the co-op," they said. "We can easily find another boy when we get there."

Zhang Seng I became a co-op apprentice, and later a Bailie boy. He was slow, but worked hard at everything; he was easygoing and able to get along with everybody. Someday he would make a good cooperative chairman.

Tough and shortsighted, Wang Qing didn't make the best of impressions on visitors. He was a native peasant lad who could make himself understood and trusted throughout all the mountains of Gansu where suspicious farmers would guard precious coal and metal ores. His favourite trick was to lie on Headmaster Hogg's bed, pleading belly-pains until Headmaster Hogg went out, at which time he would make surreptitious passes over his face with the razor of the supposedly unknowing headmaster. Walking over the mountains, returning to school after an inspection trip to Baoji, Wang Qing was all but persuaded by his fellow students that the steam locomotive they saw there had several oxen concealed within the boiler. Though Wang Qing, nicknamed "The Oaf", never became very proficient with the writing brush, he learned a lot from the sharp-witted refugees and others who were his schoolmates.

Soon after Aylwin took over at the school, there arrived a tall 18-year-old middle school student, with a letter from a Baoji co-op asking for admission. It was decided to give him a trial on accountancy; for the first month he was lazy, haughty, and unhappy, and probably stayed in the school only because he couldn't go back to his co-op and didn't know where else to feed himself. Then suddenly he began to lead school debates, attend newspaper-reading circles, and work hard at his subject. As elected captain of one of the student teams, he invented many ways in which team captains could arouse competitive spirit and encourage self-discipline. His team led in doing voluntary jobs of labour and school improvement. Later, he and another boy volunteered to take special afternoon literacy and arithmetic classes for the more backward boys and the school cook.

Problem Child Number One, for a while, was Zhu Ying Quei. He was a spoiled only son, cry baby, and piss-a-bed, commonly hailed as "Big-head, Big-head! Who doesn't need an umbrella when it rains?" His father was lost somewhere north of the Yellow River with a CIC depot, and his mother earned just enough to keep herself in a Baoji women's tailoring co-op. How to cope with the boy at the school under these circumstances was a knotty problem. In the end, nothing specific was done, but a lot of things just naturally happened.

One afternoon, Aylwin had been holding a geography lesson down by the river, after swimming. They had made a sand map of Asia with real seas and rivers. To finish things off, they all took big stones and bombed Japan until it sank into the water. Zhu Ying Quei liked the idea so much that he took to bombing the peasants' ducks, believing them to be Japanese submarines. This was strictly against orders, and Ying Quei soon found himself sunk, sitting with all his clothes on in the river. The howling was terrific, and lasted all day, but it was a milestone.

The trouble of taking his quilt out to air every morning after he had wetted it was enough to cause young Zhu Ying Quei to sit on the side of his bed at night and make water onto the floor. Various punishments were thought up for this until it became a matter of the past. Cruel jokers, however, continued to sprinkle water all around his bed and point accusingly next morning until Ying Quei began to surround his bed with a lot of hawthorn prickles to keep the jokers away. The trouble of climbing out over his own barricade in the dark soon cured him of everything, and soon his sleep was unbroken.

Whichever of the school teams had Ying Quei in it always got bottom marks for orderliness. Consequently when the time came for re-dividing the dormitory teams, "Big-head" found himself decidedly unwanted. The deadlock was solved by electing him to be school captain. After that it was easy. Dirty face, unbuttoned trousers, unmade bed, the admonition was the same, unanswerable and shame inflicting: "The school captain shouldn't do things like that you know, Ying Quei. He should set a good example."

The last time he ever cried was over the matter of the old Ford V8 truck engine that was brought up to the school for the boys to clean and take to pieces, under the guidance of Andy Braid. Somebody had remarked that it looked very much like a turtle. To Big-head, who had sweated his guts out helping to carry it up the hill to school on poles, such an insinuation was rank heresy. A fight resulted in which Ying Quei, being top-heavy, was worsted.

Without any past school tradition as a frame to build upon, a situation further weakened by the negative past spirit at the school, Aylwin had his work cut out to weld this motley crew into a true community. He gradually evolved a structure which became the school; he so frequently had to point out that the physical requirements alone of a place of learning did not constitute a school, but tradition and the school's own personality in how things were done was perhaps more important than the bricks and mortar.

Everybody had to learn to sing. Not a very difficult thing to do, as the Chinese generally love to sing. At the slightest provocation, they will burst into song. Resistance songs and folk tunes alternated. Gansu coal carriers' songs, which could not have been heard outside those mountains, songs from as far away as the southern provinces; everywhere Aylwin travelled, his keen musical ear and love of singing enabled him to note down the tunes and words of the songs that were around him. This was possibly one of the keys to his success in integrating with the ordinary people of China. As time passed and this singing tradition became established, when a new boy arrived at the school, he would find that immediately he was drawn into the centre of interest and not treated at all as an intruder to be left on the fringes. The students would gather around to ask what songs he knew to add to their repertoire. Instead of his strange accent or dialect being made fun of, the newcomer would find that his way of speaking brought richness and meaning to the songs that his new friends wanted to learn.

Everybody had to get up early in the mornings, swim in the river at least once a day, and rub sulphur ointment into his scabies if he had any. Cleanliness was not a widely appreciated virtue in the Chinese countryside. Put to the poll, it turned out that over half the students believed it natural for the human body to have lice. Health talks and swimming in the river soon cured this.

Everybody had to help with improvement on the school grounds. If someone had put a lot of time and energy, imagination, and inventiveness into some project to improve the school surroundings or facilities, he would without a doubt make sure that no harm would come to the child of his sweat from negligence, carelessness, or vandalism.

For classroom work, the school was divided into three grades. Each morning there would be about five hours of classroom work. Several of the most backward boys were put into a special afternoon literacy class, but for the rest, the afternoons were taken up in practical work. There were textile workshops, truck engines to be stripped and rebuilt, benchwork with wood and metal, a lathe driven by a small diesel engine, and there was a model steam engine. Some of them would go down to the village to do practical work in one of the co-ops.

For eating, sleeping, and self-discipline, the boys were divided into three school teams, each with an elected team captain. The teams were redivided four times a year to prevent sectionalism. Each captain was responsible for the personal questions of his team and held group discussions in the dormitory at night. He would draw up resolutions from the team to be presented to the general meeting of the whole school on Saturdays. It was recognised that self-discipline would be the only kind of training that would count for work after leaving school in a disorganised wartime or postwar society. School tasks were portioned out to team captains who gave them to whichever of his team members needed a disciplinary reminder. Two major influences came into play in promoting self-discipline. General admiration for army smartness and discipline was the first incentive for improvement. The second was the fear that they weren't attending a school at all, but a badly run crackpot foreign charity that would get them nowhere in the end. As time passed, there was a general recognition that it depended on the students themselves to prove whether that belief was true or not.

The day-to-day running of the school was used as exercise in self-management, which in turn was training for future cooperators. The weekly general meeting had six separate departments: food, the wall newspaper [notices and announcements printed or written on paper then pasted to a wall for all to read], labour service, library and newspaper reading, sport, recreation and drama. In addition, the students ran their own consumer cooperative. They could spend their allowances there of $20 a month on essential items such as soap, towels, sandals, pencils, writing brushes, and so on. A loan of $500 was secured from the Baoji CIC treasury. A further $462 was raised in fully paid-up shares from staff and students. At the end of the first quarter, the co-op declared a profit of $422.80 of which 57 per cent was distributed as purchase dividends to members. A further 30 per cent of the net profit was invested in a secure stock cupboard, and 10 per cent was the foundation of a common good fund. The first action taken by this fund was to buy pencils, which were distributed among the members. The remaining 10 per cent was paid out as a bonus for the hard-working co-op officers. Modern-style business accounts were properly kept by the students who had been elected as co-op officers, and all the accounts were gone over by the whole school as an exercise in practical accountancy.

"Democracy worked," Aylwin was able to say, "but it was far more trouble than dictatorship."

Despite the various methods employed to bring all these boys into a tight-knit community, there were three factors that influenced splits in the student body. The old reasons, which drive their wedges no matter where you might be in the world were regional differences, class differences, and the rift between groups of newcomers and the established members of the community. None of these reasons was serious on its own, but they had a tendency sometimes to coincide and form a major conflict.

The northeasterners came from an industrially developed country which had been for a long time open to influences from outside China. Being of pioneer stock, they were extremely independent and rather individualistic. Those of them who had been forced out of their homes in 1931 by the Mukden Incident had suffered a good deal of unequal treatment under Japanese Imperialism a long time before China as a whole declared war on the invader. So they learned early about standing together for good or ill.

The northwest was only recently being opened up. Its young people were called *tu bao zi*, or "country bumpkins", by outsiders. They resented the inference that they were lazy and good for nothing. They tended to be oversensitive about their own inability to speak good Beijing dialect.

The class factor was in practice, often indistinguishable from the regional one. Native peasant boys from the hinterland were suddenly brought into contact with middle-class boys from the coast. The undercurrent of tension between these two groups popped out in the most surprising places. One day, during the singing of an old Gansu folk song into which the whole school seemed to be throwing itself with tremendous enthusiasm, a native boy leapt up to shout, "They think they're clever don't they, copying our accent like that!"

One morning at breakfast there was uproar because the millet soup had been burned. Nobody would ordinarily have made any comment. It turned out that the executive head of the food department had been elected to the post by members of the rival faction with the intention of giving him a rough time whenever the opportunity arose!

All the old jokes like "how many oxen are there in a locomotive boiler?" and derisive styles of address such as "you Gansu buckwheat bag!" began to be repeated *ad nauseam*, taking on a new hard edge. The time came when the boys themselves tired of such rivalry and were glad to find a way out.

The northeasterners were easy to deal with. They had learned by bitter experience what national disunity could mean. So they were politically conscious enough to realise the parallel with their own school. Some of the older ones had already tried to lead the others to understand the dangers of disunity and so readily grasped what Aylwin had to say on the matter: "You can't expect people to listen to what you have to say about big things until you first get them to cooperate over small things." He put it to them as a question of leadership.

The northwesterners were more of a problem. "It was more difficult for us to speak the same language," Aylwin stated, recalling the formative period of the school. "They were closer with their thoughts, and referred everything to a set of social standards that I didn't properly understand. They were very polite, but less prone to accept ideas from an outsider, especially a foreigner. And of course they were very sensitive on matters concerning class or education."

"The northeastern students are very proud," one of them would say. "They look down on us because we come from poor homes. But if their own families hadn't been short of cash, they would have gone to middle school instead of coming here." It seemed to be just a matter of their lacking self-confidence.

Aylwin suggested:

> Those northeasterners look very proud to you. Actually they are homesick. They think that everybody here is against them. You should help make them feel at home. Anyhow, the school is run for people like you mostly, not for them. It's true that if their homes had had more funds they would have gone to middle school instead of coming here, and many would still go now if they had the chance. But later on, if we can build the school up properly, they will sooner come here than to any middle school.

Finally, it all got straightened out. The northeasterners developed their relationships with less pride and more politeness. The local boys became less defensive and opened up. After a few weeks, a mixed group of northeasterners and northwesterners was sent away to Chengdu to learn about some new textile machinery. A great deal of self-confidence was restored also in those who did not go, as quite a large amount of money was spent on the trip. It gave them faith in the school as a going concern.

This was Aylwin's way of operating effectively as a headmaster: the psychological way, turning situations back onto the students so that everyone would learn from the errors of others and of themselves. Rewi had a different approach. "Most of those kids are subconsciously looking for parents," he said one day. "The best thing to do is to mother them until they look on the school and CIC as family. Then they will stick by, no matter what happens later on." This became known as Rewi's Mothering Method. Its approaches lay through treatment for scabies, malaria, sore eyes, and dysentery. It involved even expensive things like sulphanilamide tablets, cod liver oil, and sending boys to have their eyes tested in Xi'an. Although Aylwin didn't altogether agree with Rewi's Mothering Method, he certainly didn't begrudge the treatment aspect. "Most people thought we were crazy," said Aylwin, laughing, "but as far as I could see there was nothing crazier than paying for boys to be trained, and then letting them get unhealthy, or go away from the school with no particular sense of loyalty."

It was found that two of the boys needed to be circumcised, so a CIC doctor was called from Baoji. He arrived with two nurses and carried a black bag filled with cotton wool and sharp instruments. One of the boys became quite frightened and began to scream, despite the local anaesthetic. Made curious by the hullabaloo, a peasant peered through the window and rushed away waving his arms in great agitation. "The foreigners are castrating the students to make them fat!" he blurted excitedly. The school's reputation slumped in the neighbourhood until a smiling victim himself was able to reassure the local population that that was not exactly the case.

At that time, an American-born Chinese lady was in the region for a few days in search of local phenomena for her social science thesis. She was questioning one of the Gansu students whom she met on the path outside the school: "Could you tell me what those boys are being operated on for?"

"They are having their 'small sides' cut," said Wang Qing, "The Oaf", helpfully.

"Please tell me what 'small side' is," enquired the young lady in her best Chinese.

"Don't you understand what small side is? Why! Small side as opposed to big side, you know."

The young lady went away more mystified than ever, and Wang Qing went off to find Headmaster Hogg. He too was puzzled. "Why did you tell me she was Chinese? She certainly looks like one, but she can't be if she doesn't know what small side is!"

The little community gradually began to mould into a solid unit. Walking together, camping together in farmhouses, swimming together in new and exciting pools, sometimes going hungry together, and often marching until they were very hot and tired, arriving in a new place together, performing their songs in front of strange people, and inspecting many of the new co-ops which were all part of their CIC "family"; all this did something for the school. One time when returning from a trip over the Qin Ling Shan to Baoji, there was quite definitely a strong community spirit. Rounding a corner on the last stretch into Shuangshipu they caught sight of their own particular mountain with the school lying snugly beneath it. A spontaneous cheer went up which made them all feel very warm and proud of themselves. "From that day," Aylwin remembered, "I knew that we would make something of the school."

There was much more trouble from the staff than there was from the boys. Aylwin found that the Chinese, who recognised themselves to be careless of details and happy-go-lucky by nature, tended to overcompensate by putting too much emphasis on the forms of things adopted from the West. So, as regards teaching, any departure from usual educational practice could only be considered by the average schoolteacher as heretic and deplorable. Never could it be regarded as a possible new step forward. The educationalists' textbook had no mention of Bailie Schools, so how was one to proceed. This difficulty was magnified by the attitude of the local petty officials who looked askance at anything different. They sent round their spies to see if any dangerous thoughts were being disseminated.

Andy Braid, the bagpiping Scots Highlander lent to the school by the Friends' Ambulance Unit, and his interpreter, Zhou Xue Yu, were of a different breed. Andy Braid was a farmer, tap dancer, cost accountant, nurse, mechanic, philosopher, and truck driver to mention just a few of his attributes. However, what was even more impressive, even admirable, about the man, as far as the students were concerned, was that he could remove his front teeth! Andy came and conquered with his bagpipes. He had soon taught the younger boys to do a passable eightsome reel. He patched up various bodily ailments, taught health and hygiene, accountancy and all about truck engines. His day began at five o'clock, leading the boys down to swim in the river, and it finished with putting drops into their trachoma-sore eyes at eight thirty in the evening.

What was undoubtedly the crowning glory of the man was when someone was needed to castrate the school piglets. Andy rose to the situation by declaring, "I used to keep pigs myself in Scotland. I suppose Chinese pigs work the same. Let me do that." The enthusiasm of the boys, most of whom had previously imagined foreigners as good for nothing but sitting in motor cars and eating with forks, knew no bounds. "He comes to China," said one 13-year-old, beside himself with admiration, "he can't speak much Chinese, but he can castrate pigs!"

Zhou Xue Yu was the same sort. Besides interpreting for Andy, he took classes of his own, coached the basketball team, and acted as treasurer for the Consumers' Cooperative.

There was a nervous, unstable fellow called Ting Qi Seng. He was always getting carried away with some grand idea or other, and was badly ragged by the pupils, but he was good at his job: teaching machine drawing.

"My mother says I'm unbalanced, the students say I'm unbalanced, and even my brother denounces me publicly as a lunatic. Deep down, I don't know myself whether I'm not crazy," he confided. His father was a brass hat in the navy but had fallen on hard times and opium. His mother got addicted to mahjong, selling all the family belongings to pay her debts. Ting himself finished technical school by borrowing from friends. Now, two years later and still heavily in debt, he was doing his best to support mother and young brother on a schoolmaster's salary. He longed all the time to run away south to drive a truck, or up north to become a guerrilla – anywhere to get away from his responsibilities. "It's not fair that a young man of my age should be weighed down with so many problems," he cried in a fit of despair.

Andy was the one who would jolly Qi Seng along on such occasions. Andy would announce him over the microphone as "Wonder Ting, the playboy of Shuangshipu," and compliment him on his English rendering of "Rainbow on the River" claiming that it was "better than the gramophone record, really. Honestly!"

Many came and went. They were entirely of the same ilk, with a common attitude that could be summed up by the utterances of a 41-year-old teacher by the name of Kang: "The boys here are unruly. They don't understand correct school manners," he said.

"That's quite true," Aylwin would reply. "I hope Teacher Kang will do his best to help them do so."

"If they don't understand manners, then there is no point in our trying to teach them," declared the educationalist. "We need hardly be expected to sacrifice our own spiritual energy to that extent."

There was an educational conservatism, supposedly based on "Western practice", which fell very short of the mark.

Writing home on 23 August 1942, after mentioning the war in Europe and what it looked like from his standpoint, Aylwin went on to say:

> Meanwhile, my private front to produce workers who understand what they are working for, and work hard because they want to, is growing bigger. One thing about having a publicity man in charge of a school is that the school quickly gets a name. People are calling out for Bailie Schools in all parts of the country, stipulating "it must be like the Shuangshipu one!"
>
> Not much to read here. That's the worst aspect, so one has to get interested in one's job, or die of boredom.
>
> Andy Braid has got a terrific passion for cleaning things. He has worked himself into a frenzy of scrubbing activity in the kitchen. The chap who "does" for us is a bit sick at the moment. He just lies in bed and watches this unwonten energy. Meanwhile, Andy makes a mental list of all the things he's going to tell him to do as soon as he's better. So you see we are improving ourselves, not sinking into the mire, or going completely native, or anything horrible like that.
>
> There is a conscientious objector here who is going to conscientiously object about conscientious objection. He came out with the Friends Ambulance Unit, but thinks better of it now. Their whole position is quite false anyway. They are being made into a valiant band of war supporters, which riles some of them, and makes others feel very grand, according to the soundness of their mental outlook.
>
> Our students all used to take a shortcut across a farmer's field, which made the latter very angry. Then other people got the habit, so that when I stopped the boys going over, it was still just as bad for the farmer. Today I got the week's gang composed of any quarrelsome, disobedient, time-wasting, or otherwise guilty boys, and had them dig up

the whole path and erect a wall at either end. The farmer is terrifically impressed, and the boys who sweated to dig up the path will make jolly well sure that no one else goes over it!

We are building new classrooms and workshops at the school, and will have a regular number of forty students soon. The original idea was to send them out to co-ops within a year, but I have another plan in mind. It seems to me that, instead of being able to change their environment when they become co-op leaders and so on, these boys may not be strong enough and may instead be changed by their environment thereby wasting all the nontechnical part of their training in the school. So we are going to set up a sort of buffer state of co-ops and machine shops, experimental textile plants, transport routes, and everything run by the school, into which to send the students after graduation. They can stay in this semi-protected area for a year or so to improve technique and cooperative knowledge, and then go out into the big bad world when their little wings are stronger. You would like my school. It is great fun.

A month later:

Our school is going along in great style. Soon we shall have a real mechanical workshop of our own for the boys to learn in, with a lathe and all. There are many problems with a school here that nobody would ever think of ... tools are almost nonexistent, and the idea that every boy should have a set of carpentry or other tools of his own, as at St Georges', would be quite unthinkable. Materials, even wood, become scarcer and scarcer. Even paper for notebooks is scarce. One of the masters taught the boys how to make their own abaci out of a few bits of old wood, some bamboo, and the digits made by rolling up little wheels of mud and putting them in the sun to dry, so that problem was solved. Toothpaste is prohibitive, so we are using salt. Clothes we are making altogether ourselves: black canvas outside, padded with cotton. One short belted coat per boy and a pair of padded riding breeches. When we get our HF wool-spinning set running – we are just buying land for that down beside the river, where there is water power – we can knit woollen sweaters too.

We have learned a lot about what kind of boys to take, and how to get them living productively and creatively together. The majority at least must be working boys, some stolid peasant natives and some quicker city lads. We can't risk more than a ten percent ingredient of student class boys, however sad the post-war circumstances of these may be, because these have bad old habits: ragging masters, long-nailed attitudes towards working with their hands, and a sneaking admiration for the non-productive bureaucrat official who can sit on his office chair and hinder people. But we should have a small ingredient, as the worker boys learn a lot from them. Some of them are more socially conscious too and act as good leaders. We've got one now who was an absolute pest of haughty, un-cooperative ways for the first month, then made a complete switch over into being easily the best boy in the school. Now I'm going to send him to help found our new school up in Lanzhou. I hope to go up there myself in a few weeks. When I come back from Lanzhou I shall go east along the line to Luoyang, where our third school is. Then maybe next year to Chengdu where they are hoping to start a fourth one pretty soon. Within a couple of years we'll have a stream of new blood going out into the co-ops. They need it. The CIC itself, by which I mean the administrative body which is supposed to organise and promote cooperatives, looks more and more like breaking up. Politics and ambitious people who try to use its publicity to get a name for themselves, all the time taking a strictly anti-cooperative line toward the co-ops, which they never even visit but pester with red tape, are getting stronger and more destructive. So, our school, putting new life into the co-ops from below, will be a big factor in saving the movement if it can be saved.

Toward the end of 1942 one letter told a little of the devastating famine in Henan, which followed the floods of August when the Yellow River burst its banks:

The cost of food here has gone up three times in the past three months. They say there is a price control on tree roots in Henan, two shillings a pound at present rate of exchange. Nobody eats much else there just now, except people who live off taxes. But of course the roots are unobtainable at the price-control rate, and there is a big black market in tree roots! In some places where the tree bark and roots are all finished, the early green shoots of winter wheat have already been carefully dug up and boiled, thereby destroying all hope of a crop next year as well.

The famine was to continue for a very long time.

Chapter 22

Beginning of the End of Gung Ho

Aylwin was going all out to develop his school way beyond what the original dream had been. He had long before seen the signs of decline in the CIC. During the previous two years, when turning up at the Chongqing Headquarters or at the various regional headquarters he had been infuriated at the frequent evidence of corruption, infighting, and lethargy; so completely different from what was happening in the countryside where the peasants and refugees were making it all work. He foresaw the collapse of the organisation and believed that the only way for existing cooperatives to survive and develop was to ease up on the organisation of new cooperatives and concentrate on the supply of new, skilled blood. It was pointless to try to start new co-ops in Kuomintang areas, as they would be sabotaged as soon as they got off the ground. This had been the demise of so many co-ops so far. There were regions of tremendous success, particularly in the northwest where Kuomintang influence was at its weakest.

Rewi Alley had been getting too much fan mail. Someone in London had done a bronze statue of him. American magazines had made a feature story of "Alley, the Man". Aylwin wrote:

> In the cave we carved the text "He is altogether lovely" from a piece of pink paper. The odd letters that dropped out fell naturally into an un-repeatable rude epithet. Text and epithet were pinned up together over Rewi's bed one morning before he climbed out of his mosquito net.
>
> The awful thing was that he did not laugh. In fact, he actually sulked for two or three days on end, wouldn't speak to us, read the newspaper over breakfast, and went out for long walks on his own. One day we came back to find the text torn down, and "The Man Rewi" himself sitting, lost in thought as usual, before his typewriter. The real trouble, as he thereupon divulged, was not so much the text as news of an attempt to channel all American funds for Chinese Industrial Cooperatives through the central CIC office in Chongqing, and to use part of them to provide "rice money" for the officials there, whom all field workers and co-op members regarded as a bunch of useless bureaucrats. On the very day when we had put up the text, Rewi had wired in his resignation to Chongqing rather than put his name to the rice money scheme.
>
> Of course his resignation was refused, for the time being. This was the beginning of a long struggle, the basic issue of which was whether American funds subscribed,

by cooperators and believers in Chinese democracy, to the CIC should be used to strengthen centralised control, or whether these funds should be used to strengthen field work in the hopes that a federated people's co-op movement would eventually become strong enough to take over the centralised functions of planning, co-ordinating, and research.

The use of Western funds in a country still suffering from the hangover of a hundred years of Western imperialism involved all sorts of hidden dangers. To administer such funds direct to the field through an international body answerable to the contributors, instead of through the central CIC office in Chongqing, would cause a good deal of ill feeling. It would appear superficially to be an arbitrary, foreign-imposed system of parallel control. On the other hand, to pass these funds over to the men in the central office, who were in no sense elected from below, and who had in many cases worked actively against genuine cooperation, was still more unthinkable, for it entailed their being used to support this bureaucracy itself. The faith and sympathy of contributors abroad would be lost. The ordinary contributor's only wish was that funds should go simply to the places where they were most needed. Finally, with internal prices going up by ten percent or more per month, the value of all funds would have largely disappeared if and when they did penetrate the red tape and get into the field itself.

For nearly a year, Rewi Alley and the other diehard Gung Ho fighters resisted centralisation and continued to distribute international funds to the Chinese people. A storm blew up denouncing the aid of Indusco Inc, CIC's collecting agency in the United States, as imperialism, an insult to the Chinese race, a reversion to extra-territoriality, a step back in the process of Chinesification. This argument, hiding the real issue beneath apparently progressive war cries, carried a good deal of weight with the more woolly species of liberal-minded Chinese and American.

The support of the American people was absolutely essential to their progress and even to their survival at the time. Funds subscribed through Indusco Inc. in New York and forwarded through the International Committee in China kept work alive in front-line depots to which the bureaucrats refused help, provided for essential training and research, and at the same time discouraged predatory politicians from taking them over in view of the unfavourable publicity that would certainly result abroad. Yet every article in popular American magazines and newspapers seemed to fuel the fire in Chongqing. They were labelling the CIC as "un-Chinese". As far as Rewi Alley himself was concerned, it was unfortunate that American publicity had necessarily to be focused on some striking personality. Every mention of him as the central figure in CIC was like the kiss of death to his reputation in Chongqing government circles.

The attacks on CIC were so vicious that many of the movement's closest allies regarded the situation as hopeless. One of them wrote: "It is no longer an uphill fight. It is a knockout, and the best elements in CIC are practically finished. CIC will remain, only it will change its nature to something quite different."

The final blow came on 21 September 1942, in the form of a telegram from the Chinese Central Government informing Rewi Alley that he was no longer required on the governing council of CIC.

Writing in his typically optimistic manner to a close Chinese colleague, Rewi expressed a wish to be allowed to work quietly away in some corner or other, to hold things together and keep the Gung Ho idea alive: "The Chinese people are ready to make the movement a success, and we should betray our trust if we left it just because certain persons have managed to get themselves into power. This game of ours is being played in the interests of the most decent democratic thing in these parts, and it is worth playing to the end."

In another letter, this time to a fellow New Zealander, Rewi told of tremendous forces behind the conflict leading to his dismissal:

> I was thinking yesterday, looking down on the Yellow River from Lanzhou's bare loess hills, how like this river the Chinese people are. From those heights, it seemed that the river was still; a yellow placid bar. But you know what a tempestuous emotional thing it is, and that only when one crosses it on a sheepskin raft does one realise how quickly it runs, how hopeless it is to go against the current, and how only in some quiet backwater can one go upstream at all. At times it freezes over and lies like a white bar of silver between the desert hills. Beneath the ice, the water races along as madly as ever. There is nothing that is really static about this country. The Chinese are an emotional people .... The bureaucrat and saboteur can put up so many skilful arguments, and the field man is left knowing that none of these will work, though not always knowing what to say in reply. ... But there is a more cooperative day looming.

After Rewi pulled out of Shuangshipu on a truck for Chongqing, Aylwin wrote:

> He left me with the consciousness of two very piercing blue eyes and several crushed bones in my right hand. Maybe it was for want of a wife, maybe it was indigestion, or the fact that the coffee supply had finished, maybe it was an overdose of the sulphanilamide tablets which our New York office had sent out to cure my trachoma, maybe it was the fact that progress was slower now that the worst part of getting the school into shape was over. Anyway, during the following weeks the usefulness of existence in Shuangshipu seemed very doubtful. Why wasn't I at home firefighting, or somewhere over Germany in a bomber? What had Shuangshipu or the CIC got to do with the battles in North Africa, the Solomon Islands, or The Don, which were being fought at the time? I felt I simply must have an "old school tie" to wear.

Letters from Rewi didn't help. One read, "In case I don't come back, I appoint you as sole heir to the cave and all that is in it." Aylwin wrote:

Hardly encouraging stuff. I thought of all the files in his big black trunks. Maybe if he was going to be executed I could make a great biographer.

> After a while, letters started to arrive from America. The way they read gave a revived reason for existence. Friends of the CIC in America had been fighting their own battle, refusing the wishes of politicians for one main stream of aid to China in the

interest of bigger and better postwar business prospects. The faithful Indusco supporters insisted on staying independent.

Letters like this conferred a newer and more satisfying kind of tie than any of the "old school" brand. After reading them I could go out with a new sense of adventure to explore water power possibilities in the mountains for our new textile machinery; I could even happily sit down to the typewriter again, though the temperature in my room was well below freezing and the wind came bursting in through paper windows.

There were, in fact, stirrings on both sides of the Atlantic. From Britain, two members of the House of Lords and two members of the House of Commons, accompanied by a host of attachés and Chinese officials were to visit the CIC northwest headquarters in Baoji. Rewi Alley was still in Chongqing. Frantic phone calls, three in all, were put through to the Shuangshipu Bailie School from Baoji, urgently requesting the help of Aylwin and Andy for the occasion.

Andy was in a dour mood, working out all the answers to an old arithmetic textbook. "If they've come to China to see the war effort," he said, looking up sternly, "let them come here and see the school. I see no reason why we should flock around them in Baoji. The Chinese have a phrase for flattering high personages: 'patting the horse's backside'. In Scotland we call it something much ruder than that. I'm staying here."

Aylwin decided to go:

I went to Baoji. Not to pat any horse's bottom, but because I remembered how previous celebrated foreign guests had been rushed through Baoji in an attempt to keep them from seeing anything, and thought that an extra "high-nose" might help with the showmanship end.

The office when I arrived was buried thick in posters and slogans of international unity, banners with co-op names in English, sheets of statistics, and women asking what kind of cakes foreigners liked with their tea. Peter Townsend, Friends' Ambulance Unit member and Ocean Secretary since my departure for Shuangshipu, was busy typing twenty copies of every report he could lay his hands on, while Bob Newell, another FAU man attached to the technical section, drew maps showing everything that an MP should know about the cooperative movement in northwest China. People snatched meals when and where they could, or forgot to eat at all. Out on the streets the police and a conscripted band of helpers were busy sweeping the streets, covering unsightly buildings with sprigs of fir trees, flags, victory posters, and the catchy and inspiring inscription: Welcome, Lord Allwyn, Lord Teviot, Mr Scrymgeour-Wedderburn, and Mr J. J. Lawson to China!

Meanwhile the telephone wires and grapevine telegraphs were busy, and various disconcerting rumours began to come in. The provincial governor, or the provincial Kuomintang Party secretary, or maybe both, had telephoned Chongqing suggesting that the mission should not visit Baoji at all! Deep depression took over, but we worked doggedly on until a reply came from Chongqing – the mission must at all costs go to Baoji and be shown cooperatives! This threw us into a state of near hysteria.

The next shock came from the provincial government's representative in Baoji. He informed the Gung Ho secretary: "The mission may be shown one or two co-ops, but must on no account be allowed to see any co-op members as they might be too dirty. In fact, the provincial chairman says that we must allow as few people to be seen on the streets as possible. The people are too dirty. Our guests will have half an hour between lunch and catching the plane for Chengdu. Please arrange for your biggest co-op to receive them."

Hoping against hope, we kept this news from the sixty or more other co-ops who were preparing parades and welcomes over a radius of ten *li*. Meanwhile the government representatives hurried away to tear down the huts of straw and mud which the most recent wave of refugees, from the Henan famine areas, had built for themselves beside the railway line. The refugees, apparently too dirty for the lords to behold, wandered away homeless once more.

It was an odd remark to make: "I'm so fed up with this country." It was odd because it was uttered by a Chinese. It took a considerable amount of provocation for a Chinese to speak discouragingly about China to a foreigner. It took even more to make him say so in a train where he might be overheard. We were on our way to Xi'an to meet the great men. My companion continued, "I can forgive the ones who are down on us because they think co-ops are dangerous. We can combat those. But these well-educated men in public positions .... Many of them are returned students from English and American universities! They try to bury us under foreign-style speeches and feasts because they think we will appear ridiculous .... What are we to do with them! And they'll poison China's relations with Westerners before they are through: to them, all foreigners are fools and babes, believing everything they are told and seeing only what they are shown. How can they believe that people can so easily be fooled?"

We arrived in Xi'an at two in the morning. Huge posters and garlanded flags hung in the electric light over the station gate. Street sweepers were out in the bitter cold. A soft light glowed from one of the windows in the Xi'an guest house. Could it be Lord Allwyn, restless with indigestion pains after a day's enforced feasting? No doubt the refugees turned out of their huts beside the railway line in Baoji were lying awake too that night. "Fine if only the refugees and Lord Allwyn could get together somehow, eh?" Aylwin thought.

In the kitchen of the CIC office I finished off the week's typewriting by candlelight, and cycled up to the guest house next morning at dawn with a package of manuscript tucked away in my overcoat; nothing dangerous, no military information, no complaints, but just plain reports on northwest co-ops. But we couldn't afford to arouse suspicion by handing them over too openly.

The guard saluted. Swing doors were opened by boys in livery. I made my way upstairs to the rooms occupied by the mission's press followers, knocked on the door of the *Chicago Daily News*, and found Art Steele smoking in bed. After a struggle, Art remembered me from Hankou days when he and I had belonged to rival organisations.

"How's news, Art?"

"Why fair, you know, fair," Art replied laconically. "Yesterday we went to the front. It was a swell trip. There was liqueur brandy and plenty to eat on the special train. When we got to Tongguan, the paths going up to the front were all nicely swept. After some more drinks there was a mock battle, done by electricity from the control house. There were pink flashes for bombs and blue flashes for shell bursts. An officer explained the whole thing to us in Chinese while another officer wound the handle of a sound machine that explained the whole thing in English. Then we got back into the train. After we had gone, the Japanese shelled the mock battlefield."

"Did the lords enjoy it?"

"As far as I can see they are just plain tired more than anything else; no time even to digest their imitation foreign meals. But I haven't succeeded in talking to them since we left Chongqing. They have their own special part of planes, trains, and dinner tables."

I worked out a plan of campaign for the next day with Art, and caught the next train back to Baoji. But not before having crashed the best breakfast I'd had since Hankou in 1938. And not before having heard well-bred Englishmen discuss the weather in a way I'd not heard it discussed since Oxford in 1937.

Baoji was still in no mean state of agitation. Bob Newell, Quaker and pacifist, was poised over a banner reading "Exterminate all Japanese from the Pacific Area" as I walked into the room.

"Don't you think that a little strong?" he asked.

"It means *South* Pacific Area," explained the Chinese secretary from the desk where he was touching up a speech of welcome to be delivered by the local general.

It was a grand speech; more clichés per square foot than I would have believed possible. Peter Townsend made such a stirring translation from it that they translated the translation back into Chinese and gave that to the general to read instead of the original. Peter was so pleased! "Think how I'll feel when all that comes out," he crowed. But in the end he didn't get the chance to hear it. Next morning, at zero hour, looking much more like the genuine lord than either Allwyn or Teviot, Peter successfully commandeered a car in which to take the newspapermen for a surreptitious tour of Baoji while the others were at lunch.

Luncheon over, the big Douglas airplane was warming up on the airfield ready for take-off. The officials were tired but self-congratulatory on having got the mission successfully onto the airfield without letting them see more than one or two tiresome co-ops for more than a few minutes each.

Lawson, veteran Labour MP, took Bob Newell and me aside under the wing of the plane for a chat. "Is there any chance of you people being pushed down under?" he enquired, turning down a meaningful thumb. We edged further away from the official hawks. "Of course, we'd heard something of the sort before," he went on, "but it's easy to see for ourselves what you're up against after today's show."

"We aren't much to look at yet," I ventured. "That's what they feel bad about more than anything. You can't blame them for being sensitive in a way."

"I'm an old man," said Lawson. "I remember when I was a lad putting my nose against a little window of a grocery store in our town. Now that store has spread all over Britain. That's the co-ops. Smallness isn't anything to be afraid of, at first. My advice is this." He waddled away further out of earshot, moving with a tough miner's gait and sticking out the chin that had brought him to the top of his league and sent him back undefeated to the House of Commons for nearly twenty years. "Hang on now at all costs. It's the people that are coming out on top everywhere in this war. Our mission has been hustled around pretty much on this trip, but I can't say I haven't learned anything. They showed me what they said was a railway workers' union in Xi'an, but I could see it wasn't a real union. The men didn't dare speak to me. In one factory I asked a worker if he had anything to complain about. He said no. I told him he was a fool. I told him that, when I was a boy, I worked in a factory like that, and I had a hell of a lot to complain of. The interpreter wouldn't interpret that at first, but I made him put it over .... And then we did see the good airy workroom of your army blanket co-op. And we did notice the co-op members at the station there to meet us but turned away by the soldiers. Hang on, I say. I've got all your reports in my pocket and I'll be writing you up when I get back home."

There was plenty of time for conversation, as Peter's car with all the newspapermen had got utterly lost. I feigned complete ignorance of course. The officials were very angry and used all sorts of unkind words to minor officials, who were supposed to have been keeping watch over the newsmen. After forty minutes' waiting, Lord Allwyn was heard to remark to the Chinese in charge, "It's a shame to keep you and me waiting like this." Poor man, it was past his teatime.

Everybody climbed into the plane which then taxied down the runway leaving the newsmen behind. I thought agonisingly of what the Baoji officials would do to Peter when they found him with the missing men, and the disappointment of millions of readers when Art Steele and the rest, stranded in the inaccessible northwest, failed to produce the daily columns. Art was thinking the same thing, judging by the beads of terror on his face as the car snorted painfully up the hill onto the airfield plateau. Too late! The plane was already five hundred yards away and moving upwind. We waved handkerchiefs and yelled hopelessly. The car charged the plane like a mouse after an eagle. The eagle swept majestically forward but then veered to one side, was overtaken by the mouse and swallowed its collection of embarrassed worms. Art stopped mopping his brow for long enough to wave his handkerchief at the window as the plane swept past us again and took off.

Peter came back sitting on the spare wheel behind the car, trying to pretend he wasn't there. I said "Close thing, Peter!" as he hopped off, visibly shaken. "You might have been locked up for that. We've renounced extraterritorial rights, you know."

"Stop being silly, and let's go for a bath," he said, shrugging it all off.

Peter, under steam heat, was still full of the enthusiasm shown by his newsmen for the co-ops. "The battle is joining, old buddy," came floating over the top of the bathhouse's wooden partition.

"The battle is certainly joining, Peter."

"It's incredible to see that kind of preserved-fowl type in Baoji though, eh?"

"If you could see yourself straight from Oxford, you'd seem to be a pretty odd bird yourself probably!"

Peter stirred in the water. "God, yes; and Oxford seems strange from here too, doesn't it? Rugger, beer in silver tankards, honeyed muffins for tea, white flannels, and music in punts on the river. Bump suppers, champagne, bonfires of lavatory seats; mortar boarded pass Mods [Mods: short form for Honour Moderations which are a first set of examinations at Oxford University during the first part of some courses such as Greats], gowns flying out behind the bicycles of those on their way to old Brether's lectures on international relations, reading about the fall of Addis Ababa in front of the common room fire, surprised on learning that a Double Blue [The Blue is the highest sporting achievement at Oxford or Cambridge Universities and is awarded only to members of certain sports clubs who have competed for their university. Double Blue is achieved through gaining a Blue in two sports] is a necessary qualification for the best colonial posts, while two college game colours (squash racquets acceptable as one) will do for the Indian Civil Service. I suppose all that's a thing of the past, now."

Silence and steam. "This is a relief, isn't it?" I continued. "First bath I've had this winter."

"The conception of relief, as such, is obsolete," said Peter. "There must be productive relief or nothing, these days. Mere distribution of food or money is demoralising."

"But you can't have productive relief in a bath."

"When you've been in China as long as I have, my boy," said Peter, handing his towel to a muscular half-naked attendant, "you'll know more. Now rub my back," he added to the man. After a short silence but for the swish of the towel, he added, "My God, if you could see the black pellicles now rolling off my hips, you'd see what I mean by production!"

"The people are dirty, Peter."

"Yes. Thank God we're dirty. It's a comforting thought."

This was how Aylwin's book ended, showing great promise for the years to come. This was just the beginning.

Chapter 23

A New Start

Now they all felt a surge of energy. With so much encouragement and support from abroad, and being independent from Chongqing, there was hope again – a reason to drive forward. As the winter progressed, more refugees from the famine-ridden Henan Province came westward. On 10 March 1943, in a letter home, Aylwin wrote thus:

We have about a hundred and sixteen refugees here in the care of the school. Fourteen are boys – good lads, about fourteen to seventeen years old. The whole bunch we picked them from were equally needy, so we had to disregard all pitiful stories and just pick the brightest ones who will make the best co-op members later on. Then we have over a hundred refugee men who we are putting to work so that even when the refugee funds give out after a couple of months or so they will be self-supporting. Some are up in the mountains cutting and carrying timber. Some are stone masons for whom we bought tools and then put them to work to make the pounders which other refugees could use to pound out mud bricks, which other refugees could use to build houses, and so on. Then we sent fifteen up to reopen a disused lime kiln. Another twenty-five or so are digging a long water ditch that will harness water power for a new wool and cotton spinning mill by the river just below the school. What with all this, and only a few staff to run the refugees at the school, I haven't been able to get down to writing anything for the *Times Educational Supplement* as they have asked, or for anyone else. I hope to do so soon.

We just had a visit from a lot of "high-nosed" people from Chongqing: the head, and his deputy, of the Friends Ambulance Unit in China, relief authorities, and others. It was funny to see so many of them at once. One of them, a British Embassy man, brought a tin of cocoa which he kindly left behind in our house. We held a big meeting with our forty boys, and all the refugees. The boys were a terrific hit; they have invented a special game of their own, which consists of an imitation English speech by one boy, and a translation by another. It is really very funny – just a string of unintelligible noises delivered very solemnly, in a portentous after-dinner manner, which they have picked up from all the various English and American visitors who have been here. The visitors were really impressed at the free-and-easy atmosphere of the place, and the natural attitude of the boys toward foreigners. They said they had never seen anything like it in Chongqing or Chengdu, where all the regular missions and other schools are. So we are really doing something special, I believe.

I want a holiday and a wife, but these are really quite minor wants these days. I might so easily want rest from shell shock, another arm or leg, or a head, as so many millions of fellows like me need now.

On a quick visit to Xi'an in June 1943, Aylwin wrote the following letter:

It wasn't Smallbone but Zhang. It wasn't "Arden Grove" but the "Building of White Happiness" on North Great Street. One didn't look out of the window at Station Approach but at a road with a well beneath some trees, and a lot of children and rickshaw pullers keeping cool there. The temperature was 104°F in the shade. The drill had to be worked by a treadle. It didn't hurt very much or for very long owing to the magnificent state of my teeth which haven't been touched by anyone since Smallbone in Harpenden. This is no doubt owing to the number of rusks you gave me as a baby. I can't think of any other reason.

The first day I went to him with toothache, he couldn't tell where it was, and I couldn't say exactly. So I went out and found a magnificent ice cream shop. After several helpings, the tooth was aching very selectively, and I went back happily to tell him, to have him put a stop to it at once. But the door was locked, and he was off duty for the rest of the day, so I had to bear the very special toothache for the rest of the day *and* night. Now all is well, and I shall be going back to our school via Baoji tonight.

I suppose you cannot get ice cream in England these days. Here you can get anything if you have money, and nothing if you haven't. The gap between those who have and those who haven't is becoming bigger and bigger all the time in a rather terrible way.

I have a magnificent system for travel between Baoji and Shuangshipu. I just ride a bicycle to a village at the foot of the big mountain range and stop there for my breakfast until a truck comes along. Then I jump on the bike and hang onto the truck up to the top of the hill. It is quite safe as the hill is steep and so the truck goes very slowly. I have done this eight times now, and six times out of the eight, the driver was so surprised that he stopped the truck and suggested I put my bike on top and ride with him free to Shuangshipu.

One time when Aylwin had been in Baoji to plead and argue for cash funds, it was late by the time he achieved his goal, enforcing a late-night bicycle ride back to Shuangshipu when no motor vehicles were on the road. On a long downhill slope he glimpsed ahead of him a group of figures at the roadside. It was impossible to stop what with the speed and the slope, and suspecting it was bandits ahead he peddled even harder, yelling at the top of his booming voice. Crouching at the last moment, making himself smaller, he careered through the astonished group like a bat out of hell.

His letter continued:

The school is turning out quite well. Now we have been entrusted with some really important small-scale machinery, which can run off water wheels, but is so efficient that its product can compete with the city factory stuff: an HF wool-spinning card with mule of twenty-five spindles, an English machine designed by Harry Fitzpatrick, and an Indian Ghosh small cotton spinning set of three hundred spindles. We are to train the mechanics for this and at the same time our machine shop will copy the machinery. The co-ops all round will club together to buy sets of these machines and will invite our students out to show them how to run them. Just now we are building the houses and digging the waterways for these sets, which will start arriving soon. The refugees from the Henan famine area are doing a tremendous job: lime burning, timber felling and hauling, brick making, building, digging .... Everybody eats the vegetables produced by another group of refugees to whom we gave a vegetable patch, and supported through their first months.

It is all good fun! But somewhat wearing, owing to lots of incredibly stupid difficulties. I am in charge of the money! Can you imagine anyone less suitable? It certainly gives me a pain in the neck, and money is practically useless these days. Soon people will be using it to light fires with, as it is cheaper than firewood.

Now we want to start a similar school for agriculture and forestry, with the boys living together as one community with the mechanics and textile boys.

A month later:

We are just beginning to get the important machinery set up here now, and to get our boys back from Chengdu, where they have been learning to use it. It is quite a moment in the school's history.

It meant a lot to us in the early days to send all our best students away to Chengdu, just as we had got them somehow licked into shape, and to take new raw ones on. Now we have got the new ones trained up pretty well, and the old ones are coming back, so the school as a whole is feeling strong. It is developing more and more a spirit of its own, which is essential. We have managed to train up one or two teachers, after a great deal of trouble, who now feel themselves as part of the school. At first, teachers tended to remain only on sufferance because they couldn't get any other job that was handy. Being a foreigner, an Englishman naturally suspected of bullying, imperialism, or at least racial prejudice, I could never attempt to be stern with the teachers or haul them over the coals when they were slack. What they didn't do, Andy and I just had to do ourselves. In the end it is working out and we have got some real interest and real loyalty to the school. There are also two graduate students who teach the backward boys very well indeed. So we have got something that will soon hold together of itself, but to get outside support is a different matter.

The tall and handsome jack of all trades, Andy Braid, is soon going to get married. His fiancée is the Hawaiian-born Chinese girl who didn't know what "small sides" were, and at present teaches social science at West China Union University. She will then come and work for our women's department in Baoji. Andy, amongst all his other skills, is an experienced nurse. He runs the CIC clinic here besides keeping all our boys so fit that they are a legend all round the neighbourhood.

August's letter told of yet further expansion:

The school is growing fast. The other day, Rewi Alley brought seven boys over from the Luoyang Bailie School, which is in the famine area and has had to be closed down. There was nowhere for these newcomers to sleep as we were very full. Taking the bull by the horns, I say to myself that we may as well be really crowded if we are going to be crowded at all, and fetched along five more good boys from Baoji – three Henan refugees and two native Shaanxi boys.

Now we have got some good new staff, and everything is getting organised. I am hoping that in another month or so I can leave this place for a bit and go to see the Chengdu and Lanzhou schools. Just now, it is my turn on the roster to be in charge of daily living and discipline affairs. That means up before light, wash in the river, morning exercises, and so on – as much as possible living with the boys right through the day till evening. They are a good bunch. We keep them in good shape with plenty of exercise and deep breathings! Also some concentrated fish oil that Madame Sun Yat-sen got us from America.

It was at the beginning of August 1943 that publication of his book became a certainty. He had titled it *Yellow River Watch*, but it was published under the name *I See a New China*.

The other day a great contract arrived for my forthcoming masterpiece, *Yellow River Watch*, from Little, Brown & Co., one of the best publishers in America. Unfortunately all the meat has to be cut out, including all of chapter seven, so it is left pretty milky. This has been done by my own wish, as I think work is more important than writing about it, and I certainly would have to take a holiday, as it were, if all that came out. This is not the time and all that! Remember what I wrote to you about France once? Remember that the bubble is going to burst horribly one day, after all this inflation with milk. When it bursts, the milk will be very sour, and no mere toothbrush will wash out the splashes. It will smell for years. That is why it would be so much nicer if the meat could be left in to *Yellow River Watch*. It is to be published on or before January 31st, 1944. English publication is supposed to be arranged, as I expect you know.

It had been under strong protest that he had agreed to the drastic cuts, and he was never sure whether to agree had been the right thing to do. He promised himself that he would make up for the diluted nature in his next book, which he had already started writing.

Already in the summer of 1942, Rewi and Aylwin had discussed the almost inevitable move north or west to ride out the rest of the war, developing the school in readiness for liberation and reconstruction. It would be almost impossible to get the school with all its pupils and equipment north through the blockade to Yan'an, so moving west would be most likely. However, they decided to put it to Zhou Enlai. If he preferred them to go to Yan'an, so be it. They sent a message indicating that if they did not hear from Zhou Enlai, they would make preparations to move west when the time came.

One summer evening in 1943, a truck belonging to the Sino-British Science Cooperation Institute based in Chengdu pulled into Shuangshipu. While a broken spring on his truck was being mended, the director of the institute, Dr Joseph Needham, quickly crossed the river and found his way through the fields and eroded gullies to the wooden-fronted cave. Corn on the cob and honey with the local bread were for supper. They talked late into the night about the resources out westward. Needham was on his way out along the Silk Road to tackle some technical problems at the Yumen oilfields. Rewi could come along to see for himself what the Gansu panhandle, a narrow strip of mountain passes and semi-desert running between high plateau of Outer Mongolia and the Tibetan Massif of Qinghai, was like. Western Gansu was one of the great underdeveloped areas of China's northwest. About ten day's drive out beyond Lanzhou brought the expedition to Dunhuang, the site of 309 Buddhist cave temples in the midst of the Gobi, beyond the last fortress outpost at the end of the Great Wall of China, Jiayuguan. Worn-out engine bearings forced the travellers to stay near Dunhuang for about a month, which allowed them to explore the cave temples thoroughly. The cave walls are covered in wall paintings showing the life and culture of China beginning with the fourth century and ending with the twelfth. Some of the pictures can be described as modern symbolic art. Others look like design sheets from a fashion magazine. There are pictures of jousting tournaments exactly like those in mediaeval Europe. There is also a Nestorian cross and a picture that looks like the Last Supper. On the return journey, they stopped at Shandan, one of a string of oasis towns at the narrowest part of the panhandle at an altitude of over fifteen hundred metres and with a long and illustrious history. In times gone by, the population of Shandan County had been as much as 240 thousand. In the 1940s, the population was a mere 90 thousand. Rewi was attracted to the place with its plentiful resources and got the idea of Shandan as a possible location for the Bailie School in the event of necessary evacuation from Shuangshipu.

On 12 November 1943 Aylwin wrote:

> The school is really getting on its feet now, and people are asking for our students all over the place. Maybe we will be able to send some to America soon. The business side still gives me a pain in the neck, but for the moment I have to manage – not only the school, but the setting up of various outside productive plants too. The refugees have discovered a new coalmine, and this is turning out well. We have just made a big cart with motor-truck wheels and pneumatic tyres. We haven't got enough money to buy mules yet, so for the moment we have to use horses belonging to the "public manager". He also burns coal, mined by our refugees. In return, he allows all our students and staff to go and bathe in his baths with fresh water once a week. This kind of friendly agreement, a personal arrangement, is still the only way of getting things done here, private or public.

This week I went on top of a truck seventy kilometres north of here, where grain and things are cheaper. I took one hundred thousand dollars with me and had a good time buying up supplies for the school, with the help of one of our older boys who is a native of the place, Wang Qing, "The Oaf", who was one of the students sent to Chengdu to learn to operate the new machinery. He has just come back full of savoir faire, and still quite unspoiled. He knows a lot and can stand up for himself, reads a lot, but at the same time is in perfect sympathy and contact with his own peasant people. This is a great thing. In fact it is real success as far as we are concerned. So I was very happy after we two had a long talk one morning there. His remarks are absolutely classic and will make good material for the next book.

On his return to Shuangshipu following the long-planned spell of travelling and inspecting, Aylwin wrote home:

The boys' classwork and practical work have come on amazingly in my three-month absence. Some of them, who were still farmers' boys until a year or eighteen months ago, can now draw intricate machinery straight from the machines themselves, and what is more, they do it better than upper technical school boys with nine or ten years schooling behind them. Ting, the unsettled young man who always wanted to run off somewhere, is now a first-rate Bailie teacher, with a heart for the job and an incredible success in teaching machine drawing to so-called "half-witted" peasant boys, to his credit. I hope we can send him to the States with a gang of boys one day, as he is the quickest picker-up of things and best explainer of things I know. He has the educational background necessary, but has the brains and rare humour and love of simple people to stand out against all the usual "foreign-returned" student mentality. Our teachers, from looking on the school as a weird place where they might as well eat until they can find a better rice bowl somewhere else, now take a real pride in the job and seem to understand that they are part of a big worthwhile experiment. Outside, local opinion has changed too, largely as a result of the sheer physical impact of the Bailie boys on the town. Maybe this was most noticeable in February when Rewi put them all into shorts, shirts, and caps and led them off to work on digging the Ghosh water race. But it began even earlier, when surprised early risers reported having seen gangs of crazy boys rushing into the river at half past five in the morning.

English classes are coming along well. In a test on ten sentences such as "I make cloth, you make clothes", "He uses a hammer and forge to make nails", "Who is he?", "Where is he going?", "What do you learn at school?", "Is that truck broken?", "Yes, can you fix it?" and so on, they scored seventy to eighty percent mostly, only two below sixty percent. In holiday classes I sometimes get them to ask each other questions, and the tone of conversation, so to speak, drops. For example, "How many wives have you?", "Is his girlfriend's neck clean?", "What did you eat for dinner?", "You smell bad", "You are a bad egg", and so on *ad infinitum*.

Lao San has lost his two front teeth and looks rather intriguing as a result. Lao Si gets rounder and redder every day, until we won't quite know if it's right that he should be so chubby. Is there a limit to chubbiness? They are both in the garden now helping put up a fence for the tomatoes. Lao Si has just found a very big bean and brings it to me for inspection, suggesting that we buy some meat and fry them together for lunch. His greatest object in life is to reach greater rotundity.

On 23 July 1944 Aylwin wrote:

I have just woken up Lao Si from his afternoon nap, washed his face, spanked his bottom, and sent him out to get an appetite for supper. I told him he did nothing but eat and sleep and that he was becoming such a fat little pig we'd have to chop him into shreds and fry him. Unfortunately he took it literally and was rather unhappy for a time. They are a good family. Today Lao San has malaria. I don't know if he gave it to me first or *vice versa*. Anyway, we jointly politely blame it on the mosquito. At lunchtime the two elder brothers came rushing in here from school waving a letter from their father – the first in over a year. Lao Si can't remember his father at all, Lao San hardly, except that mother used to spank him when father was out, which was quite a point in father's favour. It will be a good family reunion one day. Rewi and I hope we'll be in on it. Rewi has taught Lao Si a very high-sounding speech, delivered in the professional patriotic wartime speech-making screech: "*Jin tian wo men de jia zu yao chi rou.*" (Today we will eat meat.) "*Ming tian wo men de jia zu yao chi rou.*" (Tomorrow we will eat meat.) "*Hou tian wo men de jia zu yao chi rou.*"(The day after tomorrow we will eat meat.) It has just about as much form and thought in it as the average speech to which youth by the million is daily being subjected for hours by the million. But strangely, our Lao Si delivers this speech with the maximum of sincerity and hope, for such is his present aim in life.

It's so good of you and Barb to find me these wives. Don't quite know when I shall be able to come and fetch them away. How about my four sons? But, of course, maybe by that time they can go back to their original father. They are a unique quartet as a matter of fact, especially Lao Si. You would be absolutely unable to contain your grandmotherly instincts on first sight and forever more. The only thing is he wets his bed. What to do about that? Put his nose in it? Yesterday I made him hold his hand on the wet patch in the attitude of a man being sworn in on the witness stand, and make a short speech on contrition and resolution. Then he had to take his sheet down to the river and wash it. Which wasn't bad considering he is only five and rather backward in all except eating, at that. He can wash his clothes, too. I believe I learned to wash clothes at the age of seven, when you took me to Exmouth and you taught me this as a parting motherly act before I went off to school in Switzerland. Another problem is that Lao Si gets all the attention from visitors. There is simply no rule or unwritten convention in China about personal remarks. In fact the most blatant personal remarks, even to grown-ups, are considered quite the thing. This makes Lao San unconsciously jealous, so that he spends a lot of time telling Lao Si, "You're just a fat little pig. You can't do anything but eat and sleep!" Or, "You're all too small except where you're too big; and that's your head and your stomach." And so on, after the guests have departed.

Someone from Chongqing sent me a cutting from the *Central News Bulletin* – a wire from Boston, Massachusetts – "A new George Hogg book has been published by Little, Brown & Co. George Hogg, an Englishman ...." So there we are. There is the new China that we are rather doubtful about seeing. There is Ida Pruitt called timid for the first time in her life, and George dubbed forever more as a compromiser, or not? Anyway, it is really highly gratifying to have published a book in any form, isn't it? I am more grateful than words can say to Ida Pruitt for all the sweat and tears if not blood that she has spent to bring the book about, and to Peg Snow for all the help and inspiration without which the book could never have been published.

Chapter 24

Apple Trees, Goats, and Conscripts

In a letter home dated 11 September 1944, Aylwin wrote:

> Your war seems to be nearly over, but we have a sort of feeling that a lot of things are going to happen to us, and to other people, before this war is over. The Japanese may want to grab another big slice off China as they get beaten in the Pacific, and use this part of China as a buffer area to protect their real economic base in north China and Manchuria. If so, we may have an exciting time soon.
>
> Eating is good these days. Tomatoes in the garden are still going strong. Corned beef presented by Embassy friends still unfinished. Waffle machine just bought from a retiring missionary went into action today, using whites of eggs separately beaten as leavening agent. Potatoes are in season, and bean milk always a good standby, honey from the Tibetan border district very pure and white – much better than the local brand, which is largely adulterated with malt. Lao Si getting so fat he can hardly walk. Lao San more than holding his own against his various constitutional enemies. "Eat up," says Rewi, "we probably shan't be here much longer."
>
> He isn't exactly a pessimist, but he is taking a very firmly prophetic view that the Japanese are coming, and soon. Consequently my peace of mind is constantly being disturbed by such remarks as "don't forget the apple trees when you go, George; they have to be taken up carefully, roots wrapped in straw," and so forth. Or, "I wonder how the goats will stand the trip?" The trouble is we have about fifteen tons of essential machinery apart from other things, and no trucks - only two carts and not enough mules to go round. So I sometimes feel like bashing him. But of course it wouldn't do any good. His mind just works that way - in a sort of continuous nonstop stream of ideas which are seized upon and brought to the surface in a very loosely associative way. This is really a very useful kind of mind to have, as in thinking over one problem it brings up everything remotely connected, often vital details; things that ordinary people wouldn't think of, and so overlook. It is also a very accommodating mind; when it hits a rock, like "no trucks", it flows all around it and goes on to apple trees and goats. Meanwhile it would appear to have forgotten all about the rock, but actually, or I hope anyway, it is still setting about the rock with a swirling undertow like that on the beach at Newquay,

and will eventually spring a surprise on you, such as, "We don't need trucks anyway. I've got six army transport planes coming along tomorrow." So there's Rewi; he's just gone out to look at his teasels now. They are a sort of American burr with very spiky spikes, strong enough to be used to bring up the nap on woollen fabrics, blankets, and suchlike.

It isn't necessary to stir far beyond the mouth of our cave to get a fair slant on conscript life. During the hot summer months, an old moss-covered coffin is carried past our door out onto the mountainside several times a week with a fresh, or sometimes not-so-fresh, conscript in it each time. Our dog would come home very red of eye and shameful of tail until one day it died of a nameless disease. Long lines of white-eyed, taut-skinned yellow ghosts piled with firewood and other things for sale would stagger down from the Hanzhong direction of an evening, be marshalled at bayonet point down to the river, and then locked up for the night in a barn. Often one or two would be discovered by the river the next morning, dead or near dead, stripped of their clothing. The coffin would then be brought and its contents for the occasion dumped out behind our cave. Ting Qi Seng and three boys turned up at school very excited one day: "Aiya! The Baoji road is streaming with dead conscripts. Really frightening! We covered our faces with our hands, didn't dare breathe. Last night on our way up to the Ghosh quite a lot of them were alive, but this morning they're all dead." Just across the bridge, I passed a near-skeleton lying on the crest of the road in full scorching sunlight. His pack was still on his back, and a bamboo tube for water hung from a string on his neck. The skin was stretched tight across his high cheekbones and hooked Sichuan nose. Mouth gasping, white eyes rolling; nobody took any notice.

"Been there since last night," said a small boy whom I asked. "On his way down to the river, I expect. That's where most of them like to die." The flies buzzed with early morning energy around his head, crawled over the dysenteric discharge from one pant leg. I walked on, same as everybody else, but just around the corner bumped into the doctor from the Public Health Administration Bureau.

"What are all these soldiers dying of?" I asked, walking back with him. "There's one just round the corner here, and a lot more up on the Baoji road."

"Just starvation, Mr Ho," said the doctor. "I myself have seen five this morning." As we looked at the Sichuanese lying in the road, a few other "gentlemen of the bureau" strolled up.

"Are you going to take him to the hospital?" asked one.

"How can I?" replied the doctor. "We are not supposed to do anything about soldiers. We are for civilians."

"Of course, of course." The man quickly covered any impression of having suggested that something should be done. The doctor and I went to get some water. Immediately she realised to whom I was going to give it, the Henan refugee woman from whom I had borrowed a bowl snatched it away and ran off. But her husband thought differently. "I'll get you a bowl," he said, and went back into their hut for an old one.

"The Disabled Soldiers' Station ought to look after these cases," remarked the doctor.

"Where is it?" I asked.

"The stationmaster lives in that hotel opposite." I remembered then that this hotel had been built with free conscript labour and sold at great profit by the stationmaster who reserved a room for himself in one corner.

"Let's go and call on him," said I.

"No, it wouldn't do for me to suggest anything," said the doctor. "The thing to do is for us to go and call on the local government together." The head of the local government was out. We sat upstairs in his airy office and while waiting we chatted about public health work.

"I must leave Shuangshipu soon," said the good doctor. "It's getting too difficult. I'm supposed to stay on duty in the hospital all day, but the officials and their wives send their servants for me, and I have to go out to them. If I don't go, it is a personal affront, and I have then made an enemy in some bureau or other. There are so many official bureaux in this place, and with the evacuation of Henan there has been great influx of wives, most of whom seem to be in an advanced state of pregnancy. Last week I was called out to eight deliveries."

"Don't you have a midwife?"

"No, we don't have the funds. I've applied for an increase in our budget to cover a midwife's salary, but the process is very slow. Official documents dealing with rice allowances for staff have to be sent first to our Chongqing headquarters, from whence they are sent on the Executive Yuan, which forwards them to the Grain Department. After being approved by the Grain Department, they are sent to the Ministry of Finance, and from there to the National Treasury. The National Treasury then sends us another official document asking us for details. It is rather complicated, and we hope for action within six months." At that moment the head of the local government came in - a fat man in his underclothes, fanning himself and sweating. We sat down to sip tea while the doctor explained the situation: "... and so for the sake of our own moral feelings, for the sake of our country, and for the sake of humanity," he wound up, "Mr Ho and I thought that something might be done, and we came to ask your help."

The sweaty head of local government picked his teeth. From his expression you would have thought he didn't know what a conscript was. Suddenly he threw away his toothpick. "I was wondering where he had got to," he said. "Last night they made me certify fifteen dead, but this morning I could only find fourteen altogether, dead and alive. I've got them all marked and counted. Last night they were all alive but two; this morning there are seven dead out of fourteen. The rest are all up on the Baoji road. That's why I missed yours down by the bridge. It is really unbearable, but what can we do? We are only the local government after all. We can't move where the army is concerned."

"We thought if you would approach the stationmaster of the Disabled Soldiers' place," I ventured.

"No good. I've already tried. He says he deals only with soldiers coming from the front, not soldiers going to the front. The fact is, there's nobody appointed to do this job. The people up above haven't an official department to deal with the matter, so they don't know anything about it and it's no use trying to tell them. Nobody down below has received a document authorising him to act, so whoever does anything is doing it out of his private pocket at his private risk, and likely to be accused later of stepping on other people's rice bowls. It's a matter of responsibility."

"If you could get a room somewhere and put all the sick ones together," suggested the doctor, "I'll be glad to come and treat them, and if there is any expense involved, Hr Ho and I will meet it together. How does that sound?"

"Good, that's quite easy," said the head of local government, "but we don't need any money for food at least. We've had "the hundred names" [the idiomatic expression for the common people] out offering them rice gruel, and they can't even swallow that. Yes, I'll send out and have them concentrated at once." We sat back to talk and drink more tea until the report should come in from the local government underlings.

"You know," said the now-not-so-sweating head of local government, "we buried a hundred and fifteen of them here last summer. The trouble is no food. Each man is allowed one and a half catties of flour a day, but he's lucky if he sees one catty." "What about the rest?"

He shrugged his shoulders.

"Yes, and they load them up with merchandise and stuff," said the doctor. "Of course, being starved and having to carry heavy loads all the way from Sichuan, they get physically run down. Then they pick up some germ – dysentery, malaria, typhoid, kala-azar, dengue, anything – and that's it for them. There is a medical allowance of so much per head, but they never get to know anything about that."

"Why should they send Sichuanese soldiers up here, anyway?" I asked. "The climate and food are all against them."

"Of course it's not the same abroad, so you wouldn't know," it was explained. "In our China, the northern soldiers are sent to the south and the southern soldiers are sent to the north. It is supposed to stop them running away. As for starvation, an officer in charge of a company of soldiers was complaining to me the other day about the amount of sickness among his charges. I asked why he didn't feed them better. He told me I didn't know much about conscripts. If they are fed better, they'd get frisky and start running away. I told him that the opposite must be true. If they were fed better there would be no reason to run away and become beggars. The more they are not fed, the more they want to run away. He laughed at me, but it's true. The people up above never see what's going on below, or they would arrange things better. They are too far off from us down-belows. That's the real trouble."

"Speaking from a purely medical point of view," said the doctor, "those men are beaten to death more than anything else. It doesn't matter if they are sick or tired, they are just forced to keep on walking, and if they don't walk, they are beaten until they drop. I've seen it happen many a time."

"In the army," the local official went on, "conscripts are just so many items to be delivered to a certain place at a certain time. Condition is of no concern. Take accommodation for instance; that's something I know about first hand. The officer in charge always asks me for a room with no window. After supper, the conscripts are ordered out to relieve themselves. Then they are packed into the room without a window so tightly that they maybe have to sleep lying on top of each other on the floor. The guard stands at the door with his rifle, and nobody is allowed out. No matter if it's dysentery or if you want to urinate, you can't get out of that door, so you have to do it on the floor. But there's no room on the floor because everybody's packed in there so tightly. You can imagine what it is like in there on the hot nights we've been having lately. Of course it's very bad for the eyes," he concluded on a medical note, in deference to the doctor. "No wonder so many of them go blind."

"How do they get fed?" I asked. "Is that your responsibility or the army's?"

"Ah, I can tell you about that most clearly. The officer in charge of the conscripts carries with him an official document stating how many men he has and what allowance per head of flour, cooking oil, and vegetables should be given. The local government is asked to provide this from the contributions of the 'old hundred names'. But recently a new order has been issued stating that 'In order to relieve the burden on the people, the cost of grain, oil, and vegetables shall be worked out on the basis of local market prices and delivered to the conscription officer in cash.' This makes things much worse for the conscripts. In the old way, at least it was rather inconvenient for the officer in charge to sell what provisions he saved, but new payments are all in cash so he can keep what he doesn't spend right in his pocket."

"Suppose men die or run away. Do the officers still keep on drawing for the same number of men?"

"If they are given a thousand men in Sichuan, it states a thousand on their documents, and we can't go investigating; they just draw for their thousand men. The difficulty comes for them when they get to Xi'an. There they must hand in eight hundred and fifty men out of every thousand – an allowance of a hundred and fifty for dead and runaways – or pay a fine of so much per head. That is why, when they get near the end of the journey, they flog even ones who are half dead to drive them along, so as to fill the quota. If they are too far below numbers, they begin to impress. That's a lot of fun! The other day they impressed an official from our county government who had been out investigating something in the country. He showed his credentials, but it didn't make any difference. They just tore off his badges and burned his papers. He had to walk all the way to Baoji carrying a sack of flour before the mistake was discovered. Of course, if he'd not been an official, there'd have been no hope for him unless he'd had some rich friends in Baoji."

"Are the conscripts passing through here all more or less the same?" I asked.

"Not at all," he admitted. "Didn't you see the gang that came through here from Gansu the other day? They were a fine lot. Not a sick one among them. They don't have so far to walk before getting here, as we are not far from the Gansu border. Besides, they are used to the climate. Maybe the Sichuan conscripts are all right too when they leave home. Maybe their families come and give them food and stuff to take with them. But all of that would be finished long before they even got out of Sichuan. You can see the Gansu men still carrying the great cartwheels of bread their wives gave them."

The report came in – eight concentrated, seven buried. The doctor went off to investigate. I met him several hours later on his way back. "The man we found near the bridge is dead," he said, "along with two more. There are four left now, but only two of those can possibly survive. Of these, one has TB and the other dysentery, but we may be able to save them with sulfathiazole."

"What, at two hundred and fifty dollars a tablet?"

"Yes, and we've only got a few hundred tablets left now. Our drug supplies haven't come through for a year."

A few weeks after this, I happened to be offered a ride on an empty military truck going to Baoji. At a place called Red Flower Village it stopped to pick up a lot of padded winter clothes that had been abandoned there by a gang of runaway conscript carriers. While the truck went off to pick up the clothes, I repaired to a house by the roadside to eat cornmeal soup with potatoes floating in it, and fresh hot bread cakes.

"Do you send conscripts from this village?" I asked.

"Yes, we sent eight the other day," the old woman told me.

"Once a year is it?"

"You never know when they will come for conscripts. They come when they come; several times a year. We haven't many young men left here now though. They took the last young man from the family next door to here, leaving only old folk and children. If our men come back, they are runaways, and we are held responsible."

"Did you see the bunch that dropped the bundles of clothes up the road there when they ran off?"

"Yes. They were from Sichuan. All very thin." By the time I had finished more than one bowl of soup, the truck came back, piled high with retrieved clothes on top of which I bounced comfortably all the way to Baoji. The news there was that the generalissimo had visited a conscript camp in Chongqing, shot the man in charge dead on the spot, and ordered several extra dishes for the conscripts' next meal by way of celebration. "If only there were a generalissimo in Shuangshipu," I thought, "and another in Red Flower Village, one on the mountain pass between Sichuan and Shaanxi, two or three in Baoji, and another on the conscript train to order the doors unlocked when the Japanese bombers come over. Then the conscripts in the northwest might get a fair break." But by the "issimo" nature of any "general-issimo", there can only be one of them, and what's more he can only be in one place at any time.

On his next trip to Lanzhou, Rewi went to visit the Commissioner of Reconstruction, an agronomist and native of Gansu called Zhang Xinyi, who was keen on Gansu taking a leading role in the reconstruction of the northwest. The situation in Shuangshipu was explained to Zhang, and the sense in moving to Gansu was made clear. Asking Rewi to where he would like to move the school, Zhang produced a map and pointed out a few suggestions. After brief consideration of these places situated within close call of Lanzhou, Rewi pointed to Shandan and asked "How about this little place, sixty kilometres east of Zhangye?" Rewi received a doubtful look. "It has coal, kaolin, plenty of houses, water; surely no one could do us any harm on that deserted plain between two such high mountain ranges. Most of it is uninhabited." Zhang smiled, agreed, and had a travel pass made out. Zhang was later offered the post of titular headmaster of the Shandan Bailie Technical School, which turned out to be a sound political move. In the early months of the Shandan School, after a banquet at the Shandan County magistrate's *yamen*, a local official came to visit and started ranting in an inebriated fashion that everyone believed the school was just a "bunch of red hats". It became clear that they must get Gung Ho's name and blessing in this project. The Gung Ho head office should plead with the Gansu provincial authority in Lanzhou for a more sympathetic magistrate in Shandan. Zhang Xinyi's first major contribution to smoothing political waves resulted in the old magistrate being retired back to Lintao from whence he had come.

Rewi, one evening in Shuangshipu, broke through Aylwin's typewriting. He was reading about Marco Polo's travels with the idea that it was a sort of Cook's guide to their forthcoming trip. "When you are marching through the desert sands at night, George," he said, "don't be afraid when you hear bells and gongs and weeping and gnashing. Everybody will say it is ghosts, but what it really is is the hot surface of the sands contracting in the cold at night; they make that noise when they are disturbed by people kicking up the surface."

"Thanks, Rewi. I'll remember, old boy."

Chapter 25

The Clinic

In a letter home Aylwin explains about his recurring bouts of malarial fever:

I've just found a scrap of paper that just says "Malaria – fascinating" on it. No date. But I know what it means. It is really fascinating when it is just coming; first, an ache in the finger joints and an inclination to eat more than usual. Then the first spinal shivers. I always feel particularly merry around this time – sort of adventurous; like waiting for some great friend on a railway station. "He'll be here in just three and a half minutes. There's nothing I can do to stop him coming or hurry his coming. I can see the train in the distance, coming down the hill by the Bluebell Woods. And when he comes everything will be quite different." Once I was down at the machine shop when it came – a boiling hot summer's day, and they were smelting iron. I stood as close to the furnace as I could get, with the sun on my back, and I was cold! But of course when it's really got going there's nothing fascinating any more. That's when one begins to feel homesick with dark thoughts such as: "China's not really much of a place. After all, I've been here seven years now anyway. It's been very interesting, but I can't hope to do anything. They never really trust us."

I can't remember much more about that slip of paper, but have just remembered writing some notes in pencil on my bed boards, so will take the typewriter over there. Yes, the notes are still there, but rather rubbed out. As far as I can read:

Sick
Milk
Shredded wheat on Sunday evenings
Cold water
Choc-ices
Reading in front of the radio, going out afterwards to rugger or tennis
Eclipse of the moon as seen from Mother's bedroom window
Never come back to China again
Better
Would be funny to take some of these kids back home

Wonder what they'd think when they got inside a real big factory there
Wonder how they would take to rugger
Wonder how it'll feel playing rugger again
Will I be fit? How old was gaffer Bond when he used to play for Harpenden against school, anyway?

Quite better

Perhaps there's no need to be going home for a while yet!

You mustn't get the idea that I am malaria-ridden. I only have it about once a year, and can always stop it pretty quick. It is of the every-other-day variety, which gives one time to recuperate and counter attack. The clinic is now in our back cave. Theoretically we see people during the lunch hour only, but quite a lot of peasants' kids, old half-starved refugee women, children, and suchlike turn up at odd times causing confusion. Yesterday was Sunday, and poor Rewi didn't get a rest all day. First to come was the little shepherd kid who goes past our cave with eleven sheep every morning and evening. His name is Wu See, and he looks like an adenoidal anthropological ape, wears one of Andy's old jackets as an overcoat, grinning as he stutters and stammers all the time. Well, he walked in with a basket of eight eggs, intimating by various anthropoid swings and bat-like motions of the arms, combined with a more than usually expansive grin, that this was a piece of largesse on his part. "You really mustn't," says I. "Take them home to your old mother." "Don't be so polite, Mr Ho, they are for your dinner." And so on. Finally I took the eggs to get rid of him and turned back to the book I was reading. But the door opened again almost as soon as it had shut, and in walks Wu See with a smaller edition: "This is my brother," he says. "He's got a great hole up between his legs and he can't walk." The motive behind the eggs being thus painfully clear, there seemed naught else to do but to tell him to pull his pants down. The pants were sure enough covered with pus and blood. "My God," said Rewi, and turned back to his typewriter. So I guessed it was my turn.

I got back at him later by going out as I caught sight of three scabies and syphilitics walking in at the gate. Wu See and I bathed the boil for some time in permanganate of potash solution, Wu See scornfully telling his brother not to be such a "c-c-c-cry b-b-b-baby" the while. Wu See then took out the pants and wiped them off on our doorstep. "Quite cl-cl-cl-clean now", he said, mightily grinning, and handing them to his brother. "Now how about those eggs," I said at last, pressing them back. A fight of greatest politeness ensued, and Wu See won. I wasn't very wholehearted anyway as we wanted some eggs for waffles. In the end, two turned out to be addled.

So passed the Sabbath morn; I had been up at five and over to school to finish the chores before coming home to rest. "When'll you be back?" called Rewi, as he saw me sneaking out of the gate leaving him to the scabrous and syphilitic three. "Probably next month," I replied and snooped down to a room next to the school dorm for a quiet snooze. A good bed with a quilt on it and a coverlet over my head; how warm, how snoozy! This really is Sunday after all! But just at that moment came unmistakable sounds of Ma Jen Seng, the smallest and most problematic boy in the school, engaged in a high-pitched swearing competition of frightful intensity with Zhang Tian Zai, who might have come straight off the toughest of tough streets in Chicago. I yelled for them, and there was abrupt silence. Then the door opened and two no doubt angel-faced boys crept in, weeping crocodile tears of contriteness. They were foxed, however, because I didn't even take the sheet off my head to see their pitiful "please-forgive-me" expressions. "If you want to swear, please go far away somewhere else as I want to go to sleep," says I. I don't know if this was quite orthodox or moral or character building, but they went, and so did I – to sleep.

Before leaving the clinic, let me introduce you to our water carrier, Lu Keng. He is a refugee from Henan – quite a young fellow, puckish face, turned-up nose, twinkling eyes that seem, now I think of them, as blue, but they can't be of course. He loves singing Henan folk songs about such things as the sun coming out like a red melon, and so fast it seems like it's moving in jerks, and you sit by the plough watching your wife coming up the road with your breakfast, and what you do to your wife (rather crude), and how the food tastes, and how you send your wife home telling her to come back at lunch time but to leave the children at home.

Well, Lu Keng sent us quite a lot of patients to the clinic. I don't mean polite introductions from a grateful patient or anything of that sort. Under certain circumstances Lu Keng suddenly turned from a twinkling boy-blue into a ferocious sort of animal. He would snatch up a stick or a carrying pole or a bit of firewood or the kitchen knife and rush at people. What people? Just any people? Well no. I must allow that the preconditions for his attacks were quite simple and determinable. In fact, really only one quite simple thing was needed to turn him into a raging animal compared to the she-wolf protecting its young – and that was that anybody should have unlawful designs on the child of his sweat; namely, the water in the butt. Since Lu Keng himself didn't really believe in washing much, "unlawful" was often defined by him to mean washing with water. Anybody appearing near the kitchen with a washbowl had to make jolly sure that Lu Keng was out before dipping the bowl. Or else there would be a fearful roar, a clang as Lu Keng's weapon for the occasion struck the uplifted washbowl shield, and a clatter as the shield dropped to the ground and the would-be washer rushed away. We warned Lu a lot of times, but it didn't do much good. And people liked him on the whole and were apt to forgive, especially people who didn't think much of washing anyway.

A few days ago, Lu Keng turned up with a huge boil on his eyelid. Bob Newell was in charge, and Bob is very jealous of his time, though a painstaking nurse. Now Bob had been taken away from his grey iron [cast iron] foundry plans and ruminations many and oft by pathetic victims of Lu Keng's anti-washing fury, so he had a score against him. "So you are Lu Keng?" he said with rather an unpleasant look in his eye, I thought. "I think perhaps what is needed is something hot to bring the poisonous matter to the surface. Ah yes! I have the very idea! A piece of hot-pepper cut up small and applied to the affected eyelid!" Lu Keng looked askance but sat down obediently to wait. A few minutes later he was walking away as sadly as any of the patients he had sent us, but still trustfully feeling that the foreign doctor had done the very best thing for him. Such is white man's prestige. But it didn't last through that night. After twelve hours of agony Lu Keng groped his way down town to the local horse doctor.

Signs of rain bring a different sort of gleam into Lu Keng's eye. At the first drops, he rushes to collect all available pots and pans, arranging them carefully under the eaves to catch everything – leaves, bird-droppings, dead rats, old sandals, etc., that come down with the first torrent. Then he retires happily to the kitchen, reaches up for his one-stringed Chinese violin, and settles back happily for an old-time number.

A long time ago, Lu Keng worked as an apprentice in a glue sweatshop. One day the master came to him when he was by himself behind a bush where he had just finished relieving himself. "Keng," said the master, "you are a good man. If you work extra hard, I shall be able to give you an extra pair of shoes at the end of the year, and maybe a shirt too. But don't tell any of the others." Lu Keng went back very proud that the master had taken notice of his good work, and slaved away for the next six months. Just before New Year's Day, the master ran away with all the money and was never heard of again. The house and all the equipment belonged to somebody else anyway, so the apprentice couldn't get any of that. The funny thing was that, when they started talking to each other about the master, it came out that he had secretly approached every one of them with the same promise of extra fine rewards if they only kept up their good work.

I have just come upon a very professional temperature chart. The line goes sharply up and down between 104°F and 106°F from the fourth to the thirteenth day and comes down beautifully on the fourteenth; a perfect typhus chart. Notes on the case say:

(1) Rash on the arms ninth day. Muscles hurt.
(2) Gave one tablet sulpha-pyridine to prevent lung complications twelfth day.
(3) No motions of bowels after fourth day except after enemas given once every two days.
(4) Thirteenth day patient seems near collapse. Gave dose of coffee to stimulate heart; seems stronger; in evening gave enema.

Do I remember that thirteenth day! The boy on watch called us early. "Looks very bad," he said. And he was right. He looked absolutely finished. Zhou, our second textile technician, came round. He is from the same Henan town as Zhang Quei Yuan, the patient. Says Zhou: "This is not typhus at all. It is just a Chinese sickness called sheep's boils. All you have to do is to pick up pieces of the patient's flesh on a needle and cut it with a knife. Then he will get better at once. If you don't, he will certainly die."

Rewi would have none of it, and sent him away. Zhou went over to the school and got some of the teachers and boys around him. "It's just common old sheep's boils," he said. "I could cure it in a minute. Of course the foreigners don't have that in their country, so they don't know." By this time I was over at school, and one of the teachers came to me. "What about letting Lao Zhou have a go at Zhang Quei Yuan?" he said. Suppose it wouldn't do any harm, anyway. Mustn't leave any stone unturned at a time like this. It might be good psychologically anyway." So the teacher and I went over again to Rewi. "No," said Rewi firmly over the top of his spectacles. "No. Technician Zhou may be a very good weaver, but I won't have him mucking about here." That was that. Rewi even went so far in the heat of the moment as to suggest sacking Zhou from the school.

At eleven o'clock I was back again. Rewi had decided to go to Baoji. The baby, apparently breathing his near last, was mine. So was the trusteeship of the white man's prestige. What was I going to say if the guy died, and everybody half believed, or more than half believed, that he could have been saved with a needle and a couple of jabs with a penknife? It was hard to explain why we hadn't given him any medicine, too. "Typhus: there's no medicine yet invented, just careful nursing." That's all very well for a doctor with the BMA behind him or a Harley Street reputation, but rather weak coming from a lone non-medical foreigner in Shuangshipu; and to Chinese, who are apt to believe in nothing, that is not spectacular.

As a parting inspiration, Rewi suggested coffee. Having administered two spoonfuls, I went over to the school and called a mass meeting, including cook, gardener, etc. etc. Some people thought that the war situation had taken a turn for the worse. Others thought it was a funeral service for Zhang Quei Yuan. Actually it was a lecture on the history, causes, and cure of typhus, as stated in the Missionary's Medical Manual, with Zhang's temperature chart on the blackboard and a full account of all our nursing. There were gasps as the temperature chart went up on the board as a to-and-fro fight between two almost equal forces. The variations between top and bottom temperature for each day got bigger and bigger as the strength of both contestants weakened on the twelfth, thirteenth and fourteenth days. "Disease" pushed its way up, and then "resistance" made a comeback and floored "disease", only to exhaust his strength and give "disease" a chance to get up and push him back again. They had never seen it in that light before. The meeting ended, and everybody rushed out to take out their beds, exterminate mice, rats, etc. And the best of it all was that Zhang Quei Yuan had turned the corner while we were at the meeting. He never looked back. That afternoon, the father of somebody's cousin's friend turned up with a cigarette case full of silver and gold needles. "This is my sheep's-boil needle," he said. "I differ from other doctors. My method is to stick the needle far into the entrails. It is a special soft gold needle that can go round corners and arrive at just the spot required to set the *yin* and *yang* forces in motion. Some people advise letting blood. My method is to put the needle in precisely to the spot, and withdraw it at once. I have cured thousands. All along the railway from Baoji to Luoyang I am famous at every station. When I am on the train, the news travels faster than I, and crowds come down to hold up the train while I cure people on the platform."

"My dear sir," I said, "you are exceedingly welcome. Please sit down and have a cup of tea." And I went on typing very busily until he got the idea and rose to depart. "Won't you sit down a while longer?"

"Thank you, no. Please remain seated," said he understanding perfectly.

Did I ever tell you about the temples at Fengxian near here and how there came to be two of them? There was once a beautiful bride busily sewing her husband's quilt for the winter, helped by her new sister-in-law. After they had packed up and gone in for the day, the sister-in-law missed one of her rings, searched for it everywhere, and then accused the bride of stealing it. A quarrel ensued, which ended in the bride saying, "Let us go to the temple tomorrow at dawn and ask Buddha. I will burn paper and pray to Buddha that, if I have really taken your ring, he shall cause me to fall down and break my leg as I leave the temple door."

Early the next morning, they went, as agreed, to the temple on the hill across the river, and the bride burned paper and incense and put up her prayer. Then the two women turned to go, but stepping over the stone doorway, the bride slipped and broke her leg. "Ah, that proves it," said sister-in-law, and the bride, having no word to say, was carried home and refused to eat, lying on her bed until she was as good as dead. Then the husband came home and enquired anxiously into the story. Everything seemed in order. Tossing restlessly on his bed that night, he felt something hard under him and found it to be the ring. Swearing vastly, he tore up the hill to the temple, bought all the paper and incense with which the good monks could supply him, and started a conflagration. In the midst of the smoke he could be seen dancing about, waving his arms and swearing at Buddha like a madman. "So you, too, Buddha … you too are open to bribery. Your judgements too can be swayed by considerations."

Next day the monks, having overslept after their great labours to put out the bonfire of paper and incense, were horrified to see Buddha's place empty save for a pedestal! Just then a peasant came running, hardly able to speak. "Oh, good monks," he said, "Old Buddha is sitting over on that hill opposite just by my topmost cornfield, without any shelter. He looks so sad, and the rain is washing the birdlime that's been on his nose all these years, and it's running down into his mouth. What shall we do?"

"Go quickly and call the village elders," adjured the monks. "Have them bring strong ropes and carrying poles." So all the people came running down, some to see the birdlime running into old Buddha's mouth from where it had always looked like a carbuncle on his nose, others to bind him lovingly with ropes and carry him back to his home. "Old Buddha's weeping," remarked one woman. But none could say for sure whether it wasn't the rain.

Next night the same thing happened – Buddha disappeared and was found over on the hill opposite. Again the loyal peasants carried him back with soothing words, but to no avail. He seemed to think that he had no face to remain in his old temple, so the good farmers built him a straw shack to keep off the rain. And that's why there are two temples in Fengxian, one on each of the hills across the river. "Old Buddha," remarked the peasants after they had finished converting his hut into a new temple, "he makes mistakes like the rest of us, and like us has to be forgiven."

Patriotism is a funny thing. The other day, Rewi was sitting at supper with Lao San and Lao Si when strains of the national anthem came over the fields from where the schoolboys were lowering the flag. Lao San jumped up patriotically to attention, and Lao Si tumbled off his stool and nearly sat on his bottom before he too struggled into something like the correct stance. "If you're going to stand to attention, you really can't do it properly indoors," said Rewi. Lao San rushed out, followed by Lao Si. On getting out of the front door they caught sight of old cripple Wu sitting on the grassy hillside with three goats lying beside him. "Lao Wu, don't you hear the national anthem? Why don't you stand up? You're a Chinese aren't you?"

"But if I stand up the goats still won't stand up. And they're Chinese goats," said Lao Wu. "You cannot expect the goats to stand to attention, can you?" By the time the argument was over the national anthem had long finished and the flag lowered.

At long last, I have succeeded in finding someone to write down all the songs I've had in my head for the last four or five years. There are quite a lot of them. Mostly folk songs and also some modern Chinese songs which show a lot of Western influence but at the same time remain typically Chinese. The music teacher at Qin Ling College in Chengdu is an amazing person. She took them down as a stenographer takes down a letter. I would sing over one quite long phrase, and she'd jot it down, sing it back to me almost correct and get it perfect on the second singing, and so on. We had about fifteen done within three hours. Those were all the best, but there are quite a few more pretty good ones. When she has copied up, I will send you a copy by some safe means and you, Stephen, and Rosemary can play about with them. They are really priceless tunes, some of them. Did you ever realise that China had exquisite music not so very different from ours? I think that most people in the West regard the Peking Opera music as typical Chinese, whereas it is in fact artificial court music. The real music of the people is in the folk songs. Jo Needham is also rather excited about Chinese folk songs. I am giving him some copies of the songs. He is rather an extraordinary man. He can do Morris and sword dancing. The other day in Chongqing he asked me and an American folk song expert round to his room, and we had a good sing.

Chapter 26

Trouble at the Mill

Dated 22 October 1944:

This rainy season came late, just when Rewi, Bob Newell, and I had all decided it was over and separated in our various directions. Rewi came off worst. He got stuck a couple of weeks or so in a village up the road on his way to Lanzhou with the advance party to Shandan including the HF machinery and five boys. The rain flooded the courtyard and the latrine, and the mixed scent of the farmyard and other nice things rolled in under the door with the dirty water. He apparently occupied himself writing a lot of letters, telegrams, and so on. Haven't seen any poetry come out of it yet, but you can never tell. If there was any, I suppose it will be a bit more acrid than usual if not actually stinking with poetic admonitions to electrify, mechanise, and sanitise.

Bob came off best. He had got as far as Hanzhong on his way to pick up a convoy of trucks in Chengdu, and drive them back here so that we can have them to take us and our stuff to Lanzhou and Shandan. He stayed in the Hanzhong guest house as guest of the U.S. boys, reading magazines and no doubt helping to drink their coffee and chocolate rations. When the rains ceased, he donned his best, strode out onto the airfield with what was as near a Yankee swagger as he could manage, and boarded an American plane for Chengdu.

I got off all right – somewhere between the two. The rain just got me in the train on my way back from Xi'an to Baoji, and held me in Baoji for two weeks. I lived in what used to be my old "Ocean Secretary" room, since occupied by Peter Townsend, Andy Braid, and now by Bob Beshears of the Friends Ambulance Unit. I don't know if Bob enjoyed my stay as much as I did, as he nobly gave me the bed and slept on the floor, thinking that I would be gone within a day or two at the most. As the days dragged on, I was of course more and more loathe to giving up occupying the bed, and he, with true American hospitality, equally loathing for me to sleep anywhere else. His loatheness beat my slothness, so I stayed in the bed.

He has a poisonous typewriter that cuts a ribbon to pieces quicker than anything I ever saw. The said ribbons being practically unprocurable, this is a bad fault. We used it in turn, he to write letters and reports for K.M. and I to write out a lot of stuff about what's been happening around Shuangshipu for the last two years. One day the mail from America came in, and he got a letter from his sister telling him about a new book she was reading, and asking him if he had ever met the guy who wrote it – one George Hogg. Boy, did I feel bucked!

With news of the Japanese making new advances westward, Aylwin wrote the following to Ida Pruitt in New York:

You will probably be wondering how we are preparing to meet emergency; that is, if you read the newspaper closely. The first thing was to wire Chengdu for funds; if left too late, there might be no way of getting them down here, so we had to have something in hand quick. Meanwhile we had to think about a place to move to if the worst came. We have students from all up the line north of here, so it wasn't too hard to find one who could offer us all his farmhouse barns for an emergency school a little way up the road. If the situation didn't clear, we could hike on and presumably end up at Lanzhou with the school there. We had to keep all this dark, or people would accuse us of starting a panic; but we had to plan. And we had to plan alternative routes in case of the main roads being bombed. In view of our various hiking expeditions around here, that isn't so hard either. Transport is the biggest problem. We have one cart with a couple of horses. It is a magnificent cart with truck rear wheels, axle, and such, and good tyres. But even so it can't get more than a small proportion of the Ghosh machine on it at a time. We reckoned that the Ghosh can be packed into about fifteen crates, needing four or five cart loads. On top of this we have the school lathe, the HF, a truck engine, two little diesel engines, a spinning machine and four looms – all of which are absolute priority goods. Two ways remain: to get more vehicles, or to distribute the stuff in small batches with pack animals and human carriers.

The Ghosh can quite well be split up, but this has a lot of disadvantages. While working out how to split into small units, we also set about planning better transportation. First we resurrected some old truck rims and tyres, and a bit of steel tubing that will do for an axle for a cart. Taking these down to the machine co-op, we asked Engineer Kuo to make us the other parts necessary as quickly as possible. He was in rather a gloomy mood, thinking about what to do with his eighty odd tons of valuable material and machinery, but agreed to get the job done at once. The boys from Hweixian, north of here, promised to acquire horses from the farms around, so we have got over a great deal of the problem. Maybe we shall be able to get hold of a truck when the time comes (if it comes). Having thought that far, we thought one stage further: how about when we have to set all the machinery up again at the other end? We haven't a single blueprint or drawing to help us. Here, it was done entirely by the experience of one man, and he might not be available in our new surroundings.

So today we sent out fifteen boys under Ting Qi Seng, our draughtsman, to make detailed drawings of all the Ghosh machinery. I was down there this morning, and the sketches were going on pretty well, with the parts of each type of machine laid out in rows, and boys going at them with callipers and rules, sketchbooks and pencils. It is a pretty nice setup there, and I hate the idea of ever having to leave it. But at least one must be ready for everything, and we must sacrifice anything to save that Ghosh. Just think, if anything did happen to Xi'an and Baoji, our Ghosh would be the only spinning set in the whole of the northwest!

Back at school, the younger boys were having a good time. With fewer people in each class they had more attention per man from the teacher and could get more individual coaching. I noticed in the English class right away that some of the kids who had never asked many questions before were taking a much more lively interest. Same with the machine shop work. The young refugee who helped the builders of the Ghosh house and came to school afterwards as a kind of reward, got his first chance to work on the lathe. Well, well, it's a healthy life and a healthy community. I think we can hold together under anything that comes, or even if it doesn't come. Maybe better if it comes than if it doesn't.

Back in Shuangshipu, after three weeks absence, there was a lot to be done. Our democracy still has to be watched pretty closely or it gets mixed up with other things – the old gang spirit on the part of the boys, and the old gang spirit on the part of the teachers. Meanwhile the technician at the Ghosh Indian Spinning Set Co-op had gone on strike and left the twelve boys idle for three weeks. He has never really gone on anything else, so far, so I have sacked him now. It was quite a miracle to me that twelve boys left absolutely on their own for three weeks hadn't actually got up to any serious mischief. With a "hold everything" policy on the Ghosh I tried to maintain the status quo there for a week while I fixed the school.

Three days ago I moved over here to the Ghosh spinning plant. Looking rather obviously, I hoped, at the piles of machine parts strewn about the floor, I told the technician that the water wheel ought to be turning pretty soon, and then asked him if he reckoned the machinery would be ready by then. He hadn't been working for the past three or four months and had been undermining the whole spirit of the plant with his laziness and other bad habits.

"Give me a bonus of twenty thousand dollars and I'll write you a guarantee to have the plant running within a month," he offered.

"I admire your frankness," I said. "Only thing is – why couldn't you have been frank like this two months ago and asked for twenty thousand dollars then? As it is you've wasted two months of our time. I'll tell you what, you return the salary you have been drawing all this time you haven't been working; then we'll talk again."

"Oh no, that's not our Chinese way," he said.

"Where does the 'Chinese way' come into it? If you've taken our pay, you should either work for us or get out. That's the same in any country."

"Yes," he replied. "Not only have we Chinese had our ways of doing things. Don't you Westerners have your little dishonesties also?" he asked.

"Sure we have. But I never heard an Englishman, caught in dishonesty, excusing himself by saying 'that is the English way'."

"Certainly not," chimed in Engineer Kuo, our middleman, "and the Chinese people didn't elect you to speak for them anyway."

I find there is a lot of work to be done that we don't need the technician for, and we are getting along with it pretty fast now. The day he went, the Ghosh boys themselves got busy starting with the first stage machines and going through the lot, process by process, testing for maladjustments. Ho Li Zheng, one of the misfits sent back by the Chengdu school, was elected chairman of the supervisors with Xiao Jen and slow, stolid Zhou Zhang Lin to help him. Half a dozen others now back from Chengdu have set up their own shop committee to manage the production end. The cooperative was made complete by sending over three boys from the school to work as accountant, storekeeper, and housekeeper. I moved into the technician's now-vacated quarters to be close on hand. All Lao Kao's lime co-op refugee workers are back here with their picks, crowbars, and blasting powder for a couple of weeks to help us put the finishing touches to the dike, while the twelve Ghosh boys work inside on the machines.

Our senior teacher, aged only about twenty-five and supposed to be in charge of school discipline, student thought, livelihood, and all that kind of stuff, ruined his whole life the day before yesterday by trying to embezzle $60,000 in the most childish way that was bound to be found out. When I say "trying to embezzle" I mean really actually did, but hadn't time to digest before having to disgorge yesterday.

"What was that $60,000 cheque for yesterday?" Zhen Xi Quei, the school accountant, asked me as I returned to the school from visiting the Ghosh.

"A cheque?" I pondered, feeling that $60,000 should leave some impression despite being notoriously absentminded.

"You chopped it yesterday while you were at the Ghosh and sent it back to me to cash", Xi Quei kindly prompted, knowing me of old.

"Did I?" I said, beginning to wonder what kind of nightmare this was. "Did you chop it also?"

"Of course I did," he said, a bit nettled. "I couldn't very well refuse as you had chopped it already."

"By whom did I send it to you?"

"Why, Li Wang Fu. Funny you don't remember!" He went off rather upset at this new display of my outrageous muddle-headedness. I went off to look for Li and found him playing basketball.

"Did I give you a cheque for $60,000 yesterday?" I asked apologetically.

"No," he said. "What cheque?" We went in search of Zhen Xi Quei.

"Don't you remember?" Zhen Xi Quei asked Li when I brought them face to face. "You stopped me yesterday just in front of the guest house and told me that Ho-Ke had asked you to cash it and take him back the money."

"No," said Li, looking blank, "I don't remember." Zhen went off to the bank without another word, and Li went back to his faultless basketball playing. I sat and held my head in my hands and thought of all the times since my penny-a-week pocket money days when I'd had similar nightmares about disappearing money, and then found it was only something I had forgotten. But this time it was real. Either Zhen or Li had stolen my seal to chop the cheque and had drawn all that money from the bank. If it were Zhen, who was our old student, then it was just about the end of the school; he would be the classic example of the "corrupt working people" whom everyone kept telling us we could never rely on, and a perfect stick for our enemies to beat us with. If it were Li, our master of discipline and senior staff member, a leading light in the Youth Corps, a model high school graduate and son of a Christian pastor, how could he have been so stupid? Had I really given him such a poor impression of my acumen that he thought I would let the disappearance of $60,000 go unnoticed? And if Li had really brought the cheque to Zhen for his signature, how could he now have the face to deny it? It was quite incredible and quite, quite crazy.

After rushing round for clues all day, I decided to call Li over to the cave for a quiet chat. Fortified by the last of the coffee and some honeyed toast, I started by a little verbal bullying, how I wanted to help him but he wouldn't give me the facts, and he was crying within five minutes. Then I turned on some of the sob stuff by playing variations on the theme of how much we all owed him and what friends we were and how if by any possible chance it did happen to have been him, I was sure that he had the best of intentions, and that I should of course hush up the whole affair. That made him cry even more and he came out with the whole thing. "Why did you do it?" I asked. "Was your home in bad trouble?" No, it wasn't that. "Then you personally had some debts?" No, not that. "Do you mean to say that you wanted to get rich quick?" No, certainly not that at all; boo-hoo, what an idea. "Perhaps you felt you lacked security and need to buy up goods to hold against an emergency or a collapse in the currency?" No, most definitely not. "Well then, why?" Long silence, sniff-sniff. More silence. "It's a matter of my individual mental development." Ah, I thought I had it now: "You mean you wanted to use the money to go abroad and study?" No, not that either. "I was discontented with my present condition." "Yes?" "And I'm interested in music. I wanted to use it to buy musical instruments. I was dissatisfied about my mental development."

His signed confession read like a hymn. "Neither for personal profit nor from motives of individual greed for wealth, far less from any desire to hoard goods in time of national resistance, I, Li Wang Fu, withdrew $60,000 from the Bailie School bank account because of a question of my own personal spiritual interest and no other reason." But there was never any question of the martyr's stake for him. He was safe in the knowledge that prison, in China, is not yet for the sons of gentlemen, unless they have been unfortunate or stupid enough to cause personal offence in high quarters. His only concern was to keep his self-respect, which he did by means of his written confession. Of course, communications being what they are, he might be able to get a job and get along all right if he goes to some other part of the country, but, for the sake of his mental development (he's no real musician, really), he has ruined himself anyway as far as the northwest is concerned. Instability. That's the keynote everywhere. Morals rest so much on social praise or disapproval. When the society was a stable countryside and village society, this worked quite well. Everybody knew everything about everybody else in the village, so although "face" had its disadvantages, it also worked quite well. But when everything is shifting and uncertain, people aren't the same people from day to day, and what happens to the morals? I don't know really how well Western people would stand up to an environment like this. But there is something to be said for making each man to carry his own standards inside him and to hell with what other people say.

As the war dragged on, "inflation of currency" ran high, paced by its close colleague, "deflation of morals". Corruption became more and more obvious in everyday matters let alone the big-shot racketeering that one heard from all sides.

The first time a shopkeeper asked me, "This receipt – how much shall I make it out for?" I was surprised at the fellow's apparent stupidity. "I've just given you a thousand dollars, haven't I? So make it out to a thousand." But I had confused stupidity with salesmanship. It had already become conventional for storekeepers to make out receipts to whatever sum the customer thought he could get away with on his accounts – and "the customer is definitely always right". When one store starts to do this, the others must follow or else the buyers from official bureaux will go where things are made easier for them.

At the beginning of the winter of 1944, the price of charcoal in Shuangshipu suddenly shot ahead of all other commodities. Local garrison troops were patrolling all paths leading into town, forcing peasants to unload, and then carrying the charcoal themselves to sell at fancy prices. The soldiers operating this racket were careful to turn their uniforms inside out, or detach their identification badges before entering town, but it is impossible that their officers were unaware of what was going on, any more than they could plead ignorance to the charge that soldiers were fast stripping the temple mountain bare of its trees and the local farmers bare of precious faggot stores.

Motor trucks were supposed to be used only for matters of prime national military importance, yet it was common to see army trucks going through Shuangshipu on their way to Chongqing piled high with merchandise brought over from Japanese territory and guarded by soldiers in National Army uniform. The Kuomintang inspection stations set at intervals along all highways demanded a vast number of permits and documents from every truck, and took up a great deal of everyone's time; but so long as the papers were in order they had nothing further to say about a general's private spoils. The inspection stations, with their telephonic facilities for pricing goods in various parts of the country and their absolute command over the destinies of every truck on the road, carried on a roaring trade themselves.

Along the road, anything valuable had to be firmly sat on at all hours of the day and night. A relief convoy hauled several crates full of stones for a thousand miles, and delivered them proudly in Lanzhou under the impression they were medical supplies. Shops in Xi'an and Baoji displayed for sale, at terrific prices which only generals and profiteers could pay, special bottles of vitamins A and D by the name of Oladoi, which had been brought over from the USA for exclusive use in accredited hospitals and organisations engaged in relief work. A general who took a leading part in the great retreat from Henan in 1944 approached CIC in Baoji with an offer to sell us back all his stock of army blankets at a reduced rate. Since these blankets had been made by our cooperatives in the first place, they were indistinguishable from the blankets being delivered on the present contract, and so, he justly pointed out, we could hand them over to the army supply people and get the full price on them all over again. Military officials in Xi'an even acquired large personal stores of American aviation fuel.

As for those engaged in higher learning, they seemed to be as much affected as anyone by the general spirit of every man for himself. The *Ta Kung Pao* and other Chongqing newspapers carried stories of a well-developed trade in examination papers between professors and pupils, and of students sent off to America at government expense who stopped short in India to act as smuggling agents in fountain pens and watches. In Chengdu, while I was there, it was common talk that the salaries of the Chinese university staff were insufficient to feed even a small family, and so the teachers were forced into part-time business. There was widespread social decay, and Shuangshipu could not expect to keep very far away from it.

It is a point of honour among modern educated Kuomintang Chinese to dismiss all national topics with the remark that China, as a nation, is really too deplorably Chinese for words. If only such shortages as automobiles, coffee percolators, and Coca Cola could be made good in the bigger cities, these people would have little left to worry about. This attitude is common not only among the university men and foreign-returned students anxiously nursing their Western-cut suits through the duration in the bigger cities, but has spread through to the entire middle-class bureaucracy and from it to its hangers-on. The term *wo men zhong guo ti shi jian*, meaning "our Chinese affairs" covers such a multitude of sins that from listening to chance conversations one might imagine squeeze and cheating of every kind to be national Chinese inventions, and the same with inefficiency. "When foreigners say they're going to do a thing," an errand boy from the bank confided in me, quoting most probably his superiors, "they generally do it. But when we Chinese say we're going to do a thing, it just means that we want to find out what other people will say if we actually do it. We Chinese often all start off together on some affair, then someone says, 'Come over here and look' or 'Let's go over there and beat that man,' and we scatter off, east and west. We're like that." On a more humorous tone, bearing in mind his difficulties, the same kind of semi-detachment may be traced in the remarks of a Tianjin-trained lorry driver on pouring a bucketful of thick, muddy water into his radiator: "The mud stops the radiator leaking – that's our Chinese chemistry!"

Chapter 27

Ghosh! We're on the Move!

At the beginning of November 1944, Aylwin wrote home about preparations for the impending move westward:

> Today, being Sunday, forty boys have come over from the school and are swarming all over the riverbed with baskets, carrying poles, barrows, picks, shovels, ropes, and whatnot, making the hell of a noise and actually getting the hell of a lot done too. In the evenings, after work, we stage basketball matches on the new pitch we have levelled off: Ghosh v. The Rest and Chengdu v. Shuangshipu.
>
> The plan (Rewi's) for the Ghosh is to pack up the original Chongqing-made set and truck it off to Shandan, keeping the plant here for the original Nancheng set made by the Shuangshipu Machine Shop Co-op. The boys have got nearly all the old set packed up and listed, keeping out one of each kind of machine. The packing cases of machines are all stacked up high in one corner, and this afternoon we are beginning to bring in more of Engineer Kuo's Shuangshipu product.

There were enough packing cases to fully load the trucks that Bob Newell had managed to get the use of.

The waterway is finished for about two hundred yards, and we are now halfway out into the river doing the final bit that will divert the whole stream across into our channel. It is good fun, and we are all very happy doing it, as probably any boys in the world would be. Eight of the biggest boys with the horses and cart bring over huge boulders for the outside edges, workmen out blasting more stones with homemade gunpowder, and more workmen on the breakwater itself arranging the stones as they are carried over. Troops of smaller boys with baskets carrying smaller stones to fill up the centre part of the breakwater between the two outside lines of big boulders.

Day by day, Lao Kao's men push their reinforced dam further and further. The Ghosh boys in the shop work at fever pitch to get the machines fitted, cleaned, and tested, stage by stage, using a baby diesel for power. Every now and then they rush out to oil bearings on the water wheel just in case it starts turning that day.

"Why didn't you ever get going like this before?" I asked Zhang Tian Zai, who with the now less incurably gentlemanly Duan Ying Fu and a hulking Gansu peasant lad called Ko Yang Qien, formed the shop committee. "How could we when the technician was here?" he replied. "So long as he was in charge, we couldn't do anything without him telling us. It's the same in any factory – if you do anything off your own bat, the man who should have told you to do it in the first place comes and complains: 'What are you trying to do – break my rice bowl?' So then you've made an enemy, and he'll never show you how to do anything again."

Our Bailie School truck just went by on the highway above us, to Baoji, with one of our old boys who is now our school accountant and accountancy teacher, going to Baoji to buy cloth for our winter padded clothes. Work stopped for a minute as the truck chugged slowly up the hill, everybody cheering like mad. This is one of those big days, when the entire world seems Bailie School. We are already planning to have a grand opening of the waterwheel next Sunday – or maybe declare a full holiday on a weekday – to celebrate the success of ten months' blood, sweat, and broken fingers. And have we got to leave all this now and go up to Shandan where there is nothing – begin all over again? It seems as if we have to, but we'll hold on to this place for as long as possible. It's too much a part of us all just to let it go like that before any Japanese have come very near.

A great thing happened on November 10th 1944 ....

I got back here late to hear a jolly clanking and swooshing noise. I ran down the hill to find the boys in candlelight staring mesmerised by the turning water wheel and letting themselves be spattered freely by the spray blown off the paddles. At last, after a year or more of building and being flooded out just as we were nearly finished, we have got the thing going properly – a real proof that China needn't rush into slums and crowded cities to industrialise, but can do it efficiently in villages without destroying all her old basis of society, and without all the pain of the industrial revolution in England and so forth. It is done on a new design drawn by Bob Newell and seems to be very good. All last night I kept waking up to hear the strange clanking noise of the big cast iron gears, and though happily that there was no other sound I would rather be woken by. Breathing deeply of the imaginary salt sea air out on the dam next morning before breakfast, I gazed down into the deep green water on one side, and onto the nearly dried up pebbly river-bed on the other, and then back over the row of planks forming the sluice gate, and above that to where the wind blew a fine spray off the top of Bob Newell's multi-paddled water wheel. Far behind the wheel, I could see Monk's Mountain where Lao Kao and his refugees had cut timber for the dam and the water race, and for the beams and rafters of the big workshop. Inside, the power of the river was surely ours, by right of our sweat, sore shoulders, and broken fingers – and Lao Liang's body, crushed lifeless under the cart bringing lime from the kiln. The power was flowing at sixty revolutions a minute along the underground shaft from the wheel, up the broad leather drive belts to the lime shaft, and then branching off on narrow I-belts to the baby spinning machines down on the shop floor. Groups of boys in overalls were working intently round each machine. Some looked up grinning as I went by, others too engrossed to notice. Wherever there was a river, our Bailie boys and our refugees could start a community!

And now, just as we've built a nice new motor road up to the school, and got the waterwheel here running, it looks as if we'll be moving away pretty soon, and will have to start all over again in more difficult surroundings! It is rather discouraging, but our future will be better up there we hope.

A week later, on 17 November 1944:

Just at the moment I am manager, technician, and cashier of the Ghosh co-op as well as dean, cashier, business manager of the school, chief doctor at the clinic, head of household at the cave, head of the refugee committee; also trying to write a book and fight a lot of narks at the same time. I had one big awful time yesterday. It would have been enough to turn you into a raging pro-violence non-pacifist for life I should think. I will tell you about it someday.

Rewi's wire arrived from Shandan yesterday: "Houses procured. Send machinery at once."

Rewi had got to Shandan with the advance party. Most of the big houses in the city were empty. There were about fifty temples, some of which were in ruins, others still standing but not in use. The local government was as putty in the hands of the Muslim Ma Bufang bandit gang. Rewi was offered a chance to rent the disused Fatasi Temple. Ma Bufang's cavalry had some time recently stabled its horses there. The doors and windows had been taken for fuel, leaving free access for flocks of pigeons. The wooden pillars had been gnawed by hungry horses. The place seemed a wreck with hundreds of Buddhist figures lining the draughty halls. Several houses on the main street were rented for temporary quarters, which were made ready for the first contingent from Shuangshipu.

Aylwin's letter continued:

Won't be long now before Bob Newell comes along with the first of the trucks from Chengdu and we start moving I suppose. One of the teachers is taking his wife back to his parents' home today in preparation anyway. The big job is to keep everything running smoothly up to the last moment, and to send complete working units up there so that they can start right away on a definite job when they arrive. And to leave a skeleton here so that our property isn't jumped the minute we go. Well, well, quite exciting. Rewi has written more instructions about how to pack the apple trees, the goats, the cripple refugee shepherd-cum-amah, and the "babies" aged five and seven. Money? It gives me a pain in the neck. Simply isn't any use as one truck to Lanzhou from Shuangshipu costs $87,000 and a wheelbarrow costs $7,000 or so to make!

Dateline 26 November 1944:

Oh boy, oh boy, *oh boy*! The day after tomorrow we are probably starting off to Lanzhou, on the first half of our journey to the Promised Land, far from the madding bureaucrats, and today our boys on the Ghosh are actually producing good fine cotton yarn for the first time. It is a milestone, landmark, headland, memorial, fitting farewell achievement. It is enough to give us heart and hope in whatever sandy gravely foodless desert of winter we find ourselves in next. *We Did It!*

I arrived back from a visit to Baoji to find that Ting Qi Seng had packed his mother off to live with father, sold his books, shoes, spare clothes, and violin, and used the proceeds to pay a restaurant in advance for fifteen broiled chickens for consumption at the rate of one per day. Before the seventh chicken had been devoured, a phone call came through to inform that mother had quarrelled with father again, and was foodless in Baoji again. However, by this time, Ting had already volunteered for the Kuomintang's new Educated Youth Army. Newspaper articles and Youth Corps publicity on the Educated Youth Expeditionary Force Movement were vague in detail, but the general idea gradually emerged that the new army was to be flown over the Himalayas to India, equipped there, and trained in mechanical warfare by American instructors, and then would fight their way back home through Burma. Ting was the first person in Shuangshipu to join up. "The Youth Corps people have dropped all their old talk about my incorrect thoughts," he laughed. "The recruiting officer now holds me up in his enlisting speeches as a fine example of patriotic Chinese youth." Not many days later, the recruiting officer himself, with his entourage, turned up at the school to make one of these speeches. We decked the room out for him with flags and slogans. It was just after a big retreat in Henan where most of the boys' homes had been lost, so he had a sensitive audience. All our boys of seventeen and over had been automatically signed up as Youth Corps members some weeks previously on order from the Baoji Gung Ho Office, but this was the first time we'd had a real corps ceremony in our school.

"It has all been promised by the government," he enthused. "You'll be taken by plane to India. After your training there, you'll probably have about six months' actual service before you are home again. And think what a welcome will await you then! You'll be admired by everybody, and don't forget that military training is a good beginning for any kind of career. Didn't the generalissimo himself begin at Whampoa Military Academy? Come now, who will be the first brave lad? This very day I'll send a wire to Xi'an, and all your names will be in the newspaper."

A second officer, slightly more austere than the first, rose to speak. "Come now," his hands held up as in worship. "Who'll be the first?" Looking expectantly around the room and giving little tentative claps of encouragement. "Don't hesitate. Don't be afraid. There's nothing to be considered. We're not selling a patent medicine you know – this is a matter of national importance. There will be a special truck coming to take you to Hanzhong where you will get on the plane. All walking has been forbidden." Keng Si

Qin leaped to his feet, as sure now that he was bound for America by way of military glory as he had been the first day at school that he would go there to study engineering. A burst of applause greeted him as he rose and strode forward to sign. Zhang Qi Han stood up next, unable to speak, red to the roots of his hair, and very peasant like. He had grown fast in Chengdu, but he was still a long way from understanding educated people's ways. Two and a half years ago, illiterate, his father had sent him away from home to cut down the number of eligible males in the family and so to save his second brother from conscription. Now it seemed fine to him that he could volunteer as an "educated youth". A third boy stood up and spoke; a pockmarked apprentice from Laohok's soap-making cooperative. "I've wanted to enlist for some time. It's just a matter of my personal shortcomings. Would it matter?"

"You mean your imperfect complexion?" asked the recruiting officer. "That won't hold you back. Come up and sign." Others followed: some like Keng Si Qin who had fallen from middle-class families glorying now in this opportunity to retrieve lost élite status, some peasants like Zhang Qi Han who became overwhelmed by the thought of aeroplanes, officers' uniforms and the glory of being recognised publicly as educated volunteers instead of being roped up with a lot of other conscript peasants and shuffling off in the dust like Qi Han's elder brother.

Ting Qi Seng's mother soon got at him, and following days of taut, white-faced moodiness, he decided that it would be unfilial, and so immoral, for him to leave her. The recruiting officer soon heard of this change of mind through Keng Si Qin, and quickly despatched one of his underlings to escort Ting Qi Seng to his presence. There had already been a few withdrawals, and he was afraid that, if Ting too decided to pull out, many more that had followed his lead in the first place would also withdraw. Down at the corps HQ, the recruiting officer lectured away for half an hour along the old line "you won't have to fight at all. I can guarantee you a job as a musician" and so on.

"I was in the army at the age of fifteen," countered Ting. "I've worn handcuffs and I've worn shackles. I've been a soldier, and I'm not afraid to eat any kind of bitterness. But this time I simply cannot go."

The recruiting officer now changed his tune. "It's perfectly simple," he said. "If you refuse to go, all I have to do is to report that your thought is dangerously complex, that you are working on instruction from red agents to undermine the orders of the generalissimo."

Ting laughed. "You are so flattering that I should be so influential!"

"That's enough! If you do not go, many more will be influenced by you. Come now, be sensible, or do I have to make out that report about your thoughts?" As Ting pretended not to take him seriously, laughing very heartily, he was escorted to the police station. The chief of police royally entertained Ting to lunch and treated him to a violent denunciation of the corps and its recruiting officer. Meanwhile I was on my way down to the corps HQ, escorted by a recruitment minion. "My officer is in very bad humour today," he said. "You'd better do as he says or he's likely to beat you." Ready painted up for the evening, the girls of Shuangshipu's biggest brothel were sitting round the door exhibiting their wares and enjoying the sun as we passed by. "Which one would you like?" asked the minion. "Tell me, and I'll have her sent up to your cave. Very nice girls! Very good ...."

It turned out that the recruiting officer wanted me to stand guarantor that Ting would turn up for the Youth Expeditionary Force when the time came. I said that it was nothing to do with me. A compromise was reached by which I guaranteed that he would not leave school for the next ten days, and on this signed bond he was released from police custody. Since, anyway, it was now beyond his power to help his mother, Ting's mind rested easier. Whatever happened was no longer his responsibility. The remainder of the chickens were consumed, and when the day came, Ting Qi Seng was put in charge of the trucks which led the whole convoy in a shower of glory. Every house along the way had placed a table with dishes of tangerines, melon seeds, and cakes for the educated youth. Bugles blared, prostitutes cheered, and firecrackers rent the air. The first snow began to fall, and to complete the picture, a column of ragged Sichuanese conscripts, still wearing summer uniforms, pushed its way through the crowds in the opposite direction, out at the other end of town without stopping.

All through December and January 1944-5 the motor highways of the northwest were thick with the convoys of the Educated Youth Army. Tens of thousands passed through Shuangshipu within a few weeks. The generalissimo's original figure of 100,000, we learned from the newspapers, had been more than doubled. By midsummer 1945 a new drive for a third 100,000 was in progress.

Four county magistrates along the Northwest Highway between Lanzhou and Honzhang were beaten up for failing to give a good enough welcome to the volunteers as they passed through. Many restaurants along the route, whose food fell short of educated expectations, were smashed. A whole truckload of education descended on a military sentry who had asked one of their numbers to go a little further away from his doorway before urinating. The sentry was left sprawled in the newly moistened dust. The stationmaster of Xianyang, on the Lunghai Railway, was severely beaten up because the engine of the train on which the volunteers were travelling to Xi'an took ten minutes longer than it should have taken in tanking up. After a few weeks' experience of the Educated Youth waiting there for their flights to Yunnan, the bathhouses, theatres, cinemas, restaurants, and brothels in Xi'an closed their doors and fastened their shutters. It was evident that whatever anybody else thought about them, the youth volunteers themselves were determined to be an army of the élite.

The Chinese intelligentsia class had, through history, stood above the turmoil of wars and civil strife – a priesthood of calligraphers on whom the leaders emerging from each period of upheaval were forced to rely. For without their special skills in the art of writing, the system of government on which the leaders relied for their own perpetration could not be made to work. The Chinese scholars thus had no need, as had their mediaeval European counterparts, to lean on any church for support. They were supported through the centuries and unified through an often dis-unified country by their monopoly of a necessary technique which they took care to keep as elaborate as possible. It is no wonder that peaceability stands high among the virtues sung by Chinese moralists. Among the peasants, however, there is a strong opposite tradition in favour of the "merry Robin Hood brigandage". The only people who had the time to expound ethical theories and to put down their ideas in writing were the very ones who could afford to stand aloof from fighting, secure in the knowledge that their daily rice would be coming to them if they could just pass their examinations, and would be perpetuated to their families so long as their sons and grandsons had leisure enough to study the complex art of calligraphy.

New influences were coming about to cause a reversal of this ancient role. It wasn't a patriotic desire to do their bit to lick the enemy; after all there had been seven and a half years of struggle against the Japanese. Could it be a factor of mass disillusionment brought about by inflation, the breaking up of home and community, widespread undernourishment, lack of leadership, and failure to put a stop to racketeering while it was still possible to do so? Perhaps, but that was only a small group of factors in a very complex overall picture. The recruiting propaganda was hard to resist: a career starting with a trip abroad, no great exertion, no danger, no real fighting. With the help of American instructors and foreign equipment, official China may soon have had something which it never had before; namely, a mechanised army whose soldiers, closely linked by family and education with the officials themselves, can be won over by incentives other than starvation. The question was whether incentives likely to appeal to "educated youth" were compatible with those necessary to the fighting spirit of an army.

It should always be remembered that the old adage "anything may happen in China" is a reflection not so much of China's basic unpredictability as of our Western failure to get to the roots of things Chinese. We can but keep on trying, in all humility.

In late December 1944 a letter conveyed:

I am probably going to Baoji for Christmas, though I would rather stay here. We have pretty good fun these days – the school has mostly gone away, and I am here waiting for the last batch of trucks, so I am enjoying a spell of home life, writing all day and playing with the kids in the evening. We play How Green You Are, and other games. The best one is Ordering Dishes. In this, everyone is a dish, and one person orders dishes, remembering the correct names. As he places his orders, the dishes get up and follow him around the room while he makes remarks on their tastiness or otherwise. As soon as he says "I've eaten enough" everybody has to find a seat. Whoever can't find a seat, because of there being one chair short, has to order the next time. Old Four thinks this is wonderful, as eating is his favourite occupation. Sometimes he gets the names of the dishes wrong, e.g. *la zi ji* which means "peppered chicken", he usually pronounces *da zi ji*, which means "typewriter"; *suan la du si tang*, which means "sour-peppery tripe soup", he pronounces slightly differently which alters the meaning to "sour and peppery stomach ache". Then every night I have to tell stories: Old Four and the Three Bears,

The Pied Piper of Shuangshipu, and so on. I wish I had Garry's *Muddle-Headed Postman* here. I can't remember many stories, and it is very hard on the imagination.

For the past two weeks I have been writing steadily and have got over half of my new book done. I am sweating to get chapters I to V finished before leaving here. Then VI will be about the trek and VII will be when we arrive there. I'm still undecided what to call it. It is nearly all conversations and conclusions to be drawn from such. Chapter I is an introduction to Shuangshipu by way of four glimpses at what four different kinds of people – native Shuangshipu, Henan refugee, officials, our cave – do on a Saturday night. Chapter II is all about the school, student meetings, work on Ghosh, etc. Chapter III is about Chengdu, the troubles there, with plenty of conversational backchat on the bus. Chapter IV is "Home Affairs" – about our cave, clinic and so on. Chapter V is "Bankrupt" – which is supposed to be our society. Chapter VI is "On the Road", and Chapter VII is "Far from the Madding Bureaucrats", or something of the sort. I will get off I to V quite soon I hope. Maybe I can get someone to take you a copy direct.

I forgot to tell you how cold it is here. The other day I had the brilliant idea of propping my typewriter up against the fire to warm it before using. Unfortunately I put it too close, and five letters dropped off! I have sent it to Chengdu for repairs. Luckily there is another one here, or I'd be diddled.

In Lanzhou, an ancient public highways lorry was hired to help the contingent of thirty-three boys who had trekked in groups from Shuangshipu to Lanzhou on the first half of their journey to Shandan. It was loaded with various provisions that could be got hold of in Lanzhou, on top of which the boys' bedding was layered. Each student was fitted out with new padded clothes and a sheepskin coat against the severe cold wind of wintertime Gobi. The flaps of their caps were tied down over their ears, and small hand towels were tied over their noses and mouths for when the dust got too thick. The boys piled in on top of the bedding in the lorry, sitting with their backs to the cutting wind of the highland passes. It took them four days to reach Shandan from Lanzhou. Only once did a lorry wheel break through the ice when crossing a frozen river. A great deal of collective effort got them out of that predicament. In the dusk of the last evening, as they were cruising down the long gradient down to Shandan from the three thousand-metre-high Dingqiangmiao Pass on Yanzhi Mountain, following the decaying rampart line of the Great Wall of China, something flew into the driver's eye through the broken window causing him to leave the middle of the road. The outer front wheel rode up over a pile of rocks at the side of the road tipping out several of the boys onto the road. As they were so well padded against the cold no major injuries occurred, but on their arrival at the dark and cold house in the main street of Shandan, treatment of many sprains and abrasions was the first concern. On the following day, Christmas Day, classes started in the somewhat draughty second-storey room which had been set aside for the purpose. Lessons in the mornings, practical work in the afternoon: the old familiar Shuangshipu pattern of the day. The afternoon practical work consisted of organising the temple so that it could be put to use, paving the classrooms with brick found here and there, and clearing areas suitable for the all important machinery of the machine shop and textile sections. The temple and surrounding area had to be ready for when Aylwin with the second contingent and the remainder of the essential machinery would arrive in approximately two months' time.

Under the eye of Buddha

Shandan Bailie School yard with the dagoba in the background

Shandan Bailie School gateway

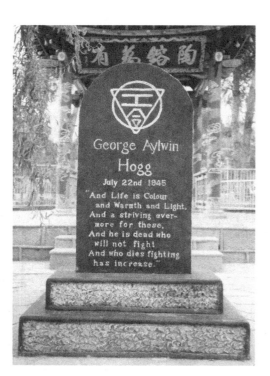

George Aylwin Hogg's grave reconstructed after the excesses of the Cultural Revolution

George Aylwin Hogg's grave within the memorial park in Shandan

Statue of Aylwin
situated in the
George Hogg
Memorial Library
in Shandan

Memorial day
procession to
Aylwin's grave
at Shandan's
South Gate, 1946

Chapter 28

Shandan

The vast areas of Northern Asia were long ago inhabited by various nomadic tribes known generally in China as *Xiong Nu* and in the West as the *Huns*. One tribe or other would sometimes settle in an area which became a kingdom, as was the case with the Yuchi tribe, in an area corresponding to modern West Gansu. The Yuchi was later disposed of by Meqhder, the *zenghi*, or leader, of the Xiong Nu. Various princes rose to power within the strongest tribes, and territories were seized, giving rise to continuous slaughter in the region. Zhangye, an oasis town founded in the Han Dynasty, about two thousand years ago, situated about sixty kilometres West of Shandan, was the scene of many struggles. Marco Polo, on his extensive travels, was held here for a year or so. He refers to it in his writings as Campichu. The name has since reverted to the original Zhangye, which is a Han word meaning "extended arm".

War continued to be the main occupation of the nomadic tribes in their many kingdoms, but then a group of Xiong Nu families with the clan name of Assena rose to dominate the area. At that time in northern China, one of the reigning dynasties was Tuoba Wei, which lasted from AD 220 to 265. The Tuoba Wei worked hard and aggressively to bring this region within the influence of China. To escape the Tuoba, five hundred families of the Assena clan fled to a natural fortress – Jin Shan (the Golden Mountain) situated right beside the present-day Shandan. Close to here, forming part of the mountain range to the north (Ala Shan) bordering onto the great grasslands of Mongolia, is a magnificent peak that the modern Chinese call Long Shou Shan (Dragon Head Mountain). As the mountain was shaped rather like a Xiong Nu helmet, the Assena people called it Helmet Mountain or *Turco* in their own language, and soon they came to call themselves *Turco-men* or Turks.

For a time, the Turks smelted iron for a prince of the Liang Dynasty (AD 502–557) at Liang Zhou, which is nowadays known as Wuwei, and they were called his blacksmith slaves. The Turks thrived and became a powerful frontier nation in the area between Zhangye and Lanzhou, and two great leaders of that nation held court close to the site of present-day Shandan.

Good horses were of paramount importance to the Xiong Nu. It is not known exactly when the horse-breeding farm of Da Ma Ying, near Shandan, came into being. It is known, however, that this farm supplied eithty thousand horses a year to the armies of the Tang Empire (AD 618–906), so it can be safely assumed that the farm is well over one thousand years old, and it is still, to some extent, in operation today.

During the Tang Dynasty, the main currency for the horse trade was silk, and it was during that period that Shandan, or Jin Shan as it was then called, developed into a very large and rich trading city on the Silk Road. The walled city had fifty-eight streets. Water from mountain streams was lifted up by great water wheels into channels running along the top of the city walls to irrigate the vegetable gardens. A Tang prince was situated there to welcome and deal with the foreign traders coming from the West. Indeed, the city was so splendid that Arab traders thought they had arrived at the capital of China. The real capital at that time was Chang'an, today's Xi'an.

The splendid city of Jin Shan was completely destroyed by the Tanguts when they conquered the area, but then, as they needed a regional capital, they founded the present-day Shandan opposite a pass through the northern mountains giving access to their capital in the kingdom of Xia, which is within today's Mongolia. The name *Shandan* came from the two characters spelling its name, shining out quite clearly on a cliff face in the golden sunset. The Xia kingdom was overthrown by the Mongols of Genghis Khan in the early thirteenth century, and a Mongol prince made Shandan his capital.

In the Ming Dynasty (AD 1368–1644) the city began to grow in size and splendour despite damage done by frequent earthquakes. A large temple called Fatasi (Temple of the Hair) was built and, a *dagoba* [type of Buddhist shrine] constructed which housed a box containing the alleged hair of King Asoka of India – the first Buddhist ruler of India. The Silk Road was one of the major routes which brought Buddhism to China, and during Shandan's prosperous years many temples were constructed. By the time my uncle went to Shandan in 1945, many of these temples were still standing but were in a bad state of repair. Some of them had recently been used as stables by the army of the warlord Ma Bufang.

Workshops and laboratories were set up by the school in some of the temples including Fatasi, and the pupils would work away at their lathes, looms and lab benches under the guardian eyes of the gigantic temple statues. These are all gone now, but a temple of the same period still stands in nearby Zhangye. This temple houses China's largest reclining Buddha made entirely of wood and measuring some 34.5 metres from head to foot. This Buddha was documented by Marco Polo during his year-long house arrest there.

A county magistrate by the name of Huang, during the Ming Dynasty, brought into operation an amazing project which diverted the Datong River through the pass at Bianduokou from the Qinghai side of the Qilian Mountains to bring plentiful irrigation water to Shandan's arid lands and the neighbouring Yongchang area. The system was so successful that, after his death, Huang was worshipped as the City God. In the 1990s the government of the day was exploring the possibility of reactivating the system to bring plentiful water once again to the desperately dry Shandan.

Slaughter was commonplace throughout West Gansu during the years of the great Moslem Rebellion in the late Qing Dynasty era. In the more modern Kuomintang era, the Fourth and Fifth Red Armies, under the misleadership of Zhang Kuotao, tried to open a way to a base on the border with the Soviet Union. The Moslem Ma warlords from Qinghai, backed by the Kuomintang, attacked them ruthlessly. At that time, Shandan was a Red Army base where Long March youngsters froze and starved through the fierce Gobi winters. Yet the young reds fought back heroically until the Ma cavalry finally mowed them down. Slaughter of a different nature was always close by in the 1940s and 1950s. Rewi recalled the poor people of Shandan in scant clothing, or even naked, out on the sparse grasslands gathering *fa cai*, a hair-like plant that had a market value for export to eastern and southern China. Their only defence against wolves would be a short stick they carried. Wolves in the area were plenty and fierce. One cold mid December day, an old man and his grandson trudging along with a donkey carrying their load were all three killed and devoured by wolves. Within the walls of the city, wolves had come through the water gate and snatched a baby whose mother was washing clothes nearby. She turned to chase the wolf, leaving the way for another wolf to come in behind to grab her other child who was playing nearby.

The Shandan of the early 1940s was quite a beautiful place in its own way. The small walled city of the 1940s was the original temple city, and most of the temples still standing were built during the Tang and Sung Dynasties (AD 618–1279). Long ago, the hillsides were covered in dense forest, and fast flowing rivers passed by. Great flocks of sheep and herds of horses grazed the steppe, and many crops were grown in the rich fertile valleys. Now the hills are denuded, and rivers run dry. At about 2,000 metres altitude, and about five thousand kilometres from the coast, the climate varies from extreme cold to intense heat. It rarely rains, the average rainfall being only a few inches a year. The northern mountains, fifteen kilometres distant, form the border between Gansu and Ningxia, one of the provinces of Outer Mongolia. About seventy kilometres to the south is the snow-topped Quilianshan range of mountains bordering onto Qinghai and the Tibetan Massif.

The city wall was huge and earthen, thirty or so feet high with gates north, south, west, and east. The north gate was in name only as it faced the northern mountains from which direction Genghis Khan with his Mongol horde had swept through the Great Wall of China to take the city. In building these walled cities, each entrance was in the form of two gates at right angles to each other. One reason for this was to deter invaders; another as protection against sand storms. A third was based on superstition. It was believed that travellers were invariably followed by evil spirits that could not turn corners. So, on entering the city at a right-angle bend, the traveller was cleansed, and the evil spirit left outside. The manoeuvre was difficult, however, with a modern lorry. From the east gate, which was the main entrance, the road first passed the magistrate's *yamen* then went on to the market square at Da Shihtzu or Great Cross, which was the meeting of four main streets. Around the square, on the roadsides, the merchants each day would set up their wooden trestle tables to sell vegetables, meat, bread, and course local cloth. The main street had a certain charm. Behind the avenue of sizeable trees were small, beautifully carved gateways which were the entrances to each individual courtyard. Tang dynasty tiles, lions' heads, and fearsome dragons topped the elaborately carved doorposts. This elegance was sadly missing in the other towns on the Silk Road where some years previously the Kuomintang had ordered a clean-up campaign during which such gateways had been torn down and replaced with uniform black-painted wooden doors and shuttering. Outside the south gate, the small Muslim city stood with its mosque, its inns, and food stalls. To the north of the city the terrain was bleak and barren, strewn for a couple of kilometres with thousands of burial mounds up to the crumbling remnants of the Great Wall, some bearing headstones hewn from rock hauled from the mountains. To the south of the city, the land was fertile with elms and poplar bordering cultivated fields where farmers grew wheat, potato, and millet. Beyond this was parched desert toward the mountains on the border to Qinghai.

The major exports at the time were opium and young girls. The sordid side was greatly evident: the beggars at the gates, the stench of opium from the shops selling it, the Kuomintang soldiers passing through, the local administration in the hands of the landlords and gangsters with no pity for the crudely exploited populace. A small girl could be bought for half the price of a donkey.

Aylwin arrived in Lanzhou in February where he collected stores and equipment, and hired some trucks for the last stage of the trek to Shandan. The horse carts were already on their way from Lanzhou. By this time another major Gung Ho crisis had blown up in Chongqing requiring Rewi's presence there to ensure continued International Committee funds for the Shandan project. On his way down to Lanzhou from Shandan, Rewi came across Aylwin in an inn yard at Yongdeng, about 110 kilometres north of Lanzhou, sitting atop a laden truck typing away to his heart's content at his book while the lads played basketball in a field opposite. They had met many adventures walking beside their horse carts from Shuangshipu to Lanzhou. Ice-bound mountain pass roads were made even more treacherous by a layer of loess dust blown from the Gobi, disguising the slippery surface. Some had nearly been killed as one horse and cart fell to the bottom of a steep gully. Some, when riding on a truck that collided with a munitions vehicle, amazingly escaped death when both trucks burst into flames and exploded. The sixty boys came through it except for one who died of heart trouble in Lanzhou. Five boys had been in the advanced party with Rewi Alley, thirty-three in the first contingent, and twelve in the last contingent.

Aylwin wrote home on 2 April 1945 for the first time from Shandan:

> No, we didn't have to push barrows – they were for an emergency in case we couldn't get transport and the Japanese came quickly. But in the end, things went off well without barrows. However, we did have to use a couple of mule cart fleets, comprising pneumatic-tyred carts, carrying up to two tons per cart with three or five mules each. My truck overhauled one of these fleets at Tianshui, about halfway from Shuangshipu to Lanzhou, and I got off the truck to go with the carts for a bit. In five days we made fifty-seven kilometres over the mountains, and two carts overturned! It was the worst time of the year over high mountains in the coldest winter for twenty years (I see from your letters that you had it too), and the roads were covered in snow and ice. From Lanzhou we hired a fleet of six ancient (1936) Mercedes-Benz diesel trucks. Old age had robbed them of the use of their self-starters, so the fleet of these over-age darlings has to have a cocky young Dodge petrol truck in charge. Each morning the Dodge tows No. 1 diesel up and down until it snorts painfully into action, then No. 1 tows No. 2 until No. 2 comes to life, and so on down the line. Then they all start off together, with the Dodge shooing along at the back in case any of the old boys drops out of line.

Now that we are here, the barrows are all in full daily use – on the job of clearing out the muck from the old (now most new-looking in many respects) temple that is our school, and pushing in building material from the houses we have bought all around for wrecking purposes. The nearest timber available in any quantity is about sixty kilometres away in Minle on the Qinghai border, so we have to be content with wrecking old houses and using the timber and bricks from them.

A barrow is an object of great curiosity here. The people hadn't got as far as inventing the barrow yet, though many hundreds of years ago they build a wooden Buddha about a hundred feet high, with a many-storied house all around him. One story consists entirely of ears, eyes and nose. The ears are the height of two of our tallest boys. No barrows, but Buddha statues. Rather a waste of wood (a rare commodity in these parts).

Nearly all the Buddha statues have been carried out of our school temple, though with much misgiving on the part of the local people. Three of the biggest had to be left, by terms of our contract, plus two baby pagodas and two watchmen. These are all in our spinning shop. The three big fellows are gold leafed and very handsome. They stand at the back of our shop, towering up to a high ceiling, and watch us work. The pagodas were supposed to be full of precious documents, but turned out to be empty. The two sturdy watchmen, whom we laid to rest and covered with matting, now guard the entrance to our store.

We are still busy fitting up our various workshops. The whole of one side of the compound is given over to work: carpentry, steam engine, electric generator, lathes, planer, milling machines, benchwork, and wool spinning. In the centre, the biggest temple holds our Ghosh cotton spinning machinery and the three remaining Buddha statues. All down the other side are classrooms. At the back there are dorms. The temple bell, slung high above the classrooms, summons us to our various tasks. Unfortunately the clapper is missing, and someone substituted a sledgehammer, which has cracked the bell. But it is still loud enough to be heard all around town.

I forgot to mention the toothbrush machine, which was made by a co-op in Jiangxi and presented to us. Though all necessary materials (ox bone and pig bristles) are available for toothbrushes here, people who want to brush their teeth all through this province either use Japanese toothbrushes or buy from Xi'an or Hanzhong. We will make a "common man's" toothbrush. The machine is fixed up already, and we are willing to pay them for bristles if they will only take the trouble to save them.

The boiler and steam engine are our future lifeline, together with the generator. We can give electric light to the whole town with it, in return for which they will give us free coal. Meanwhile, we can have light in our classrooms and power for our machine shop and spinning shops. There is still something wrong with the boiler, but we will have that fixed soon.

All the opposite side of the compound are classrooms. Another big temple in the middle we have cleared out and painted up to be our Dr. Sun Yat-sen Memorial Hall.

This will house our library and reading room on one side, and machine-drawing desks on the other. It will also be used for meetings.

Of course all the local people and officials are rather pleased to have us come, and their attitude is a tremendous contrast to Shuangshipu. In fact, life here in general is a lot more hopeful. There we were battling all the time and not making much headway. Here we have only ourselves to blame if we don't make out.

Another advantage here is the compactness. My little room, overlooking a tall, half-wrecked pagoda, opens onto a single compound containing the whole of my Shuangshipu setup and a lot more besides. I can do in an hour what would have taken me a very tiring day in Shuangshipu.

We have just sixty boys here now, with another twenty smaller ones coming on from Lanzhou in the summer, and perhaps some local kids. They have been to Bailie schools in Luoyang, Baoji, Shuangshipu, Chengdu, Chongqing, and Lanzhou and are now collected here to see if they can't really make a go of things. A good nucleus bunch of teachers too.

Our back door overlooks the mountains on the other side of which is Mongolia, and our front door overlooks the mountains on the other side of which is Kokonor [Qinghai], which is part of Tibet. Last night five of us teachers and twenty-five boys started our first lessons in Mongolian conversation. We haven't been able to get hold of a Tibetan teacher yet, but will do soon.

In a few days' time we expect George Woods, MP, his technical adviser, and some other people up here. They are making a trip from Lanzhou specially to see us, which is quite a distinction and gives us a lot of "face". I will try to get them to take this letter back to you, and send a copy by post. Peter Townsend, Rewi, and some of my pals are coming with the party, so I am looking forward to it very much. They should also bring some coffee, cake, and suchlike, which will be welcome.

We have machine drawings done by the boys in Chinese ink all over our newly whitewashed wall, and the refugees have just finished painting all our pillars red. A local craftsman has come in to paint us a huge sign in red and gold to put over our Sun Yat-sen Hall – the signboard is an ancient one we discovered in a back temple roof over a Buddha's head. It has golden dragons all round the edge. So I think they will be impressed.

It was very good to hear that my book was chosen for Victor Gollancz's Left Book Club; quite encouraging. I haven't had much time to look at the second book since leaving Shuangshipu, but have collected quite a bit of new material – enough to complete if I could get a free two or three weeks some time. A letter came from Little, Brown & Co. asking for one on just the subject I would like to write about. But that will have to wait a bit longer I'm afraid.

I have just finished setting up two large bookcases made of packing cases in my room, and filling them with books. It looks very good. Unfortunately (for me not for the school) they are nearly all technical books. Of the other books there was only one that

I hadn't read. I settled down to that yesterday in the first free time since coming here, but after the first page, which was quite good, it turned out to be appalling stuff. No newspapers, no nothing, in this place. A letter to Lanzhou takes a week, and strangely enough a telegram seems to take two weeks at least!

A lot of feasts and so on here, but mostly consisting of different kinds of fat meat. For ordinary fare, beef and mutton is quite cheap and good, as this is largely a Muslim population. Eggs are about half the price of Shuangshipu. Poached eggs in beef soup makes a good Sunday breakfast.

The kids Lao San and Lao Si accompanied me on the truck; Lao Da and Lao Er came on before with the first batch. Lao San and Lao Si both go off to primary school happily each morning (Lao Si begins here for the first time). They seem to take a rather morbid delight in the various devil idols in the Taoist temple next door. After daily entreaties for two weeks from Lao San, I accompanied him to see the "hanging-dead devil" in the Taoist temple next to the school – a fearsome object, dripping blood from eyes and protruding tongue. A box of ashes and joss sticks is in front of it, so I suppose the local people pray to him to keep suicide from their family doors. Nothing seems to stop Lao Si from wetting his bed. Perhaps fear of "hanging-dead devil" in the night prevents him from emerging to do his stuff in the pot provided. You haven't sent me the correct remedy yet. I'm waiting for it. Last night before sleeping I asked: "Will you wet the bed tonight?" "No," he said. "What if you do?" "No eggs for breakfast, no bean sauce."

A month later, on 5 and 9 May 1945, he wrote:

I wonder if you got the letter I sent you by the hand of George Woods, MP? I recently got two letters from you – one dated December 20th, 1943, and the other June 22nd, 1944. I wonder how it all happened. Better late than never! You seemed at both periods to be involved in a lot of family domestic struggles, twins [Aylwin's brother Daniel's daughters], more twins [his sister Barbara's sons], mumps, measles, dishwashing, and children who insist on sleeping in their parents' bed. You don't need to worry about the latter, which is the rule rather than the exception here; but still no reply to what to do about Lao Si's bed-wetting. George Woods brought a book on psychology with him for our man in Lanzhou. The theory, according to this book, is that kids wet their beds as some form of revenge on their mothers. Don't know if this answers the case, but it may do as Lao Si's mother used to hit him quite often.

I wonder what has happened to Wayfarings by now. As I get older I remember more and more about Red Gables. You may be interested to know that I have spent part of the last few Sundays reading Joseph Needham's *Time – the Refreshing River*, published by Allen & Unwin in 1943. I wonder if you have read it. There are not many books worth reading here, as I told you before. The Woods' party brought an advance copy of my Gollancz Left Book Club edition.

Rewi is in Chongqing with the Woods' party. He should be coming back here at the end of the month if he can. Meanwhile we are still struggling to get things fixed up and organised, which I seem to have been doing ever since we started in Shuangshipu. The thing is not yet on a smooth-going basis. The reason is partly difficulty in finding men, partly the difficulty of the chief administrator being me, who is very far from understanding how things work in this complex and ancient-modern environment, and partly the environment itself which is on a completely different wavelength to ours and so often nearly manages to blot us out but always manages to give us severe atmospherics. Now we have simply got to get things fixed. If we don't, it may be too late.

Your war seems about over. Though our news is very patchy and two weeks late here, it seems that the Russians and the Americans have got Berlin, and Goebbels is shot. No news of Hitler yet, or Goering. Ours will last quite some time yet and may take some peculiar new turns I expect.

I've just had four fried eggs for breakfast. Chinese eggs are a lot smaller than yours, so don't be alarmed. I wonder how soon you will be enjoying such things. There is an advertisement for shredded wheat with realistic pictures of same in a *Picture Post* brought by Woods. It makes my mouth water very much. Our boys, and me on weekdays, live on steamed bread, millet soup, and potatoes almost entirely. This place doesn't produce vegetables, but we have already planted our own vegetable gardens, which will probably be enough to last us from next July or August through winter. We also eat meat twice a week, which is considered extravagant.

As Ralph Lapwood is going home soon, it might be okay to write to the above address (Shandan Bailie School, Shandan, Gansu, China), but perhaps it would be safer to write c/o Andy Braid, International Committee for AACIC, 1 Medical Building, Hua Xi Ba, Chengdu, Sichuan.

Since getting to Shandan, I haven't had time to do a thing on the book until last Sunday. Perhaps I can find a few hours every week, plus all day Sundays, and have the thing finished by summer hols. Not sooner I'm afraid.

Lao San and Lao Si live just down the road with a refugee and his wife to look after them. Last night I got back after dark from visiting them and was surprised to find the flag still flapping on its mast. I was told thereupon that Germany had capitulated, and that all flags were to fly continuously for three days; sounds good, but no details as yet. I had just been reading an article in an American magazine *Free World* which said that Germany could never capitulate as there was no one with enough credit to sign the pact, so that we would be forced to role tanks through every village in Germany.

On 31 May 1945, Aylwin wondered how Europe was getting on free of Hitler:

I suppose the egg rations and so forth have been raised, and you are revelling in all sorts of good things. Don't quite know what will happen here. Maybe there could be another six months or a year of formal war, and something of a different nature after that. I think this school will be fixed up all right and on its own feet within a year, unless something untoward happens.

I've just finished entertaining Xu Weilin, the CIC secretary general and other big shots. A bit of a sweat to try to fix things up, keep things going, arrange entertainment, and smooth the way for the visitors all at the same time. Jo Needham may be up here with his wife next month. He has sent us a lot of equipment and literature of a technical kind.

Five or six skilled workmen for our machine shop turned up the day before yesterday. The shop itself is about fixed up, but the steam engine and boiler are short of a lot of things which we have to make ourselves. Maybe within a few months we shall have our own electric light and power for the spinning machines and so on. That will be a great day. We have an epidiascope [opaque projector] from Needham which we can use to pass the long winter evenings with.

We have a good staff of young fellows with a "now or never" attitude about the school. Together we are working things out and trying to set up a system that other people can work when necessary. The difficulty is to have a watertight system that does not, at the same time, become a bureaucracy and so defeat its own ends.

It's difficult to find time to write. Last Sunday all wasted by a stupid feast at the bank. You have to attend such things or word gets round that you are proud, standoffish and suchlike, and that would be the end of everything. In China there is almost no division between personal relations and business relations. If you are on personal good terms, everything is made convenient; if not, you can never get anything done at all.

I wonder if Dan'l has gone off to Europe yet.

General Secretary Xu Weilin and his entourage from CIC headquarters had been suitably impressed with what they saw in Shandan, and so the Gung Ho seal was well and truly set upon the Shandan Bailie School.

A month later, on 3 July 1945:

Just got your letter with all the reviews of the English edition of my book. Quite encouraging! I was surprised to get reviews in the *Spectator* and all those upstage papers, and especially such a good one from *The Times*. I think this is my first letter since your war was definitely over. Ours isn't, and nor is my personal war; maybe another year or two yet. I suppose that Dan'l has been flown to some international hot spot by now to put over the peace. His languages will be very useful at this point; but to whom? No doubt he has thought about that.

Our own she-goat had a litter or whatever it is that goats have, so the supply of milk for us ceased until I met a farmer on the street carrying a vast array of different-sized pots, each filled with goat's milk. Now I buy a pot from him every day, and so we are all getting very pink, and Lao Si is plumper than ever.

No, don't send me any money. It can only buy about one quarter here of what it could buy in England, and I have enough. I can't come home until this school gets going on a permanent basis. I don't know when that will be; maybe next year. Don't worry. When I come, I'll maybe hop into my private plane and be with you in no time.

Someone tried to send me twenty dollars the other day. I don't know if it was you or the agent. Anyway I don't want it. It is worth about one hundredth here of what it would be in England at the present rate of official exchange. Besides, I have a fairly fattening salary, which looks after all my wants. I could even save some of it back in New York quite easily, but at the moment I am building a house! It is built at the foot of a high mound, called a *lei tai* meaning "alter of thunder", which had been a platform used for wrestling matches in centuries gone by. This is made of earth and bricks and stands maybe thirty or forty feet high. The victor used to throw his opponent over the edge. This was in those long-ago days when the people of Shandan had leisure and initiative to enjoy such things. Later, bandits of various kinds and in various guises reduced them to such a state of poverty that leisure today means squatting on one's *kang* in the winter, or outside on a broken-down porch in the summer.

We are now in the middle of a drought, and if it doesn't end soon, the wheat crop will be about thirty percent, and I don't know what we shall eat, I'm sure. Long processions of school children, peasants, village elders, and all headed by the government officials and gentry, go down the street several times a day to one or other of the temples to pray for rain. They beat a lot of gongs on the way, and sometimes keep it up all night too. It is rather hard on the government officials who may themselves not believe in this method of getting rain but have to make very zealous pretences of doing so in order to keep in the good books of the gentry and local peasants. One *xian* magistrate some years ago knelt continuously for several days until it rained.

The present magistrate led a procession walking on his knees and burning incense. He stayed down for about three hours only and is rather unpopular locally as a result!

About three Sundays ago I finished the only difficult chapter in book number two – about seventy pages of meat, conclusions, prognostications, and so on. That is Chapter V. The first three chapters were finished some time ago in Shuangshipu. Chapter IV, an easy one about our cave and family life, is now in progress. I can finish it in two or three more Sundays. Little time to write on any other day of the week as there are usually lots of other things to do, and anyway no chance of consecutive thought. Just now I am manager of our machine shop! I will send you I-V and the rest later.

I went up with George Woods' party to the famous oil wells at Yumen. A good trip, and he is a good fellow. No time to write more as they are just about to leave.

Shandan 8 July 1945:

I think you will like Chapter IV, which I am doing now. It is all about my family, life in the cave, our clinic, Rewi, Bob Newell, the boy who nearly died of typhus, and suchlike. Yesterday was a holiday, so I got a bit done, and today is Sunday, so I got a bit more done. It is turning out much longer than I expected, which is a good thing.

Yesterday was (a) the eighth anniversary of the Marco Polo Bridge Incident that began this war, (b) International Cooperatives Day, and (c) the birthday of the patron spirit of our neighbouring temple. This is very lucky as (a) is July 7th on the foreign calendar, (b) is the first Saturday in July, two years ago July 4th, last year July 6th, and (c) is the twenty-eighth of the fifth month in the Chinese calendar. Only once in a blue moon would they come on the same day. There was a big meeting with speeches by the *xian* magistrate, me, local gentry, and so on. My speech lasted about forty minutes, which is quite short in China, with a lot of stuff about the connection between all three of these significant days: cooperation and the war effort, cooperation and the peace, cooperation and local customs, local customs and the war, the Rochdale pioneers and their four simple principles which shook the world, cooperation and Dr Sun Yat-sen's Three Peoples' Principles, as well as various pious hopes and exhortations. At the end of the meeting, our boys all sang five songs – two resistance songs, one "down-with-profiteers" song, and two cooperative songs. They really sing quite well now. They open their mouths and pronounce their words so that people can hear quite plainly what they are singing about, which is something quite extraordinary in these parts. Their mouths all move together, which looks very good. Brown faces, white teeth, brown necks and arms, white cotton sports vests, blue shorts, brown legs, sandals; quite a good impression of clean strength. After the meeting, the local officials and gentry called at the school to make me a special bow, which is very good, not because one wants to be bowed to but because it means they will help the school.

In the evening we gave a long four-act play about underground patriotic life in Shanghai from the beginning of the war to the entry of Britain and the US as China's allies against Japan. When I tell you that the boys only rehearsed for about a week, and that they were quite nearly word-perfect, you will understand that Chinese people have good memories. This possibly comes from the old tradition of the learning of whole books of the classics by heart, in the not-so-long-ago days. This was the common form of schooling until about ten years ago, and still goes on quite a bit in the country places. During our play, on an outdoor stage, the wind blew fiercely filling the air with Gobi dust; the peasants, who are crowding the city from fifty miles around to take part in the temple celebrations, all crushed in to hear better. The police and finally the army were called out to keep order. One of the two lamps blew out. The *xian* magistrate and all the big shots failed to arrive until the beginning of the second act. But, all in all, it was quite a good show.

The previous year, an American visitor to Shuangshipu thought that Aylwin was looking too thin for such a big fellow and so suggested to the Indusco Committee that they increase Aylwin's salary, to which the reply was given, "It is never any use raising George Hogg's salary; he would only adopt some more sons."

Aylwin's letter continues:

We have a new kid in the family. His name is Zhang Weisan and he is the young brother of one of our boys. Their whole family was evicted and expropriated to make an airfield. He speaks rather a queer dialect which almost nobody can understand except Lao San and Lao Si, who have fortunately made very good friends with him. All three of them sleep crosswise on a big wooden bed. On Mondays and Tuesdays Lao San tidies the bed in the mornings, puts out the chamber pot, sweeps the floor, and tidies the cupboard. On Wednesdays and Thursdays Xiao Zhang does the same, while on Fridays and Saturdays Lao Si does his bit helped by one of the others. This is their own arrangement, not mine, and it seems to work out quite well. "On Sundays," Lao Si tells me with great emphasis, "we *all* do the tidying!"

Today I ate the top off a whole washbasinful of goat's milk that had stood for twenty-four hours; thick, creamy, and slightly sour, very refreshing and very nourishing.

Rewi is due here any day with a gang of geologists to make a survey of Shandan's mineral resources. We are expecting a lot of new teachers too, which will make things easier.

Rewi had been away from Shandan most of the time since February, tied up with crises in Gung Ho, popping in briefly with special visitors on various occasions. By July, the temple and its surroundings was a school. The cotton mill was turning out yarn, and the looms were turning out cloth. The machine shop was in full swing, and classes well established. The older students were taking more and more responsibility, and new local boys were coming in to work.

The spectacular bottle-shaped *dagoba*, built over a thousand years previously, dominated the city and had become the central point of the Shandan Bailie School. Beside the *dagoba* was the Fatasi Temple in which was housed the chemistry section where soap for the washrooms and chalk for the classrooms were produced. Next to that was the electrical section, providing light for the school and power for the welders. Electric light was a great fascination to the natives who came from far afield to stand and stare at the illumination coming from the roaring generator. One day an agitated peasant came to say his wife was having a baby, and could the generator be turned off, as he feared the noise made by its evil spirits might harm his wife and child. As soon as he had asked, and before Rewi had time to speak, the generator's noise ceased as the welding had come to an end for the day. The power of the man to silence the roaring monster without moving from his seat became a legend.

In the transport compound, the boys worked day and night to keep the trucks on the road for bringing supplies from far afield. Across the road was the machine shop, where a large steam boiler provided power for the Ghosh spinning machinery housed close by, overlooked by three more gigantic images of Buddha. On the other side of the courtyard was the school's general store, behind which were dormitories, classrooms, and the library. Along the road past two Taoist temples still in use by the locals was the *lei tai* where Aylwin's house was being built. Behind the *lei tai* was the construction department, and in front a small clinic, which later became the accountancy department. Beyond was the printing shop where all the textbooks were produced, the knitting department where jumpers and socks were made from local wool, and the tailoring department where all the cotton summer clothes were produced as well as the thick padded winter suits. Further down the road, the geological and survey department was housed. Within the next two years, an area of industry sprouted outside the south gate beyond the Muslim city. This area included a leather tannery where skins were prepared for making leather jackets for the students. Gazelles abounded in the desert, and their skins were used a lot. Fox and wolf pelts provided material for fur hats. Sheepskins were used to make long winter coats, fleece inside and hide outside. The textile section was later put up there where wool was spun and dyed for rug and blanket making. The papermaking department used the long dry *jiji* grass from the desert to make paper for the classrooms. Next door to papermaking was glassmaking, which used the abundant suitable sand from the nearby desert. A large range of excellent clays could be found in the area ranging from kaolin to terracotta. The pottery department made all the bowls, plates, cups, mugs, and teapots that the school required, to mention only a few of the products.

On 9 July, Rewi arrived with Joseph Needham and a group of geologists led by the Brian Harland. Writing in his report dated the same day, Brian Harland informed:

> George Hogg is in charge of the school and, along with Rewi, is perhaps one of the few foreigners in China really making a big contribution .... It seems an anomaly – and I know Rewi and George would actively disclaim it – but they are succeeding in getting across what is of real value in the English public school system without the secondary things like academic specialisation and class snobbery. They are training leaders, but leaders who will lead in the factories from where they have been recruited. It is an expensive form of education as it means running full-scale machine shops, textile machinery, leather tanning, and whatnot to train the boys practically. They get to quite a high standard in mathematics and machine drawing and do essentials in the three Rs. But first of all there is a team spirit which is quite essential if they are to be cooperatively inclined. I must say it is one of the most hopeful things I have yet seen in China and something with which I keep feeling tempted to throw in my lot, though perhaps I shall be of most use helping on the sidelines; for to throw in one's lot really does mean giving up almost everything else as George Hogg has done.

Chapter 29

The Great Blow

Aylwin was feeling very much under the weather. He had been working very hard, and the diet available in Shandan wasn't at all sufficient. He was possibly quite severely run down. It seemed like just a cold or summer flu.

Rewi recalled an afternoon in July soon after his return to Shandan:

> We were together in one of the big old Shandan houses which we had taken from among the many available at the time for purely nominal rents. I had chosen it for my home, as he was building his cottage at the *lei tai* in the school grounds. He was feeling sick and rather grouchy. He handed me his proposed Chapter V. "I've posted a copy off to a friend in Chongqing who will add it to the rest of the manuscript and send it to the publishers," he said, "but you had better read it and tell me what you think." His much beloved Lao Si, was finishing his bath and waiting for George to tip the basin of water over him, and then to be picked up and thrown over his shoulder. When George complied, Lao Si's shout of joy was so catching that he [George] laughed his old laugh – the last time I was to hear it.
>
> No one can be absolutely sure, but the common belief is, and was, that Aylwin injured his toe when playing basketball with the boys. He always wore the Chinese peasant sandals which were comfortable and convenient; but he could never find any that were quite big enough for his Western feet. Consequently, his big toes always protruded and could easily be stubbed.

On arrival in Shandan from Lanzhou, Rewi noticed that Aylwin's big toe was swollen. Aylwin said that he had hit it and that a blister had formed under the nail. Rewi had brought some outsized sandals with him from Lanzhou, which Aylwin put on and said they were better. He was very busy and looked tired. He said that he thought he would take the chance of Rewi's return to go to Lanzhou and get one or two essential men. Rewi, who was hardly ever in Shandan, was amazed at the tremendous progress that had been made since February. The spirit of the boys was good, and the technical progress striking. The place was beginning to look something like the kind of school they were striving for. Aylwin was evidently not eating properly though, skipping meals and going on with work. On being asked when he would go to Lanzhou, Aylwin said that he would wait until after the school's sports meeting and their summer excursion hike to the mountains, which was all the summer holiday that was planned, and that he would see the summer term started and then go.

On 15 July, Aylwin went over to Rewi's house on West Street and said that his foot was sore. He put it in hot soapy water and then tied it up with boracic ointment as there was no iodine in the house. Remembering his other injuries to his feet, in particular the one when a rusty nail had gone through the sandal, it did not surprise Rewi to see Aylwin this way again. He had been very busy carrying the sports through, getting things fixed here and there, inviting the local gentry to a feast to thank them for their help and to straighten a number of human problems. He seemed more tired than usual.

Rewi read through more of Aylwin's typescripts and talked to him as he bathed and dressed his toe, which was swollen and sore. Rewi told him that he did not think the Kuomintang would let Aylwin stay in Shandan if this was ever published. He thought that so direct a sermon for the United Front would hardly be appreciated by the followers of Jiang Jieshi whose ideas were now completely opposed to those of the communists. Jiang felt that the entire communist army should submit to him in everything, even to non-resistance to the Japanese and, if he wished, they should suffer the same fate as the New Fourth Army in Anhwei. The communist idea was one of working together in order to defeat a common enemy, not to combine with him as Jiang had more than once tried to do. There would be no Kuomintang-dictated popular front, but Kuomintang oppression, which became more ruthless as it neared its end. Although they were only two foreigners "on the left", they had set themselves the task of holding the school group together and were therefore an easy target for the enemy to eliminate. Aylwin answered Rewi's remarks somewhat moodily. "I've toned it down a lot. Smoothed it out no end, can't you see? Not said half of what is on my mind to say. It's my effort for a real popular front, isn't it? I've mentioned no names, just nicknames for Liang, Zhao, Tieh, Fu and the rest."

"Well, you have sent it off, and that's that," said Rewi, as Aylwin went off to look round the machine shops before the end of the afternoon.

After he had gone, Rewi carefully read the chapter through again, selecting a few pages which were too hot to have around the house in Shandan. He pinned them together, and with other dangerous documents, he locked them away. Some years later, just before liberation in 1949 when Rewi was informed that the school would shortly be raided, he felt it necessary to destroy the pile of documents.

The first three chapters, which Aylwin had not shown to Rewi, had been sent down to Chongqing from Shuangshipu. The next two chapters from Shandan had been sent also to the same friend. Twenty or so years on, Rewi was unable to find out to whom the typescripts had been sent as no record was left. Certainly no typescript had reached a publisher. No one had heard anything of it. Rewi was forced to conclude that it had been taken from the post office by Kuomintang agents and had not made the first lap of the journey. There was no copy of any of the earlier chapters among Aylwin's effects.

On 18 July, Aylwin said that he would join Rewi for lunch but did not turn up. He turned up later and said that he was tired and would have a nap. He woke up, said that he must have caught a chill, as his shoulders and neck were stiff, and went back to school. Dr Du, the head of the local health station, was called in. His main interest was to put the patient's mind at rest: "Nothing is the matter, nothing at all." He was sure it was nothing more than summer flu, curable with rest.

The following day, again Aylwin did not turn up to lunch. Rewi went looking for him and found him sitting in front of cold cabbage soup and steamed bread, holding his jaw. He said that he did not feel up to much. "I think I'll turn in. This flu is making my head spin." Later in the afternoon, Rewi found him in the machine shop with his head on his hands and looking miserable. Dr Du was called, who laughed at the suggestion that it might be tetanus. The wound on the toe had now healed and looked normal. He said that flu was very prevalent now and that it was just this together with some dust making a bad throat condition. He advised sulphathiazole and two aspirin, which Aylwin took and went to bed.

The boys came to Rewi at three in the morning to lead them on their three-day hike to Yanzhi Mountain. He went to see Aylwin first, who seemed to have perked up. "You go along," he said. "I'll be all right by the time you get back." The hikers got an hour out on their way when Brian Harland of the geological survey came bounding across the countryside and suggested that he would take the lads, as Rewi should go back. Aylwin had had a spasm. It was clearly tetanus. Rewi cursed for not having serum to hand. The old houses and the temple where horses had been kept were perfect places for tetanus to thrive. Telegraphs were sent to places near and far; to Zhangye, Wuwei, and Lanzhou. No reply from Zhangye. A telegraph came from the Wuwei Border Mission offering assistance, but they had no transport. A lorry was sent off. The following morning was bad, but improvement showed towards midday. Dr Xu arrived from Wuwei with the returning truck, but no serum, only magnesium sulphate and some minor drugs. He took over from Dr Du. Aylwin's condition improved in the afternoon. His jaw eased so that he could drink a bit when held up. Spasms were shorter in duration. Everything looked more hopeful. Aylwin asked Rewi to read some passages from Edgar Snow's *Red Star over China*. Smiling at some of it, Aylwin said, "That's when I did a lot of thinking." Later, he got Rewi to pick out the *Communist Manifesto* to read. "That makes sense," he said after a couple of readings, and then fell asleep. Another spasm woke him. Some senior boys who had returned with Rewi took it in turns to be with Aylwin. Fan Guo Quian and Fan Wen Hai slept while Jen Zung Yuan and Sun Bi Doong took over for the day duty. A telegram came from Lanzhou saying that Zhang Xinyi was bringing a doctor and serum. That night was better than the previous night. The boys were very good and soon learnt how to make things easier all the time. Fan Wen Hai and Fan Guo Quian were there when Aylwin asked for a pen and paper with which he wrote "my all to the Bailie School". The two boys witnessed the will, with Rewi looking on, as Aylwin said, "I think I'll pull through, but one has to be prepared."

A doctor had been found in Lanzhou, but delay followed delay: for a car, then for a driver, for fuel, and finally for the drugs and serum. The doctor was fairly confident, if only the patient could hold on for a couple of days; and Aylwin was putting up a good fight. However, the party had to spend the night on a mountain pass, and although they set off again at daybreak, they were not in time.

The morning of 22 July was not so bad, but after eleven o'clock, Aylwin began to be much weaker. By this time, his jaw was set. The boys managed to give him liquids by way of a straw through an extraction gap in his teeth. Shortly after midday, a long spasm lasted for one hour followed by a short spell before the next spasm. Aylwin became a lot calmer and relaxed. He drank a little, but choked. The hikers were returning, and many of the boys tried all the life saving techniques they had learned for drowning persons. Du An Fang and Nie Guang Chun (Aylwin's oldest adopted son Lao Da) came in to help with the process. Breathing did not return. As the truth dawned, the boys each in turn quietly slipped away to cry.

Rewi wired Chengdu, Lanzhou, and Chongqing. The *xian* gave a bit of ground outside the South Gate. In the afternoon Rewi went with the magistrate and the local gentry to survey this. Brian Harland helped get things in order.

It had been a poignant relief for the boys and teachers to express some part of their love and devotion by working hard all through the night preparing everything for the funeral.

The day of the funeral, 23 July 1945, was a brilliant day. The Qilian Shan in snow looked very majestic. The clear waters of the stream sparkled as they flowd through the poplars behind the grave. The grave had been well prepared and lined with brick. At ten o'clock the magistrate came, and they set off. Before putting the body in the coffin, the boys had put a CIC army blanket in there and then laid a school-made blanket over him. They had prepared a big flag with their names on it with various characters – *Lao Shi*, Beloved Teacher, and so on. The school flag was also put on the coffin, which was draped in black cloth. Sixteen boys carried the great heavy coffin, and twenty boys with two long lengths of cloth pulled it from the front with the local officials following behind. The rest of the boys brought up the rear. Around the grave, they did not have too long a ceremony, as too much emotion was feared. His school – his family – sang the school song, bowed three times, and lay bunches and wreathes of flowers. The boys stood around in their white shirts and blue shorts. No one could say a thing. Suddenly, the boys grabbed shovels. The grave was covered with timbers, and the boys threw on the earth, building the mound with tremendous energy and covering it with brick.

They had just finished when Zhang Xinyi and Drs Pu and Sun arrived in the car from Lanzhou. Dr Xu had returned to Wuwei in the morning. They called on the local gentry and the magistrate in the evening to thank them for their help. The magistrate felt that the pathos was in Aylwin being so far from home. Rewi said that he was sure that, as far as leaving us was concerned, to be carried by the lads he had worked with and to be laid in the place which he had decided to work for was a privilege everyone envied him for. The tragedy was that it was all too early and no one would possibly be able do as much as Aylwin could have done.

Rewi then started to make arrangements to start classes the next day.

The day after the funeral, in the early morning, the children Lao San and Lao Si went to the grave with Lao Yu, the cook, to burn paper and bow. They placed coffee and bread there for Aylwin's breakfast. Lao San asked which way was England, as he wanted to bow to Aylwin's father and mother. A little later, Rewi went out to see the grave and wrote in his diary: "It stands so lonely in the amphitheatre of valley and mountains – difficult to look at ...."

A visit was made to the magistrate again, and arrangements were settled for the ceremony next day to which all the locals would be invited and the proper rites observed. The boys rigged up the big covering for the gate, and the Sun Yat-sen Memorial Hall for the ceremony. The following day, 25 July, the hall and gate were all in order. There were hundreds of wreaths hung up. Some of the boys had painted a large picture of Aylwin, under which wreaths were placed. The workers who had been helping at the school ask to be allowed to help fix the grave. Melons, raisins, tea, melon seeds, and such light refreshment were served in the main school office, with boys looking after everything very well. Rewi recorded in his diary:

> The ceremony was very good; speeches restrained and sensible. *Xian* magistrate, Zhang Xinyi, Fan Wen Hai for the boys, myself, twice, second time thanking on behalf of his family, party man and others. Official eulogy read. Incense and the usual wine cups with proscribed offerings. All was very dignified. Sung school song and bowed. It finished at 12.15 p.m. starting at 10.30 a.m. Only one boy fainted – Su Quing Ho. Many local people came. Zhang Xinyi spoke well on the meaning of his life. Man of the new age, his happiness in his work. I simply gave his history as I knew it. The boys looked well. Had hair cut and were very good on looking after visitors. In the afternoon we had a school meeting with the help of Zhang Xinyi to get things into order for the next stage of work. The boys went to the workshops in the afternoon to work. The lack of rain worried the local people.

Rewi wrote a short time later:

> George has not left this place, and everything is still full of him. His name comes up at every meal in the boys' talk. They have made a pact never to refer to him as being dead; and his orders about whose turn it is to sweep, wait at table and so on, are as iron. Lao San says "George Hogg" in English; Lao Si says "Ho Sien Siengo", and Xiao Zhang chimes in with his version. Yesterday I came home from the pottery and had a dip in the river at the back of his grave. I looked towards it and saw three black heads under the poplars looking down on the grave. It was Sunday afternoon, and his three sons had trekked out there by themselves.

And a few weeks later:

> The boys in school have been excellent, but the show is very much George's show. They have so much of him in them in the way that they evaluate things and so on. I am doing my best to carry on and hold things together. George would never forgive me if I did not stay and do my best with this most basic work. The children he left are well, but they miss his strong parental hand.

From the burial plot there was a magnificent view of the snow-covered Qilian Shan to the south, and the tree bordered Jueh Shui, a tributary of the Edsin Gol, runs close by. To keep his memory fresh, a garden was planned there with a small *ting-tzo* pavilion to cover the gravestone with its English inscription. A basketball and volleyball pitch was prepared nearby on either side, which Aylwin would have liked. A little later, various production units surrounded the memorial. This was the best kind of memorial. Every 22 July after that was a holiday. The students would play games and swim in the river, having a fun time among their fond memories.

On the headstone to his grave was inscribed the last four lines from the first verse of the soldier-poet Julian Grenfell's poem "Into Battle" which Aylwin was fond of:

> And life is colour and warmth and light,
> And a striving evermore for these;
> And he is dead who will not fight;
> And who dies fighting has increase.

At first, Aylwin's closest associates kept wondering, "if only ..., if only ..." But one who knew him well wrote: "The rules of life do not permit any *ifs*, and I think George would not wish such idle speculations. He took things as he found them, he took people with their sorrows and tragedies, he saw his friends die and their hopes shattered. This was the kind of world he lived in, and he was part of it, in life and in death."

Another, who lived in close contact with him, wrote: "He abhorred dealing with officials, as corruption and chicanery were rife; though he would laugh his way through such interviews, they left him spiritually exhausted. He would become depressed, and his face would take on the people's sorrow which he worked hard to erase."

The same person wrote of the fundamental differences between Rewi and Aylwin: "Rewi's way of overflowing kindness was replaced by George's way of balanced rebuke and encouragement; Rewi's *Quanyin*, Goddess of Mercy, with her ten arms and hands, gave place to George's Saint Paul, with his robust, loving zeal, meeting all men – and children – on their own ground. Peasants sought him out for help and protection in all their troubles and oppressions and came to rely implicitly on his word. He never failed them."

It is significant that so many of the tributes to his memory stress Aylwin's gift for identifying himself with the people he lived amongst: "George Hogg was one of the few foreign friends of China who really penetrated into the life of the Chinese people. Though he was called "Ocean Secretary" by his colleagues and friends, they never treated him as a foreigner because they never felt that he was in any way foreign to them. He really set one of the best examples of the new type of missionary." (Lu Guangmian)

"George Hogg spoke excellent Chinese and worked as one inspired. He knew the problems of all the boys in his charge and helped them individually. George was always there within reach, ready to help them. Now that he is gone, his life and teachings are even more appreciated by his pupils and colleagues. His physical presence is no longer with us, but the memory of his inspiring leadership is forever treasured by those who were fortunate enough to come within his influence." (Zhang Fuliang)

Sometime in the spring of 1945, Aylwin had written a song "In Shandan we are born again – we will stay in Shandan till we die." His love for the Shandan School was intense. Rewi wrote these words for the school's wall newspaper about the meaning of Aylwin's life:

So we look and wonder; this life, so short. So much preparation for the seven years he spent with us. It is not easy to produce a man like him. It is not easy to replace him, for he belonged to the new age of the creative common man. Few men have the capacity for affection. He had learnt how to live for the group he had built up, and in them he found great happiness. His notes on the lads in the school were full of understanding. He hoped to live to see the result of his work in the happier China we all want. People have asked me what memorial we would like to remember him with. Certainly he had a host of things he fought for. But we know that what he would have liked most would be to see the spirit of the school kept at a high level, to know that its work was being carried on and foundations for this College of the Common Man were being strengthened so that there would be no fear of its falling down on its promise to the new age. George Hogg was a successful man. He learnt how to find what he wanted to do, and when he had found it he had the strength to make his work a success. He is still a part of us all, and what we have gained from him will, I hope, carry us to success also.

Rewi adopted as an epitaph a sentence, which he had written in the introduction to Aylwin's book, *I See a New China*. This sentence caught peoples' imaginations, and I heard it repeated many times during the memorial ceremonies more than forty years later:

Through his being and working,
many blades of grass will grow
in places where none grew before.

Lao Da and Lao
San with Rewi Alley
in 1986

Lao Er and Lao Si
with Xiao Ren
in 1986

The author in Lanzhou in 1988 with his "cousins"
Lao Da, Lao San and Lao Si together with Ni Caiwan,
the headmaster if the Shandan Bailie School

Aylwin's sister Rosemary with their mother Kathleen Hogg in 1966

Epilogue

Rewi Alley stayed on in Shandan to develop the school, and it thrived despite many difficulties from all quarters. In 1947, as part of a solution to major financial difficulties in Gung Ho, the Lanzhou Bailie School was closed down and moved to Shandan, bringing an increase of sixty students and much good machinery and equipment. In addition, nine girl students were brought from the Baoji Gung Ho orphanage when it was disbanded. By the autumn of 1947 they had two hundred pupils at the school. The school developed into a complex of small industry, and agricultural production was developed on a large scale, which entailed construction of an extensive irrigation system, bringing into use wide areas of semi-desert land.

With more recruitment from neighbouring areas, a peak of four hundred pupils was reached. The staff also increased accordingly, and temporary workers were employed on building projects, on the farm, and in the mine, bringing a total of over another two hundred. It was an extraordinarily sizeable complex for anywhere in China at the time, but especially for Gansu. There were, of course, a hard core of loyal Chinese teachers, but it was very hard to persuade enough to come and work in the wild northwest. The school would not have been successful without the assistance of over thirty foreigners of a vast range of skills and professions from eight different countries, sent by different organisations at various times. The stories from the years up to and beyond Liberation concerning the development of the school into the industrial complex it became, and of the throng of foreigners involved could fill another book, if not several.

Even before 1944, the Gung Ho headquarters begrudged the money sent by the International Committee for the school. As the anti-Japanese war ended and Gung Ho prepared to move its headquarters from Chongqing to Shanghai, they wanted even more strongly to divert these funds to pay the salaries of office staff. The Lanzhou Gung Ho promoters too felt that the Shandan project was a waste of money and thought that everything to do with Gung Ho in Gansu should be in Lanzhou under close Kuomintang supervision. The situation in Shandan became even worse when the Kuomintang passed the whole of Gansu into the hands of the warlord, Ma Bufang, who already controlled Ningxia, Qinghai and Xinjiang. As a result, some exciting and on occasion dangerous times ensued, right up until the area was liberated in 1949.

In 1951, the government took over the school with Rewi Alley as headmaster. Rewi was called in 1953 to work permanently in Beijing, and it was decided to move the school to Lanzhou to become part of the Oil Technical School there. The last trucks laden with the final shipment of school equipment were moving out of Shandan as the disastrous earthquake of 1954 struck with its epicentre in Shandan County. Another legend was born. The peasants wondered how Rewi had known that the town would crumble. There seemed no end to his powers.

During the disastrous so-called Cultural Revolution, a period referred to by most Chinese as the Ten Years of Madness, the Association of Industrial Cooperatives of China and everything to do with it was broken up. During this period, the Gang of Four made demands of the foreign-born Rewi Alley, George Hatem (Ma Haide), and others that they should write criticising this and that. They refused, and consequently they were despised by the Gang of Four. The foreign-born group felt that this madness would pass, but it was an alarming ten years through which time they managed to meet quite regularly to encourage and support each other. Through the protection of Zhou Enlai they survived physically. Through their maintenance of composure, sense of values, and sense of history they survived spiritually, their love for the Chinese people remaining unfaltered. In 1980, some of the old Gung Ho promoters made a proposal to the Chinese People's Political Consultative Conference that the Chinese Industrial Cooperatives movement, known as Gung Ho, should be restored as quickly as possible, and in November 1983, Rewi Alley's dream of revival came about.

The Lanzhou Oil and Technical School, when celebrating its fortieth anniversary in 1982, resumed the name Bailie Oil and Technical School.

In September 1984, Rewi Alley visited Shandan for the last time in order to open the Bailie Library in memory of George Aylwin Hogg. It stands opposite the museum, which was built in 1982 by the provincial government at the suggestion of the Chinese People's Association for Friendship with Foreign Countries, an organisation with which Rewi Alley was closely associated. The books for the library were purchased with funds raised by the old Shandan School Alumni and some funds from foreign friends. A considerable celebration was held at the opening, attended by the local people, officials from Lanzhou and a sizeable group from Beijing including Rewi Alley, all four of Aylwin's adopted sons, the Nie brothers, and Xiao Ren, whom, everyone had believed up to that time had been killed during the war. Aylwin's grave, pavilion, and memorial stone had been restored after having been swept away in the senseless madness of the Cultural Revolution. Beside it is now a primary school of two thousand children.

The region of Shandan has been for centuries an arid and fragile land, exposed to erosion and desertification by overgrazing and mismanagement of woodland. A few years before his death, Rewi Alley put the wheels in motion to establish a new Shandan Bailie School of Agriculture, Forestry, and Animal Husbandry. The Gansu Provincial Government has been strongly behind the scheme, and money from New Zealand, Britain, and America has been donated for special projects and equipment to get the school off to a good start. Building work started in April 1987, just a few months before Rewi Alley's death on 27 December 1987. The first batch of students started in the partly built school during the autumn of 1987. When I made my first visit to Shandan, at the time of Rewi Alley's Memorial events, the school was still under construction, and farmland with buildings had been acquired. By the autumn when I was next there making the television miniseries, the farm was under development and a second batch of students had started. The school was taking shape under the able hand of the Principal Ni Caiwang, who had been a pupil of the Shuangshipu and Shandan Bailie Technical Schools.

The school in Shandan continues to develop, as do the activities of the new Gung Ho (Gonghe) cooperatives movement all over China under the auspices of ICCIC (Gonghe International). Those blades of grass mentioned in Rewi Alley's epitaph to my Uncle Aylwin certainly continue to multiply.

George Aylwin Hogg's old school in Harpenden, St George's, has adopted in no small way the story of their old boy as a source of inspiration for its pupils. Through the school's various and ambitious activities, they are helping to bridge the gap between Britain and China.

A further and most recent noteable acknowledgement of the value of my uncle's life work has been made by The Society for Anglo-Chinese Understanding (SACU) in their launching, in November 2016, of The George Hogg Fund in order to promote educational exchanges between Britain and China with special emphasis on the Shandan Bailie School. Further information on this fund may be found on the society's web-site www.sacu.org

Acknowledgements

My first and foremost thanks go to my aunt, Rosemary Baker, her husband, Cyril, and to my extended family who collectively elected me to represent the family and attend the unforgettable memorial events in China in the spring of 1988 where I came to realise the stature of George Aylwin Hogg. Also, again, thanks to Rosemary, for her encouragement in my acting the part of her beloved brother, Aylwin, in the Chinese television miniseries by reassuring me to "just be yourself; you are so much like him." Those experiences in 1988 inspired me to write Aylwin's story from the perspective of his family.

My thanks also go to James MacManus who, in 1984, in a bar in Beijing and as a journalist for the *Telegraph*, came across an extraordinary story regarding my uncle, and on his return to the UK got in touch with Rosemary Baker. Out of this was born his screenplay, which finally became the feature film, *The Children of Huang Shi*, directed by Roger Spottiswoode, and his own book *Ocean Devil: the Life and Legend of George Hogg*. James's dedication to the story of my uncle was also an inspiration for me to get the family story out there.

I am indebted to all those who are mentioned in the list of sources. As I started to write and research this book over 25 years ago, many of these people have by now unfortunately but inevitably passed away. Somehow, life got in the way for a long while but now, in my retirement, I have been able to concentrate on getting the thing published.

At St George's School in Harpenden, the story of my uncle is being kept very much alive. My heartfelt thanks go to Pam Bainbridge and all the staff there involved in working for better understanding between China and the UK and inspiring today's young people through what my uncle was able to do before his untimely death at the age of only 30.

My very warm thanks go to my cousin Vanessa Dingley, the daughter of Stephen Hogg, for her encouraging words and wholehearted support in finalising this work.

Last, and by no means least, my thanks go to Liu Guonzhong for his speedy checking of my occasional phrases of Mandarin that each complied with modern Pinyin useage, and for helping immensely with networking prior to the book release.

Recommended further reading

Ocean Devil: the Life and Legend of George Hogg
by James MacManus. Published by Harper Collins, 2008.

Dr Bethune's Angel, the Life of Kathleen Hall
by Tom Newnham. Published by Graphic Publications, 2002.

Mother of Worls Peace: Life of Muriel Lester
by Jill Wallis. Published by Hisarlik Press, 1993.

Sources

My grandmother Kathleen Hogg's own cathartic manuscript which is an unpublished piece that, in the writing, helped her work through her grief of the untimely death of her youngest son, which was closely followed by the death of her husband Robert.

Books

Airey, Willis, *A Learner in China* (Christchurch, 1970).

Alley, Rewi, *Leaves from a Sandan Notebook* (Christchurch, 1950).

Alley, Rewi, *Yo Banfa! (We Have a Way!)* (Beijing, 1952).

Alley, Rewi, *Sandan: An Adventure in Creative Education* (Christchurch, 1959).

Alley, Rewi, *Our Seven–Their Five–A Fragment from the Story of Gung Ho* (Beijing, 1963).

Alley, Rewi, *Fruition: The Story of George Alwin Hogg* (Christchurch, 1967).

Alley, Rewi, *At 90: Memoirs of My China Years* (Beijing, 1986).

Chang, Jung. *Wild Swans: Three Daughters of China* (London, 1991).

Chapple, Geoff, *Rewi Alley in China* (Auckland, 1980).

Hogg, Dorothy, *Challenge of the East* (London, 1938).

Hogg, George. *I See a New China* (Boston, 1944).

Lester, Muriel, *It Occurred to Me* (London, 1942).

Lester, Muriel, *It So Happened* (New York 1947).

Newnham, Tom, *He Mingqing, The Life of Kathleen Hall* (Auckland, 1992).

Snow, Edgar, *Red Star Over China* (London, 1937).

Spencer, Barbara, *Desert Hospital in China* (London, 1954).

Archive

George Aylwin Hogg's letters and manuscripts which, in 1991, had been passed in their entirety to the author by his aunt Rosemary Baker for safekeeping and use in writing this book. In 2010 these papers were passed to the archivist at St George's School, Harpenden, UK and at the time of publishing are in the process of transference to be archived at the Bodleian Library in Oxford, UK.

Bulletins and Reports

Indusco Bulletins 1944-49
Shantan Bailie School General Report 1947

Letters to George Hogg's parents

Rewi Alley   Ida Pruitt

Muriel Lester   Brian Harland

Interviews and correspondence

Rosemary Baker née Hogg   Ruth Robins née Thomas

Winifred Hunter née Nelson   Lü Wanru

David Proctor   Duan Shimou

Roger Hunter   Bob Spencer

Nie Guang Chun   Courtney Archer

Nie Guang Han   Walter Illsley

Nie Guang Tao   Max Wilkinson

Nie Guang Pei   Alan Green

Ren Li Zhi   Derek Bryan

Fu Bin   David Somerset

Fan Wen Hai   Tom Newnham

An Wei   Elizabeth Frankland Moore

Map of China

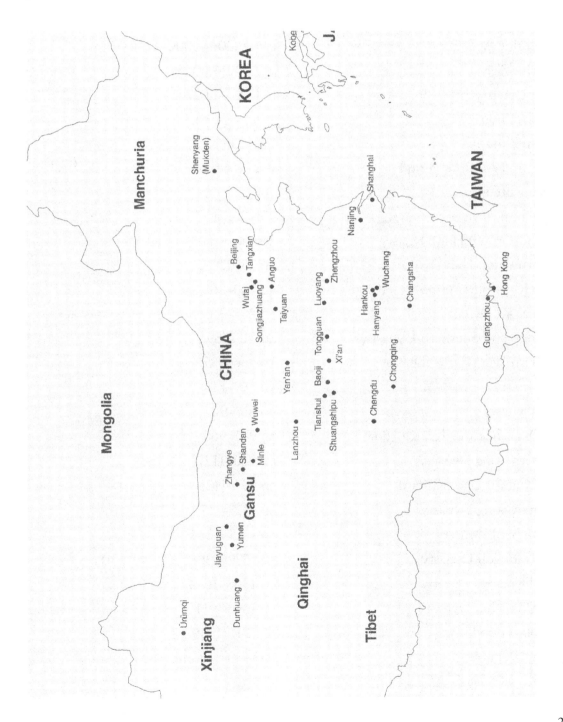

Chinese History Timeline

Palaeolithic Age	c. 600,000–7,000 BC
Neolithic Age	c. 7,000–1,600 BC
Shang Dynasty	c. 1,600–1,027 BC
Western Zhou	1,027–771 BC
Eastern Zhou	770–256 BC
Spring and Autumn Period	722–481 BC
Warring States	480–221 BC
Qin (Ch'in) Dynasty	221–206 BC
Eastern (former) Han Dynasty	206 BC–AD 25
Western (later) Han Dynasty	AD 25–220
Three Kingdoms Period	AD 220–265
Western Jin Dynasty	AD 265–316
Northern and Southern Dynasties	AD 317–589
Northern Wei (Tuoba) Dynasty	AD 386–535
Sui Dynasty	AD 589–618
Tang Dynasty	AD 618–907
Five Dynasties and Ten Kingdoms	AD 907–960
Northern Song Dynasty	AD 960–1127
Liao (Khitan) Liao (Khitan)	AD 907–1125
Southern Song Dynasty	AD 1127–1279
Jin (Jurchen) Dynasty	AD 1115–1234
Yuan (Mongol) Dynasty	AD 1279–1368
Ming Dynasty Dynasty	AD 1368–1644
Qing (Manchu) Dynasty	AD 1644-1911
Republic Period	AD 1911–1949
People's Republic	AD 1949–present

Transliteration of Chinese Sounds

The Wade-Giles system of transliterating Chinese sounds into Roman script was devised by British scholars about one hundred years ago and has never been regarded by the Chinese people as satisfactory. The system known, as Hanyu Pinyin (*pin* meaning "assemble" and *yin* meaning "vowel sound") was devised by the Chinese, and in the 1950s it was decided by China's State Council to bring it into general use. Throughout this book, in the interest of consistency, I have tried to use the Pinyin spelling for names of people and places, as this has become the standard in recent years; for example, Beijing instead of Peking and Jiang Jieshi instead of Chiang Kai Shek, even though in some cases the Wade-Giles spelling may still be in common usage. There are one or two exceptions, however, one of which being *Gung Ho*, which in Pinyin should be written as *Gonghe*. These exceptions have been accepted by the Chinese as permanent deviations from the rule due to their wide usage in the West. It should be noted that, although Pinyin is a great improvement over Wade-Giles, the English sound equivalents can still only be regarded as *approximate*.

Wade-Giles	Hanyu Pinyin	Pronunciation
a	a	far
p	b	be
ts	c	as t plus s in **its**
ch	ch	as t plus sh in **ch**at, (aspirated)
t	d	**d**o
e	e	h**er** (silent r), or the German umlauted ö
ei	ei	w**ay** (a diphthong)
f	f	**f**oot
k	g	**g**o
h	h	h**er** (aspirated)
i	i	**ea**t
i	i	s**ir** (when beginning with c, ch, r, s, sh, z & zh
ie	ie	**ye**s (a diphthong)
ch	j	**j**eep

k	k	kind (aspirated)
l	l	land
m	m	me
n	n	no
o	o	law
p	p	part (strongly aspirated)
ch	q	cheek
j	r	retroflex (not rolled) or like ʒ as in azure
s, ss, sz	s	sister
sh	sh	shore
t	t	top (strongly aspirated)
u	u	too and as the German umlauted **ü**
v	v	only used in foreign words
w	w	want, a semi-vowel only in syllables beginning with u when not preceded by a consonant
hs	x	as sh in **she**
	y	yet, a semi-vowel only in syllables beginning with i or u when not preceded by a consonant
ts, tz	z	zero
ch	zh	jump

Index